ed Books *showing the way*

OUNTY STREET ATLAS

WILTSHIRE

39 TOWN CENTRE STREET MAPS

ROAD MAPS PAGE LAYOUT

Every effort has been made to verify the accuracy of information in this book but the publishers cannot accept responsibility for expense or loss caused by an error or omission.

Information that will be of assistance to the user of the maps will be welcomed.

The representation on these maps of a road, track or path is no evidence of the existence of a right of way.

Street plans prepared and published by
Red Books (Estate Publications) Ltd, Bridewell House, Tenterden, Kent, TN30 6EP.
The Publishers acknowledge the co-operation of the local authorities of towns represented in this atlas.

Ordnance Survey

Crown Copyright
Red Books (Estate Publications) Ltd

ISBN 978-1-84192-425-0
184-10/09-06

VO2007

... 1

... 2

& Distance Guide 3

Tourist Information Centres 4

Local Street Atlases 5

Administrative District Map .. 6-7

Road Maps 8-19

Street Maps
Aldbourne 20
Amesbury 21
Avebury 20
Bradford-on-Avon 23
Bulford 24
Calne 25
Chippenham 26-27
Corsham 28
Cricklade 29
Devizes 30-31
Downton 32
Durrington 24
Highworth 34
Hilperton 63
Holt 29
Ludgershall 35
Lyneham 36
Malmesbury 37
Marlborough 38-39
Melksham 40
Mere 36
North Tidworth 41
Pewsey 42
Potterne 42
Redlynch 33
Salisbury 45-49
Swindon 50-61
Tisbury 43
Trowbridge 62-64
Warminster 66
Westbury 65
Wilton 44
Winsley 22
Woodcock 67
Wootton Bassett 68
Wroughton 43

Index to Streets
inc. Tourist Information 69

ROAD MAPPING

1 : 200,000 - 3.16 Miles to 1 Inch

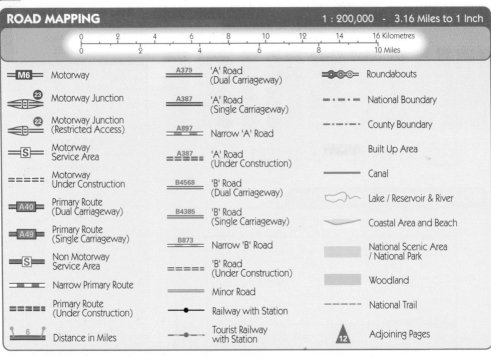

M6 Motorway	**A379** 'A' Road (Dual Carriageway)	Roundabouts
23 Motorway Junction	**A387** 'A' Road (Single Carriageway)	National Boundary
22 Motorway Junction (Restricted Access)	**A897** Narrow 'A' Road	County Boundary
S Motorway Service Area	**A387** 'A' Road (Under Construction)	Built Up Area
Motorway Under Construction	**B4568** 'B' Road (Dual Carriageway)	Canal
A40 Primary Route (Dual Carriageway)	**B4385** 'B' Road (Single Carriageway)	Lake / Reservoir & River
A49 Primary Route (Single Carriageway)	**B873** Narrow 'B' Road	Coastal Area and Beach
S Non Motorway Service Area	'B' Road (Under Construction)	National Scenic Area / National Park
Narrow Primary Route	Minor Road	Woodland
Primary Route (Under Construction)	Railway with Station	National Trail
6 Distance in Miles	Tourist Railway with Station	**12** Adjoining Pages

TOURIST SYMBOLS on road maps

✈	Airport	⊞	Entertainment Centre	⌂	Prehistoric Monument
⛴	Hovercraft	✳	Garden		Roman Remains
⛴	Hydrofiol	▶9 ▶18	Golf Courses (9 & 18 holes)	⬥	RSPB Reserve
♨	Passenger Ferry	▶	Golf Driving Range, Pitch & Putt		Ski Slope Centre
⛴	Seacat	⬛	Holiday Centre		Sub Aqua Activity
⛴ 🚢	Vehicle Ferries	⚘	Horse Racing		Surfing
		⬛	House / Building of Interest		Theatre
※	Ancient Fort	⬛	House and Garden	🛈	Tourist Information Centre
🐴	Animal Attraction	⬛	Industrial Interest	🛈	(Seasonal)
	Aquarium	✳	Leisure / Theme Park	🛈	(National Trust, National Park)
✕	Battle Site	✖	Lighthouse		Tourist Railway
	Bridge of Interest	▲	Monument, Folly		Viewpoint
▲	Camping Site		Motorsports Centre / Venue		Vineyard & Cider Producer
⊘	Caravan Club Site	⌂	Museum / Art Gallery		Water Skiing
🚐	Caravan Site	⬥	National Nature Reserve		Watermill
🏰	Castle, Tower	⬥	National Trail	Y	Wildlife Park
✝	Cathedral, Abbey, Priory	★	Other Place of Interest	✕	Windmill
⌂	Church of Interest	⊞	Outdoor Pursuits		Working Farm
⌂	Country Park	⊓	Picnic Site	⛰	Youth Hostel
⬛	Craft Centre	⚘	Place of Natural Beauty		Zoo

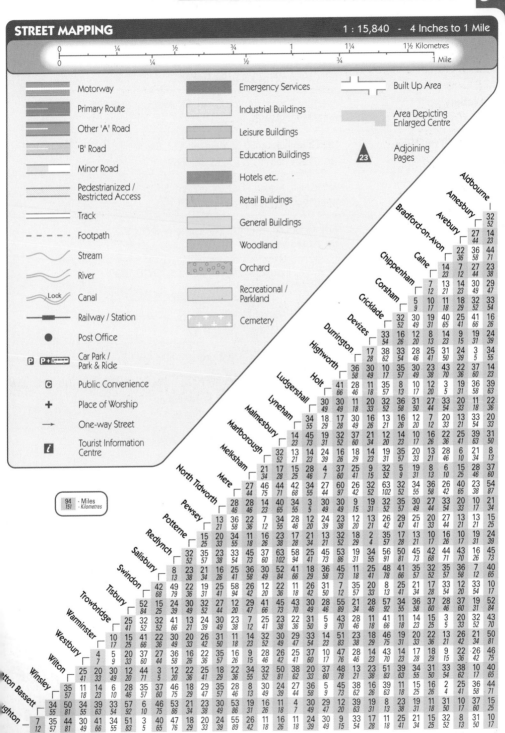

Amesbury 21 C2	Library, Smithfield St, Amesbury, SP4 7AL Tel: 01980 622833 & 01980 623255
Avebury 20 C4	Avebury Chapel Centre, Green St, Avebury, SN8 1RE Tel: 01672 539425
Bradford on Avon 23 F3	The Greenhouse, 50 St Margaret's St, Bradford-on-Avon, BA15 1DE Tel: 01225 865797 & 01225 868722
Chippenham 27 E4	Yelde Hall, Market Pl, Chippenham, SN15 3HL Tel: 01249 665970
Corsham 28 E2	Arnold House, 31, High St, Corsham, SN13 0EZ Tel: 01249 714660
Devizes 30 D4	Cromwell House, Market Pl, Devizes, SN10 1JG Tel: 01380 729408
Malmesbury 37 C4	Town Hall, Market La, Malmesbury, SN16 9BZ Tel: 01666 823748
Marlborough 38 D4	The Library, High St, Marlborough, SN8 1HD Tel: 01672 513989
Melksham 40 B3	The Round House, Church St, Melksham, SN12 6LS Tel: 01225 707424 & 01225 706068
Mere 36 B5	The Library, Barton La, Mere, BA12 6JA Tel: 01747 861211 & 01747 860341
Salisbury 49 E1	Fish Row, Salisbury, SP1 1EJ Tel: 01722 334956
Swindon 59 H1	37 Regent St, Swindon, SN1 1JL Tel: 01793 530328 & 01793 466454
Trowbridge 62 D6	Saint Stephen's Pl, Trowbridge, BA14 8AH Tel: 01225 777054
Warminster 67 E3	Central Car Park, Station Rd, Warminster, BA12 9BT Tel: 01985 218548
Westbury 65 C3	Edward St, Westbury, BA13 3BD Tel: 01373 827158

This COUNTY STREET ATLAS contains street maps for each town centre.
The street atlases listed below are LOCAL STREET ATLASES,
with comprehensive local coverage.

CHIPPENHAM & CALNE

including: Box, Corsham, Draycot Cerne, Hullavington, Kington Langley,
Kington St. Michael, Lower Stanton St. Quinton, Malmesbury,
Rudloe, Stanton St. Quintin etc.

SALISBURY & WILTON

including: Alderbury, Amesbury, Bulford, Bulford Camp, Downton, Durrington,
Idmiston, Larkhill, Mere, Porton, Quidhampton, Redlynch, Shrewton,
Tisbury, West Grimstead, Winterbourne Gunner etc.

SWINDON & CHIPPENHAM

including: Aldbourne, Avebury, Box, Broad Blunsdon, Calne, Chiseldon, Corsham,
Cricklade, Dorcan, Draycot Cerne, Gorse Hill, Haydon, Hook, Highworth,
Hullavington, Kington Langley, Kington St Michael, Lydiard Millicent,
Lyneham, Malmesbury, Marlborough, Purton, Shrivenham, Sparcells,
Stanton Fitzwarren, Stanton St. Quinton, Rudloe, Stratton St. Margaret,
Toothill, Upper Stratton, Walcot, Wanborough, Watchfield,
Wootton Bassett, Wroughton etc.

TROWBRIDGE & FROME

including: Atworth, Berryfield, Bowerhill, Bradford-on-Avon, Bratton, Devizes,
Dilton Marsh, Heytesbury, Heywood, Holt, Melksham, North Bradley,
Potterne, Southwick, Sutton Veny, Warminster, Westbury, Westwood,
Whitley, Winsley, Woodcock, Yarnbrook etc.

For a complete title listing please visit our website
www.redbooks-maps.co.uk

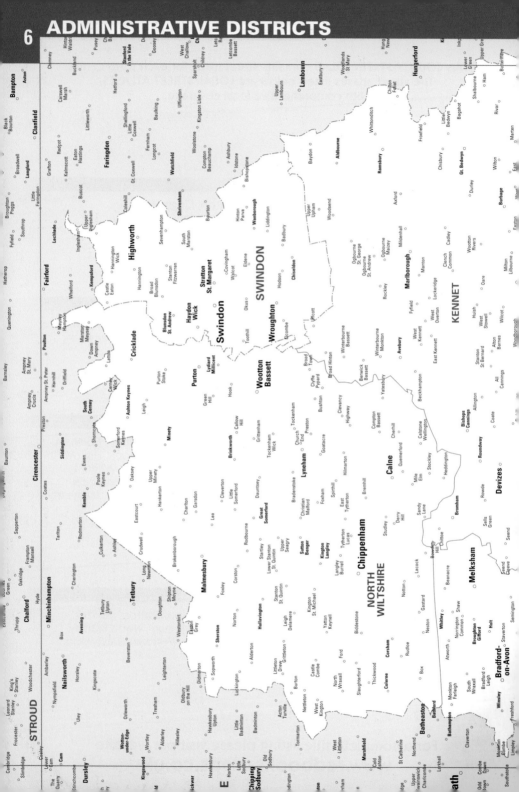

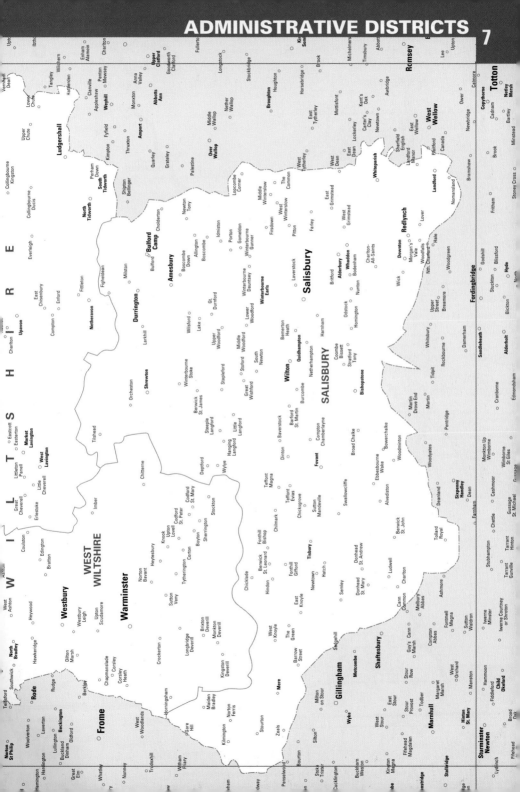

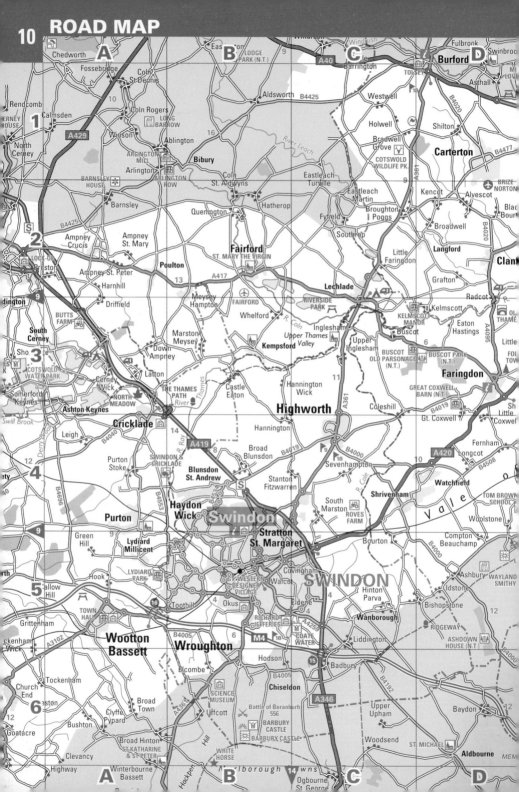

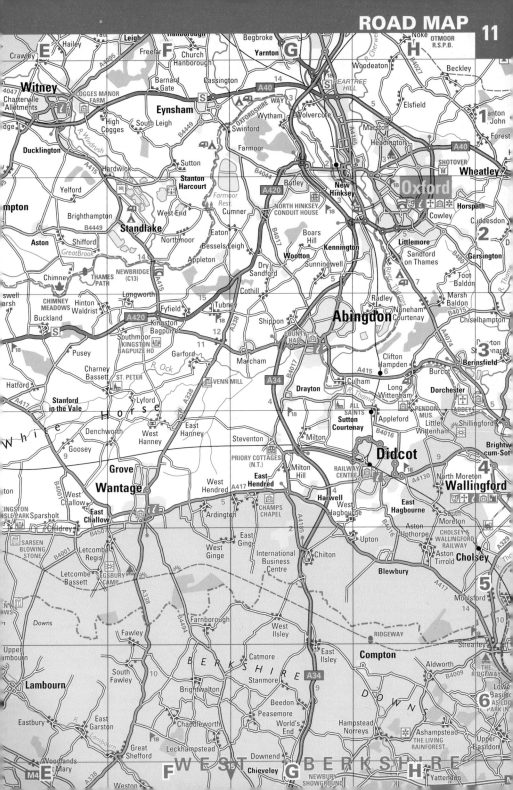

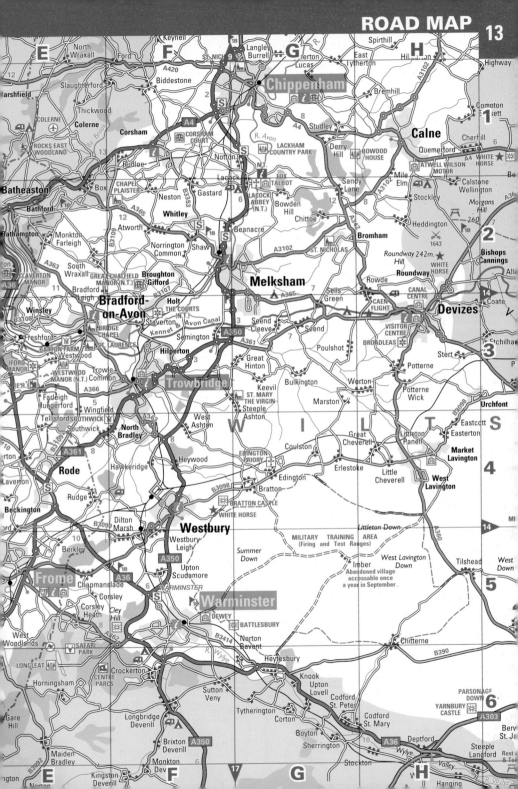

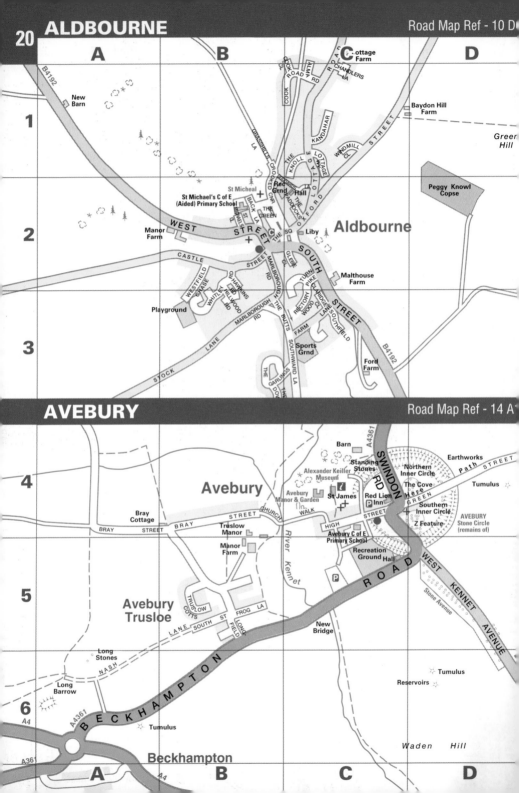

ALDBOURNE

- B4192
- New Barn
- Cottage Farm
- COOK RD
- CROOKED CNR
- CHANDLERS LA
- KANDAHAR RD
- ROAD WITH
- Baydon Hill Farm
- WINDMILL CL
- Green Hill
- THE KNOLL
- LOTTAGE
- FORD
- GRASSHILLS LA
- St Micheal
- St Michael's C of E (Aided) Primary School
- Rec Grnd
- Hall
- THE PADDOCKS
- BACK LA
- WEST STREET
- Manor Farm
- THE GREEN
- LUKES ST
- PHILLIPS LA
- THE SQ
- THE GREEN
- Liby
- Aldbourne
- Peggy Knowl Copse
- CASTLE
- WESTFIELD CHASE
- OLD HAWKINS
- WHITLEY
- HILLWOOD RD
- STREET
- MARLBOROUGH RD
- GLEBE
- SOUTH STREET
- TURN PIKE
- Malthouse Farm
- Playground
- MARLBOROUGH LANE
- THE BUTTS
- SOUTHFIELD
- BRIDGE LANE WOOD
- RECTORY
- Ford Farm
- STOCK LANE
- SOUTHWARD LA
- FARM RD
- Sports Grnd
- THE GARLINGS
- THE DOWN
- B4192

AVEBURY

- A4361
- Barn
- SWINDON RD
- Earthworks
- Path STREET
- Standing Stones
- Northern Inner Circle
- Alexander Keiller Museum
- The Cove
- Tumulus
- Avebury
- Avebury Manor & Garden
- St James
- Red Lion Inn
- Southern Inner Circle
- AVEBURY Stone Circle (remains of)
- Z Feature
- CHURCH WALK
- Bray Cottage
- STREET
- BRAY STREET
- Truslow Manor
- HIGH STREET
- Avebury C of E Primary School
- WEST KENNET AVENUE
- ROAD
- Manor Farm
- River Kennet
- Recreation Ground Hall
- Stone Avenue
- Avebury Trusloe
- TRUSLOW COTTS
- FROG LA
- LONG FIELD
- New Bridge
- LANE SOUTH ST
- Long Stones
- NASH
- Tumulus
- Reservoirs
- Long Barrow
- BECKHAMPTON
- A4361
- Tumulus
- A4
- Beckhampton
- Waden Hill
- A36
- A4

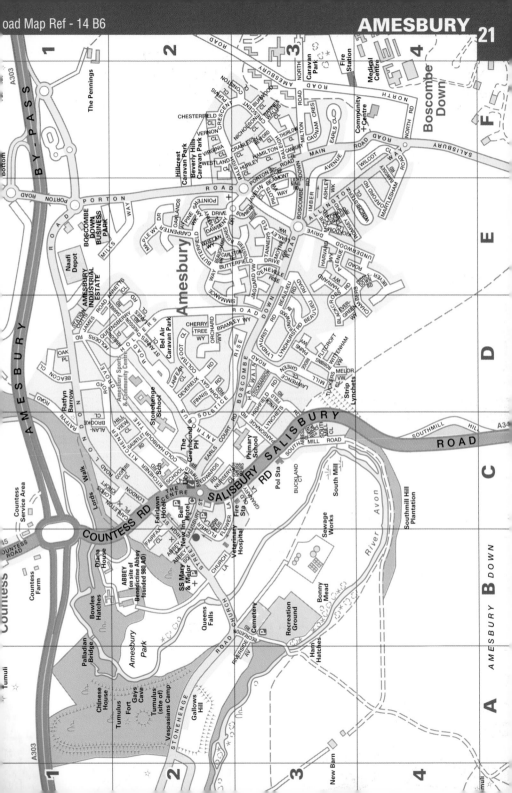

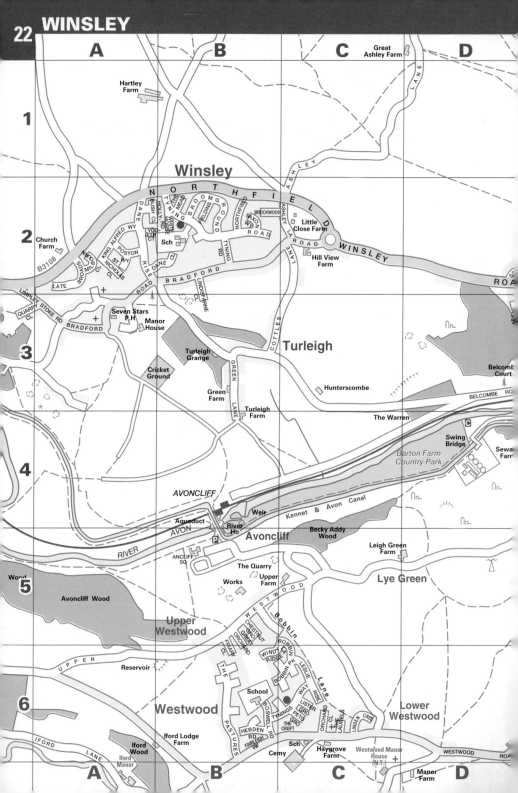

A   B   C   D

Great
Ashley Farm

ASHLEY   LANE

Hartley
Farm

1

Winsley

ASHLEY

NORTHFIELD

Church
Farm

2   BUSH CL   THE MEAD   WHITE HORSE RD   TYNING   HOLLY CL   BROOMGROUND   FELDNS   NORTHFIELD   SAXON RD   ROAD   BROCKWOOD   ASHLEY LANE   LARA ROAD   WINSLEY   Little
Close Farm

B3108   HENLEY CL   BROWL   BRADFORD   PYLE   KING ALFRED WY   NICHOLAS   POSTON WY   ST WY   LYDD ETH CT   Sch   RISE   TYNING   ROAD   Hill View
Farm

LATE   BRADFORD   CL   DENE   BRADFORD   LINDISFARNE   ROA

LIMPLEY STOKE RD   QUARRY CL   BRADFORD   Road

Seven Stars
P.H.   Manor
House

3   Turleigh
Grange   GREEN   COTTLES   ## Turleigh   Belcombe
Court

Cricket
Ground   Green
Farm   LANE   Hunterscombe   BELCOMBE RO

Turleigh
Farm   The Warren   Swing
Bridge

4   Barton Farm
Country Park   Sewa
Farr

AVONCLIFF   Kennet & Avon Canal

Aqueduct   Weir   River
Ho   Becky Addy
Wood   Leigh Green
Farm

AVON   ANCLIFF
SQ   P   ## Avoncliff

RIVER   The Quarry   WESTWOOD   Lye Green

Wood   Works   Upper
Farm

5   Avoncliff Wood   WESTWOOD   BOBBIN

Upper
Westwood   CHESTNUT GRO   Bobbin
Lane

ORCHARD   FRIARY CL   WIND   BOBBIN PK   LESLIE RD

UPPER   Reservoir   THE   BOBBIN RD   WAY   RISE   LISTER GRO   ORCHARD   CL   LAUREL G   LINDEN   CRFS   ## Lower
Westwood

6   School   TYNINGS   GRO   PETO   THE CROFT   Sch   WESTWOOD   ROA

Westwood   PASTURES   BOSWELL RD   HEBDEN
RD   FAIRO   Cemy   Haygrove
Farm   Westwood Manor
House
(N.T.)   Manor
Farm

IFORD   Iford Lodge
Farm   Iford
Wood

LANE   Iford
Manor

A   B   C   D

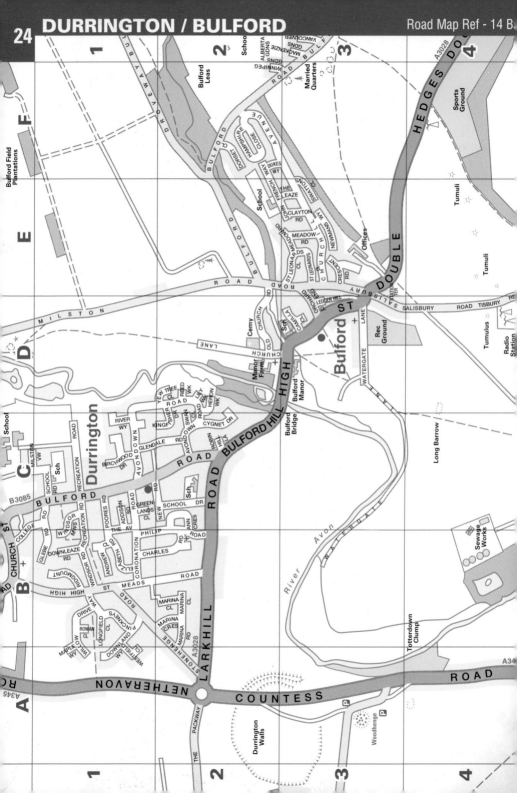

Bulford Leas

Married Quarters

School

Sports Ground

Bulford Field Plantations

School

THE LEAZE

CLAYTON RD

MEADOW RD

Offices

Tumuli

Tumuli

Tumulus

Radio Station

MILSTON

Cemy

Bulford

Rec Ground

SALISBURY ROAD TISBURY RD

LANE

CHURCH

OLD LEDGER HILL

ORCHARD END

STATION

Manor Farm

Bulford Manor

Bulford Bridge

Durrington

YEW TREE ROAD

RIVER WY

KINGF

HERON WK

CYGNET DR

BIRCHWOOD DR

GLENDALE

AVONDOWN

ROBIN WK

Long Barrow

River Avon

Durrington Walls

Woodhenge

Totterdown Clump

Sewage Works

School

MILSTON VW

Sch

B3085

BULFORD ROAD

RECREATION

WINDSOR RD

POORES RD

GREEN LANDS CL

NEW SCHOOL

Sch

PHILIP RD

CHARLES

ANN CRES

THE AV

DOWNLEAZE RD

GLEBE RD

RICHMOUNT RD

CORONATION ST

MEADS

ELIZABETH

ANDREW CL

ADDISON RD

COLLEGE

CHURCH ST

HIGH ST

HIGH

MARINA CL

MARINA CRES

MARINA RD

ROWAN PL

LONGFIELD

MAPLE WY

WILLOW WY

WESTFIELD

DOWNLAND

PINCKNEYS

DRIVE WAY

THE PACKWAY

NETHERAVON

STONEHENGE

LARKHILL ROAD

A3028

COUNTESS ROAD

A34

A345

WATERGATE

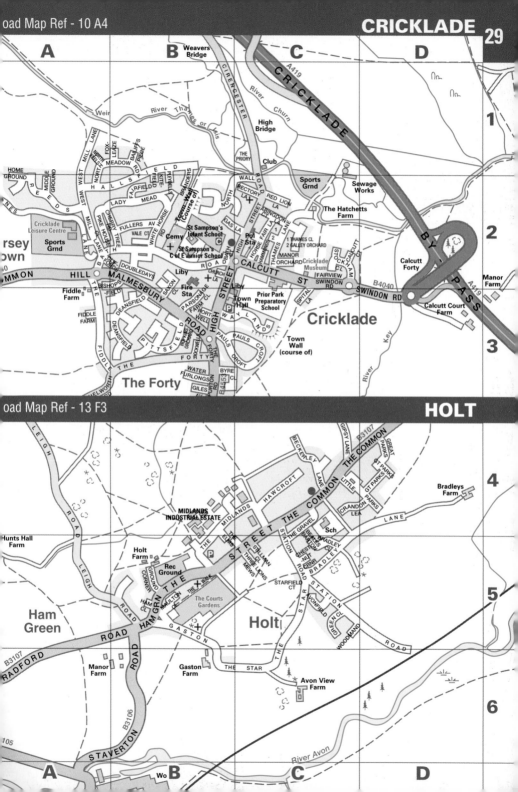

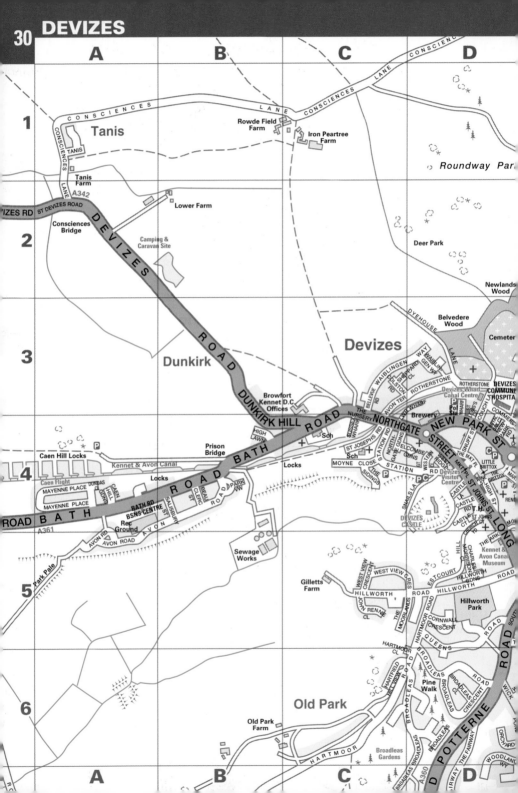

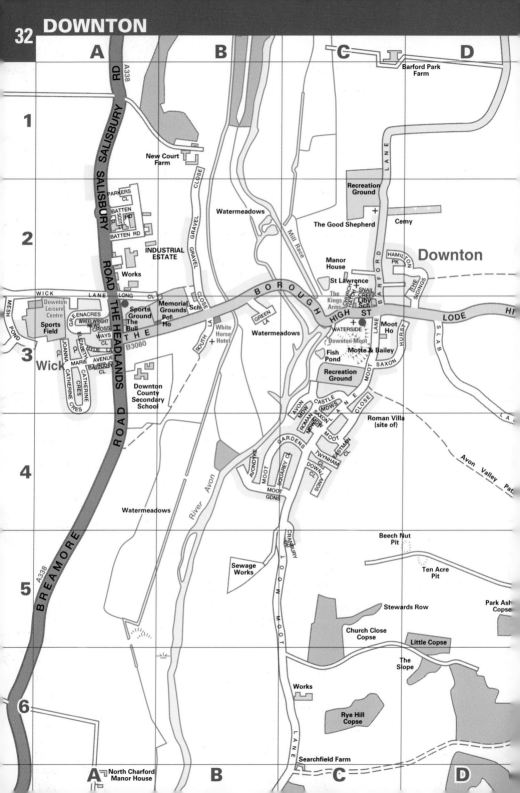

E F G H

1

Barford
Down

LANE

Paradise
Copse

Tumulus Templemans
Farm

Mitchells
Row

2

Down
House

Linchets
Copse

The
Green

LANGFORD

MUDDYFORD RD

THE

Grove Copse

O D E

Paccombe
House

Paccombe
Farm

LANE

SANDY

3

HILL RISE RD

Redlynch
House

GROVE

CHALKS
CL

THE MORGANS

APPLETREE

DOWNTON HILL CL

LIME TREE CL

THE CLOSE

ORCHARD

BOWERS HILL

PRINCES

KILN

ROW

BOWERS HILL

Cemy

LANE

Sch

ROAD

St Birinas
Hall

Beckfords
Copse

PRINCES HILL
CL

LANE

Morgans Vale

LANE

PRIMROSE

BENNETT
CL

VICARAGE
PK

Redlynch

Pensworth
Farm

4

SLAB

LANE

MORGANS

VALE

CASTLE
WOODS

HERBERT RD

RD

RIDGE

QUAVEY ROAD

ROSEDEAN

CHAPEL
RD

GOGGS

Milkhills
Park

Little Nursery
Copse

ST BIRINS

MITCHELLS

SLAB

VALLEY CL

GREENS
MEADE

Police
House

HARTHILL DROVE

CHURCH

5

Woodfalls

ELMFIELD CL

ROAD

Hall

Hart Hill
Firs

Street
Copse

HILL

CHURCH RD

Woodfalls
Farm

DAIRY
CL

KINGSFORD
CL

The Old
Inn

THE DROVE

DROVE

Sch

LANE

HIGHFIELD
LA

Lover

ST MARY'S
CL

SCHOOL RD

SCHOOL RD

Dark Copse

SPRINGFIELD
CRES

FORDERS
CL

BESOMERS CL

LITTLE WOODFA

PINE VIEW CL

Tinneys Firs

LOOSEHANGER

6

TINNEYS
CL

LODGE DROVE

THE

Playing
Field

WHITESHOOT

HILL

WHITESHOOT

FOREST RD

B3080

E F G H

A   B   C   D

Everslea

BLACKWORTH

Bromley
House

PENTYLANDS LANE

Victoria
House

ROUNDHILLS
SEVENFIELDS
EDENCROFT
KNOWLANDS
WESSEX MEAD
MEAD

Haresfiel

BLACKWORTH
INDUSTRIAL
ESTATE

Sewage
Works

CRANE FURLONG

ROAD A361

1

Highworth

SKYE
ARRAN WY
KILDA RD
LISMORE
STROMA RD
BARRA CL
ST MICHAELS

PENTYLANDS CL

HENLEY

DRIVE

FOLLY DR
FOLLY CRES
FOLLY WY
FOLLY RD

QUEENS

VORDA RD
QUEENS AV
TURNPIKE RD
ORCHARD

Northview
Primary
School

THE DORMERS
CULLERNS
SPA CL

2

AVENUE
POUND ORCHARD
GROVE
BUTE CL
ISLAY CRES
POUND RD
HOME FARM

BROOKFIELD
GROVE

WESTROP

Westrop
Primary School

Pol
Sta
RIVERS

Youth
Centre

WESTROP HILL
WESTROP

LECHLADE

MIDDI
HAYNES
DOWNS
ORANGE

THE CULLERNS
PRIORY
GRN
SPA
PRIORY GRN

ST MICHAELS
WINDRUSH
HOME FARM WY

NEWBURGH
PL

FARM WY

MICHAELS
WINDRUSH
NORTH

QUARRY
CRES
STATION
FAIRVIEW
ARCH
ELMS
THE

STAPLETON
CL

BEEBEY
GLEBE

ROAD
CHURCH
AVENUE

CHERRY

VICARAGE

CHERRY
THE
ORCHARD

ROUNDHILLS

PARSONAGE

THE
PRIORY
GRN

THE
WILLOWS

3

Hampton
Hill

OAK
CL

COPPER BEECHES

SHEEP ST

HIGH

BLANDFORD ALLEY

MANOR
HO

Liby

**Eastrop
Roundabout**

Hampton
Farm

Cemy

BYDEMILL GDNS

ROAD

BEECH
DR

GBD
THE ELMS

SWINDON STREET

KINGS
AV

PARK AVENUE

Eastrop
Infant School

GRANGE
CL

Hampton

WESTVILL
ROMAN WY
WIDE HILL
BOTANY

THE GREEN
Rec
Centre

**The Fox
Roundabout**

**Southfield
Junior School**

**Eastrop
Grange**

Highworth
Recreation
Centre

Recreation
Ground

Pavilion

Bowling
Green

STONEFIELD
STRANKS CL

**Warneford
School**

4

CRICKLADE
B4019

Club
House

Golf   Course

SHRIVENHAM

Golf

Club
House

5

Red   Down

Redlands
Court

Golf   Course

6

Red Down
Farm

SWINDON ROAD
A361

Reddown   Hill

Reservoir

A B4

53

A   B   C   D

LUDGERSHALL

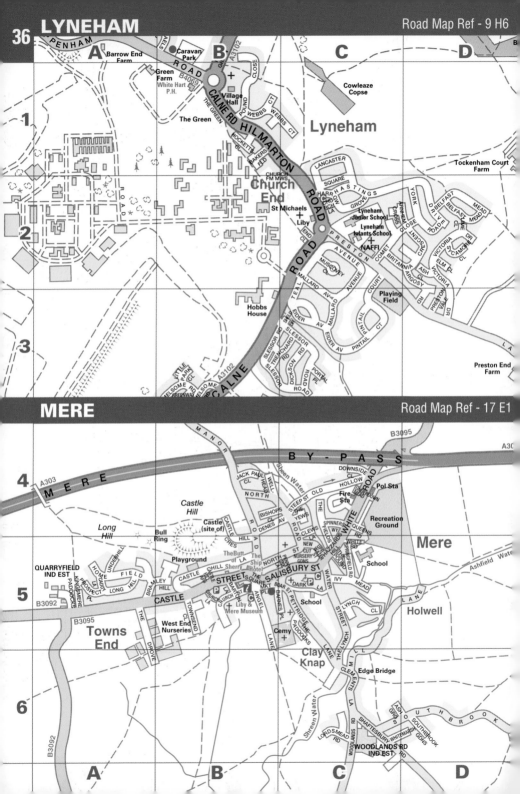

A   B   C   D

CHIPPENHAM

Barrow End Farm
Caravan Park
ROAD
B4069
Green Farm
White Hart P.H.
A3102
CLOSE
GRA
Village Hall
POUND
THE GREEN
WEBBS CT
WEBBS CT

1

The Green
HILMARTON

Cowleaze Copse

Lyneham

Tockenham Court Farm

CALNE RD
HOCKETTS
BAKERS
CL

CHURCH FM MWS
LANCASTER
SQUARE
HASTINGS
HARR BCH
GROVE
YORK
CLOSE
BELFAST
BELFAST RD
MEAD
MEAD

Church End

St Michaels
Liby

Lyneham Junior School
Lyneham Infants School
NAFFI
ARNHEM CROSS
VICTORIA ROAD
SYCAMORE CL
ELM CL
VICTORIA RD

2

ROAD

ROAD
PRESTON
END
COMET
BRITANNIA
ARGOSY
ASH
PRESTON VALE RD

MUSCOVEY CL
MALLARD AV
PRESTON AVENUE
COURT
Playing Field

Hobbs House

TEAL
MALLARD
EIDER AV
AVENUE
PINTAIL
CT
PINTAIL

3

LITTLE PARK CL
A3102
WELSOME RD
GREENWAY
WELSOME
CALNE
SLESSOR RD
SLESSOR
TRENCHARD
SLESSOR
DICKSON RD
RICHARD RD
PORTAL PL
EIDER AV
PORTAL ROAD

Preston End Farm

B3095
A30

MANOR
BY - PASS
A303

4

A303
MERE

JACK PAUL CL
WELL HEAD
NORTH
Sheen Water
DOWNSIDE
HOLLOW
MEADOWN
WHITE ROAD
Pol Sta
Fire Sta

Castle Hill
Long Hill
Bull Ring
Castle (site of)
Playground
BISHOPS
CL
DENES AV
CASTLE CRES
CASTLE HILL
STEEP ST
OLD
THE YEWS
CLEVES
SPINNERS
WHITE
Recreation Ground
QUEENS
School

Mere

5

QUARRYFIELD IND EST
B3092
HOMER
UNDERHILL
PROSPECT
LONG HILL
FIELD
BRAMLEY HILL
CASTLE HILL
CASTLE
CHILL STREET
TheButt of LA
Sherry
The Ship Hotel
NEW CUT
NURSERY GDNS
ST NORTH
BARTON
SALISBURY ST
THE SQUARE
MKT PL
ANGEL
Liby & Mere Museum
DARK
BOAR ST
BARNES PL
PETTRIDGE LA
WATER
IVY
School
MEAD
THE LYNCH
Holwell

Towns End
West End Nurseries
CASTLE
TOWNSEND
THE DROVE
BARTON
Cemy
PADDOCKS
LANE
Clay Knap
Edge Bridge

6

B3092
Sheen Water
LORDSMEAD RD
SHAFTESBURY RD
WHITEMARSH
WOODLANDS RD
WOODLANDS RD IND EST
ASH GRO
SOUTHBROOK GDNS
SOUTH BROOK

A   B   C   D

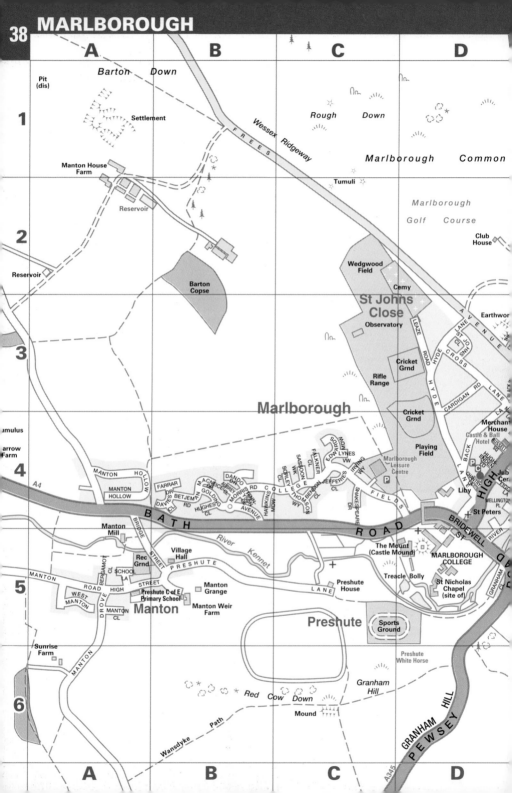

A **B** **C** **D**

Barton Down

Pit (dis)

1

Settlement

Wessex Ridgeway

Rough Down

Marlborough Common

FREES

Manton House Farm

Reservoir

Tumuli

Marlborough

Golf Course

Club House

2

Reservoir

Barton Copse

Wedgwood Field

Cemy

St Johns Close

Observatory

Earthwor

Reservoir

3

Cricket Grnd

Rifle Range

LEAZE

HYDE

LA CROSS

AVENUE

LANE

Marlborough

Cricket Grnd

CARDIGAN RD

HYDE ROAD

umulus

arrow Farm

A4

MANTON HOLLOW

MANTON HOLLOW

FARRAR

MACNEICE DR

DANDO DR

MORRIS RD

SASSOON CL

SCHLEY WK

FALKNER CL

EDW LYNES CL

SOUTH ROW

IRVING WY

JEFFERIES CL

SHAKESPEARE DR

Marlborough Leisure Centre

Playing Field

Merchant House

Castle & Ball Hotel

BACK LANE

HIGH ST

RUSSELL SQ

Jub Cer

Liby

St Peters

WELLINGTON PL

4

DAVIES RD

BETJEM

HUGHES CL

GOLDING

AVENUE

HAWKINS CL

BENSON CL

THOMSON WY

FIELDS

DROVE

BERDAMOT CL

BRIDGE STREET

River Kennet

ROAD

BRIDEWELL ST

ST MARY

RIVER

GRANHAM

Manton Mill

Rec Grnd

Village Hall

PRESHUTE

The Mount (Castle Mound)

MARLBOROUGH COLLEGE

5

MANTON

WEST MANTON

ROAD HIGH

SCHOOL LA

STREET

Preshute C of E Primary School

Manton Grange

Manton Weir Farm

Manton

Manton House

PRESHUTE LANE

Treacle Bolly

St Nicholas Chapel (site of)

CL

MANTON CL

Preshute

Sports Ground

Preshute White Horse

GRANHAM HILL

PEWSEY

Sunrise Farm

MANTON

Red Cow Down

Mound

Granham Hill

6

Wansdyke Path

A345

A **B** **C** **D**

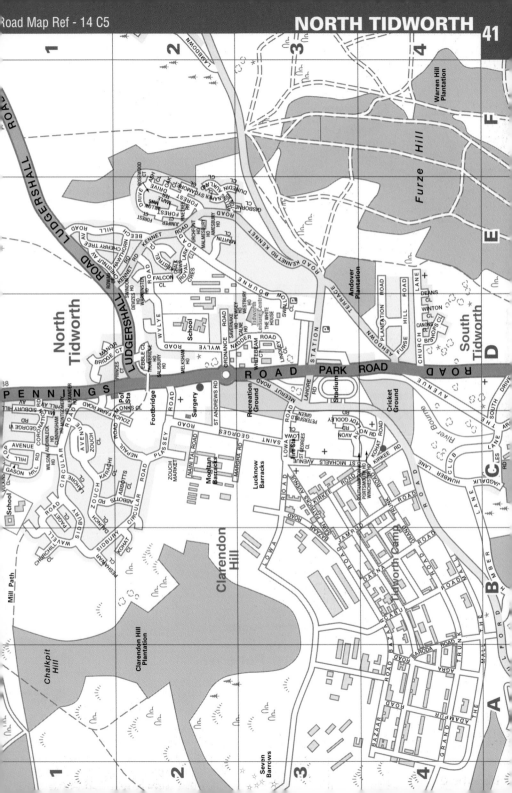

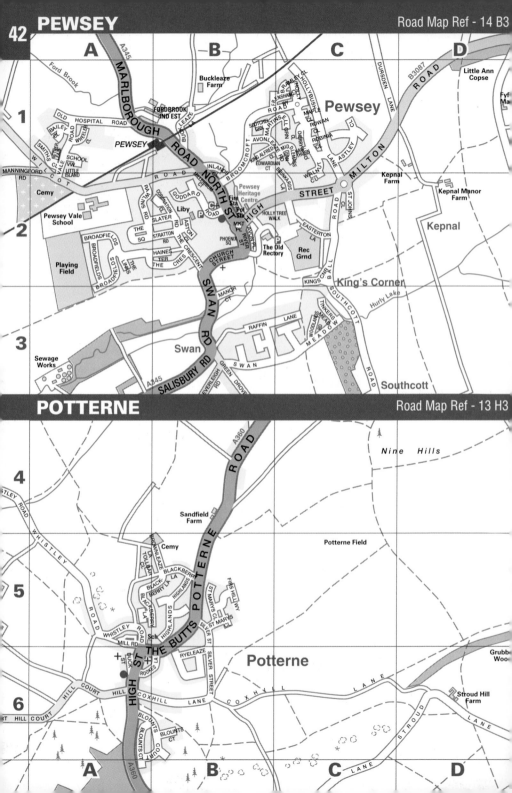

PEWSEY

A B C D

Ford Brook

Buckleaze Farm

Little Ann Copse

Fyf Ma

FORDBROOK IND EST

MARLBOROUGH ROAD

OLD HOSPITAL ROAD

BAILEY

WHITER

SMITHS CL

VALE RD

VW

SCHOOL

LITTLE ISLAND

PEWSEY

Pewsey

BRAMLEY CL

HOLLYBUSH

DURSDEN LANE

B3087 ROAD

MAPLE CL

ROWAN CL

CHERRY

ROBINIA CL

ASTLEY

SPOTCHE GDN

AVON

MARTINS

KING ALFRED RD

WALNUT CL

Kepnal Farm

Kepnal Manor Farm

MANNINGFORD RD

W I COT

BUS ROAD

INLANDS

NORTH ST

BROOMCROFT

EDWARDIAN CT

BRINKARDS

HIGH STREET

MILTON

ST JOHNS

Cemy

Pewsey Vale School

RAVENS RD

CORONATION

GODDARD CL

SLATER RD

ASTON

Liby

P

Pewsey Heritage Centre

Fire Sta

Pol Stn

HOLLY TREE WALK

EASTERTON LA

Kepnal

THE SQ

STRATTON RD

HAINES TER

THE CRES

BROADFIELDS

PHOENIX SQ

MKT PL

RIVER ST

CHURCH STREET

The Old Rectory

P

Rec Grnd

CANAL

BALL

KINGS

SOUTHCOT

King's Corner

Playing Field

BROADFIELDS

THE LIMES

MANOR CT

SWAN RD

RAFFIN LANE

WOODLANDS

TINKERS

Hurly Lake

MEADOW

Sewage Works

Swan

SALISBURY RD

A4445

EVERLEIGH RD

GREEN DROVE

SWAN

Southcott

1

2

3

POTTERNE

A360

POTTERNE ROAD

Nine Hills

STLEY ROAD

WHISTLEY

Sandfield Farm

Cemy

Potterne Field

BROWNLEAZE

TOLBARY CL

BLACKBERRY LA LA

BLACKBERRY

HIGHLANDS

POTTERNE

ST MARYS

FRS HILLWY

Grubb Woo

WHISTLEY ROAD

BLACK BERRY LA

BLACKBARN

HIGHLANDS

THE BUTTS

ST MARYS

SILVER ST

Sch

MILL RD

HIGH ST

BUCK ST

LA LA

ROOKES

RYELEAZE

SILVER ST

SILVER STREET

Potterne

HILL COURT

COXHILL LANE

COXHILL LANE

LANE

STROUD LANE

Stroud Hill Farm

T HILL COURT

BLOUNTS

BLOUNTS CT

BLOUNTS COURT

A360

4

5

6

A B C D

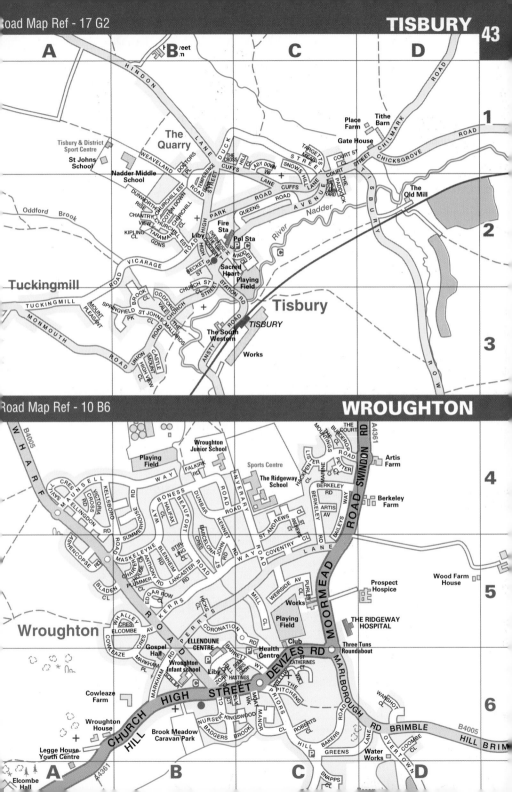

TISBURY

A   B   C   D

HINDON LANE

The Quarry

Tisbury & District Sport Centre

St Johns School

Nadder Middle School

WEAVELAND

DOCTORS PL

DUNWORTH RISE

CHURCHILL EST

COTON DOWN

CHURCHILL

CHANTRY VIEW

KIPLING CL

TARAMAH GDNS

TEMPERANCE STREET

HIGH ROAD

DUCK STREET

THE CROSS

CUFFS

LADY DOWN VW

LANE

CUFFS

QUEENS ROAD

PARK ROAD

SNOWS HILL

COURT ST

TARGETS MEAD

STREET

COURT ST

THE PADDOCK

GATE FARM CTYARD

Place Farm

Tithe Barn

Gate House

CHICKSGROVE ROAD

CHILMARK ROAD

TISBURY ROAD

The Old Mill

River Nadder

1

2

Fire Sta

Liby

Pol Sta

Sacred Heart

Playing Field

Tisbury

VICARAGE ROAD

Tuckingmill

TUCKINGMILL

MONMOUTH

MOUNT PLEASANT

SPRINGFIELD PK

BROOK CL

ODDFORD

ST JOHNS CL

VALE

MALLARDS

ROAD

UNION ROAD

CASTLE

MOUNT

HIGH VIEW CL

BECKET ST

HIGH ST

CHURCH ST

NADDER CL

OVERHILL

WEB HILL

STATION RD

ANSTY ROAD

ROAD

TISBURY

The South Western

Works

3

WROUGHTON

A   B   C   D

B4005

WHARF

Playing Field

Wroughton Junior School

FALKIRK RD

WAY

Sports Centre

The Ridgeway School

THE COURT

MOORINGS

BLUEROAD ROAD

PETTER

A4361

ROAD SWINDON RD

Artis Farm

Berkeley Farm

4

SAVIL CRES

MAUNSELL CRES

VICTORIA CROSS

ELLINGDON RD

KELLSBORO RD

BONESS RD

BEAUFORT

HALIFAX

SUMMERHOUSE WAY

STIRLING CL

INVERARY ROAD

KENNET ROAD

DUNBAR

BARCELONA RD

ST ANDREWS CL

COVENTRY RD

LISTER AV

MARINE

HACKPEN RD

BERKELEY RD

BERKELEY

ARTIS AV

WAY

BAILEYS

Wood Farm House

ASPENCOPSE

BLADEN CL

MASKELEYNE WAY

CHARTER

ANTHONY RD

BLENHEIM

PLUMMER RD

EDGAR ROW

LANCASTER RD

KERRS

WAY ROAD

MILL

WEIRSIDE AV

PURLEY

LANE

Prospect Hospice

THE RIDGEWAY HOSPITAL

5

Wroughton

WHALLEY CRES

ELCOMBE

COWLEAZE

CRES

ROAD

ELCOMBE AV

Gospel Hall

ELLENDUNE CENTRE

Wroughton Infant school

KERR

PERRY

CORONATION RD

Works

BARRETT

HALL

Playing Field

Club

Health Centre

Liby

THREE STREET

ST CATHERINES

THE PITCHENS

Three Tuns Roundabout

MARLBOROUGH RD

WANSHOT

BRIMBLE HILL

BRIM

B4005

6

Cowleaze Farm

Wroughton House

Legge House Youth Centre

Elcombe Hall

CHURCH HILL

A4361

HIGH STREET

MARKHAM PL

MOAT

NURSET

BADGERS

KINGSWOOD

BROOK

DEVIZES RD

ZOAR

HASTINGS

WILLOW WY

PRIORS

HILL

MANOR

CL

ROBERTS CL

BAKERS

GREENS

SNAPPS

Brook Meadow Caravan Park

Water Works

OVERTOWN

COOMBE CL

A   B   C   D

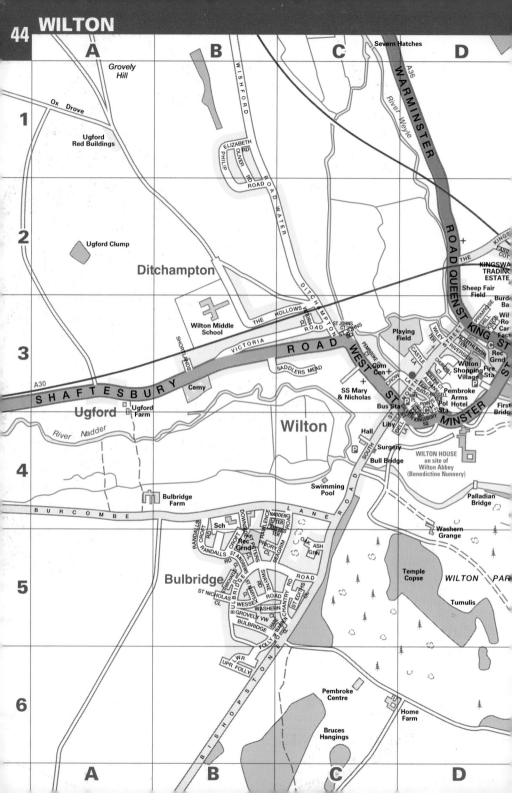

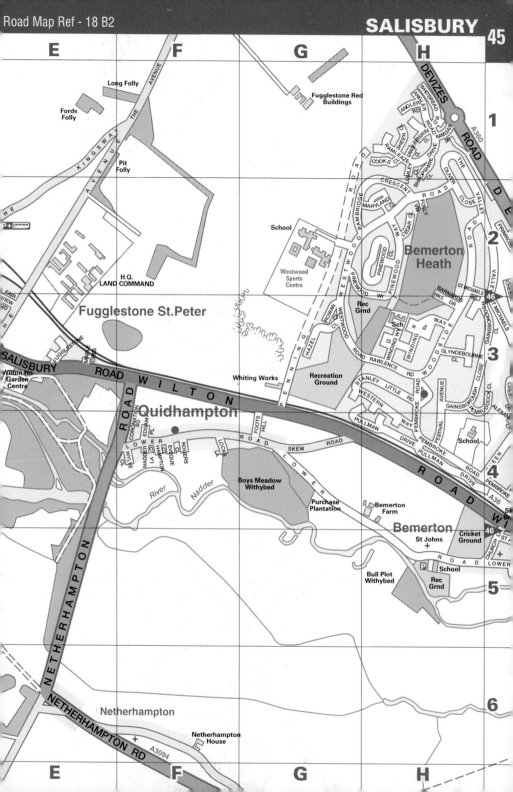

E   F   G   H

Long Folly

Fords
Folly

Fugglestone Red
Buildings

DEVIZES ROAD A360

1

THE AVENUE

KINGSWAY

AVENUE

THE AVENUE

Pit
Folly

WHITBREAD

ANGLER
RD

ANGLER ROAD

RAMLEAZE RD
CL SHEEN

LUMLEY CL
DRIVE
COOK-S CL

LAKE
ARKSHIRE

SHOPSHIRE DRIVE

RAMLEAZE

OLIVER ROAD

THE VALLEY

OLIVER CLOSE

THE VALLEY ROAD

CRESCENT

MARYLAND
CL

RAMBRIDGE

FOLLY WAY

CEDAR CL

School

Westwood
Sports
Centre

WESTWOOD

PINEWOOD

PINEWOOD WY

PINEWOOD

PINEWOOD WY

Bemerton
Heath

ST MICHAELS

BARNARDS
HILL DR

VALLEY

2

THORNBRIDGE

ST MICHAELS CL

46

H.Q.
LAND COMMAND

Fugglestone St.Peter

ROWAN CL

PENNING

HAZEL CL

WESTWOOD

WESTWOOD

Rec
Grnd

ROAD RAWLENCE

Sch

WINDING WAY

WINDING

WAY E

GLYNDEBOURNE
CL

WOODSIDE

GAINSBOROUGH CL

3

FAIRVIEW RD H

FUGGLESTONE CRES

MARLE

ROAD

SALISBURY ROAD

Quidhampton

Whiting Works

Recreation
Ground

ROAD RAWLENCE

STANLEY LITTLE RD

WESTERN

PULLMAN

WAY

AVENUE
FESTIVAL

PEMBROKE ROAD

PEMWOOD CL

ALEXAN

4

WILTON ROAD

WILLOW
CORONATION SQ
EDGAR
NADDER
TOWER PL
HAMPTON LA
EVEQUE CL
ROGERS
LOCKS LA

ROAD

FOOTS HILL

SKEW ROAD

LOWER

ROAD

Boys Meadow
Withybed

PULLMAN WAY

DRIVE

PEMBROKE

PULLMAN

School

ROAD WI

A36

GREEN

PEMBROKE RD

NETHERHAMPTON

River   Nadder

Purchase
Plantation

Bemerton
Farm

Bemerton

St Johns
✛

ROAD LOWER

CHURCH RD

Cricket
Ground

46

St B

4

Bull Plot
Withybed

P

School

Rec
Grnd

5

6

Netherhampton

Netherhampton
House

NETHERHAMPTON RD   A3094

✛

E   F   G   H

A345

A   B   C   D

1

Woodford Road

Avon Farm

The Manor House

Durnford Road

Middle Barn Farm

Monument

Avon Bridge

Stratford Bridge

Deans Farm

PHILLIPS   LANE

Cathedral (Remains)

St Johns Hospital (site of)

CASTLE ROAD

2

Stratford

Road

Mawarden Court

School

SORVIODVNVM

OLD SARUM

Castle (Remains)

Holy Cross Church (site of)

Castle Hill

Tumuli

OLD CASTLE ROAD

45

A360

ROAD

THE CLOSE

THE VALLEY

Mill

PARSONAGE CL

MILL LA

ST LAWRENCE CL

Stratford sub Castle

Parliament Tree (site of)

Engraved Stone

Hudsons Field

Paul's Dene

PAULS DENE

SNOW HILL

JUNIPER

3

River   Avon

ST MICH

DEVIZES

PRIMROSE RD

EAGLE FIELD

HEATH CL

CHESHIRE CL

Playing Field

Primary School

CASTLE KEEP

STRATFORD RD

SHAKESPEARE CL

SHELLEY DR

Playing Field

RFC Ground

FAIRFIELD RD

Wks

ST FRANCIS

4

THE VALLEY

WOODROBBINS CL

ST MICHAELS RD

QUEEN MARY RD

HEATH RD

HATHAWAY CL

HAVERONA RD

CARLILE CL

CHATHAM RD

HUDSON RD

WATERS ROAD

PARK LANE

Victoria Park

BEATRICE RD

45

SBOROUGH CLOSE

EBOR

CREST MOUNT RD

TOURNAMENT RD

HERBERT RD

ROBERTS RD

WELLINGTON RD

CROWN

LADYSMITH

CORONATION RD

PHILIP

WARWICK CL

Tennis Courts

STRATFORD

Victoria Park

QUEENSBE

CORNWALL RD

5

School

QUEEN RD

ALEXANDRA CL

CENTURION RD

ALEXANDRA DR

Cemy

Cemetery

SARUM CL

HARPER RD

INDIA AV

Butts Sports Field

School

Salisbury Leisure Centre & Athletics Track

Black Well

HULSE RD

HAIG RD

DOUGLAS RD

School

BUTTS

MOBER

VICTORIA RD

6

Cric Ground

Skew Bridge

WILTON

PEMBROKE

Labour Hall

EMPIRE RD

Bemerton

NEW ZEALAND AV

AUSTRALIAN

CANADIAN AV

CHRISTIE MILLER CL

HIGHBURY AV

MACKLIN RD

MACKLIN RDE

PALMER

School

WESTMINSTER RD

KENSINGTON RD

KINGSLAND RD

EVERS RD

Recreation Ground

Fire Station

Studio Theatre

Superstore

Castle

NELSON

SCAMELLS RD

School

ST ANDREWS

SKEW BRIDGE

GRIMSHAW RD

ORCHARD RD

Bemerton Lodge

Police Station Divisional HQ

CHANCERY

MONTGOM

HIGHFIELD

CHARNWOOD RD

NURSERY RD

FINCHLEY

Playing Field

RUSSELL

BEDFORD RD

CLIFTON

THE MAPLES

HARTINGTON RD

AVON TER

MARSH

COLD HARBOUR

MIDDLETON

ST GEORGE

MILL

STREAM APP

HADRIANS CL

LOWER

Sch

TED

HERRY ORCHARD

CHERRY GARRINGES

LAND

A36

WILTON   ROAD

48

St Pauls

D   A   B   C   D

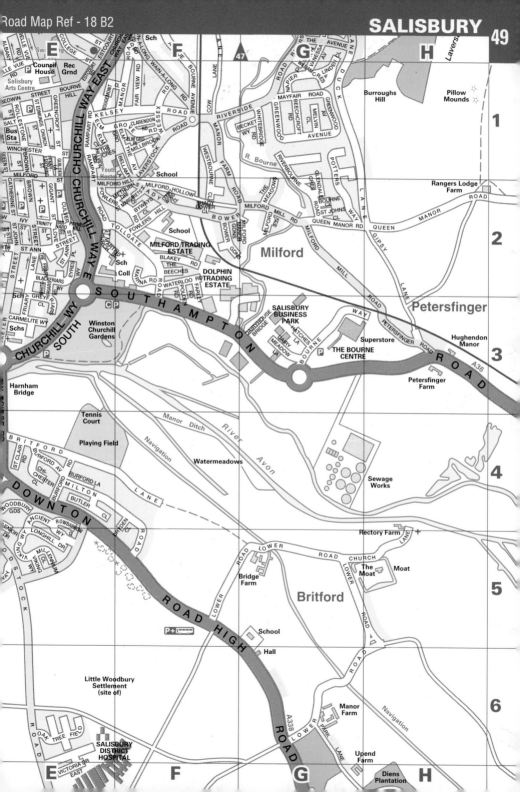

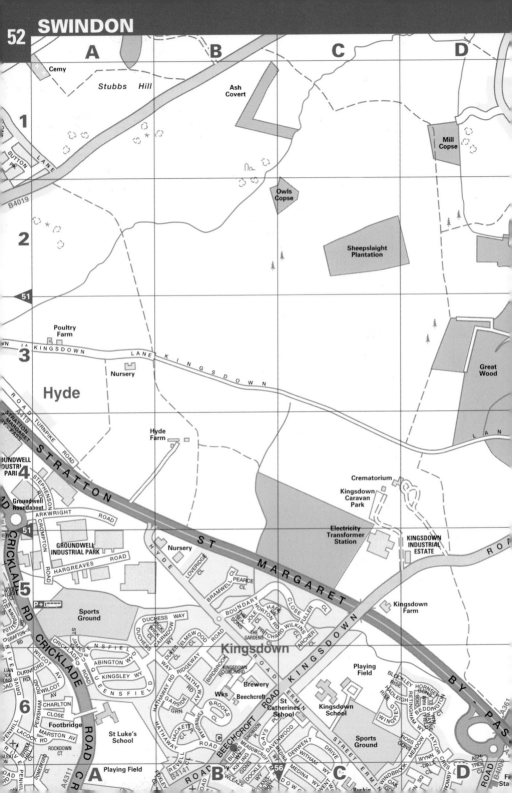

Cemy

Stubbs Hill

Ash Covert

Mill Copse

Owls Copse

Sheepslaight Plantation

51

Poultry Farm

KINGSDOWN LANE KINGSDOWN

Nursery

Great Wood

Hyde

STRATTON MARGARET BY-PASS
A419 TURNPIKE ROAD

LANE

Hyde Farm

Crematorium

Kingsdown Caravan Park

Electricity Transformer Station

KINGSDOWN INDUSTRIAL ESTATE

STRATTON

GROUNDWELL INDUSTRIAL PARK

Groundwell Roundabout

STEPHENSON

ARKWRIGHT ROAD

CROMPTON RD

51

HARGREAVES RD

ROAD

HYDE ROAD

Nursery

LOVERIDGE CL

BRAMWELL RD

PEARCE CL

BOUNDARY RD

HARK CL

HORTON RD

JOLE CL

WILKINS CL

FULLER CL

ARCHER

ST MARGARET

KINGSDOWN

Kingsdown Farm

Sports Ground

DUCHESS WAY

DUKES

ELMSWOOD

RIDGEWAY

THE GARDENS

PRITCHARD

Kingsdown

Playing Field

BLOCKLEY RISE

HORNSEY

RETINGHAM WY

HADLEIGH RISE

BEDDINGTON CT

WINDER

ST JAMES

ENSFIELD

ABINGTON WY

KINGSLEY WY

QUEENSFIELD

CAIRNDOW WY

HATHAWAY RD

BIRDBROOK

KINGSDOWN ROAD

ORCHARD

Brewery

Beechcroft

Wks

St Catherines School

Kingsdown School

Playing Field

Sports Ground

STREET ERMIN

WYNDHAM RD

WILCOT AV

DURNFORD

CHARLTON CLOSE

PEWSHAM

Footbridge

MARSTON AV

ROCKDOWN CT

St Luke's School

HATHAWAY RD

GARSIDE

HACKETT CL

BROOKS CL

BEECHCROFT

REVELL RD

MEADOWCROFT

KILLING GDNS

DOCKLE

GAYS

DANEKWOOD

DERWENT

WITHAM WY

MEDINA

DRIVE

WINDBROOK

ROSS MEADOW

CRICKLADE ROAD

Playing Field

A4311

B4141 ROAD

56

Kingsdown School

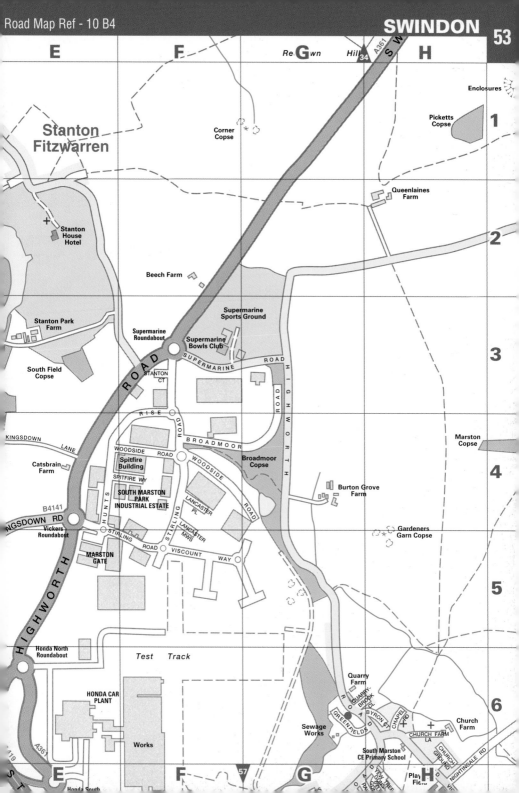

E F G H

Re**G**wn Hill

A361 S W

SWINDON

Enclosures

Picketts Copse

1

Stanton Fitzwarren

Corner Copse

Queenlaines Farm

Stanton House Hotel

2

Beech Farm

Supermarine Sports Ground

Stanton Park Farm

Supermarine Roundabout

Supermarine Bowls Club

ROAD

SUPERMARINE ROAD

HIGHWORTH ROAD

3

South Field Copse

STANTON CT

RISE

ROAD

BROADMOOR

Marston Copse

KINGSDOWN LANE

WOODSIDE ROAD

Spitfire Building

SPITFIRE WY

Broadmoor Copse

4

Catsbrain Farm

WOODSIDE ROAD

Burton Grove Farm

B4141

HUNTS

SOUTH MARSTON PARK INDUSTRIAL ESTATE

LANCASTER PL

NGSDOWN RD

Vickers Roundabout

STIRLING

LANCASTER MWS

Gardeners Garn Copse

HIGHWORTH

MARSTON GATE

STIRLING ROAD

VISCOUNT WAY

5

Honda North Roundabout

Test Track

HONDA CAR PLANT

Quarry Farm

QUARRY

BROOK

6

BYRON CT

CHAPEL RD

Church Farm

Works

Sewage Works

GREENFIELDS

CHURCH FARM LA

CHURCH GROUND RD

A361

ST

E

F

57

G

South Marston CE Primary School

NIGHTINGALE RD

Play Field

H

Honda South

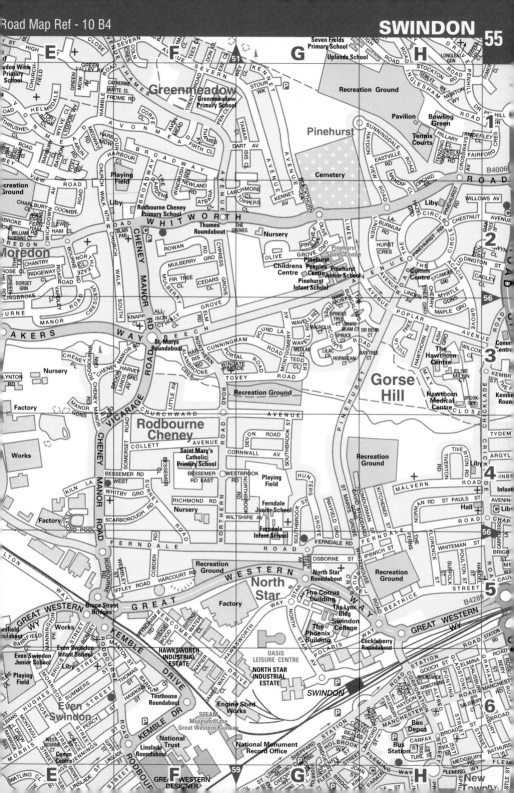

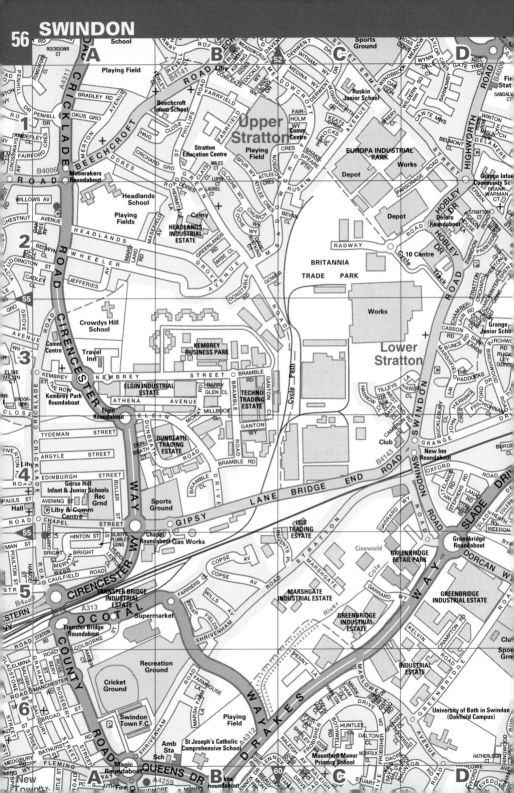

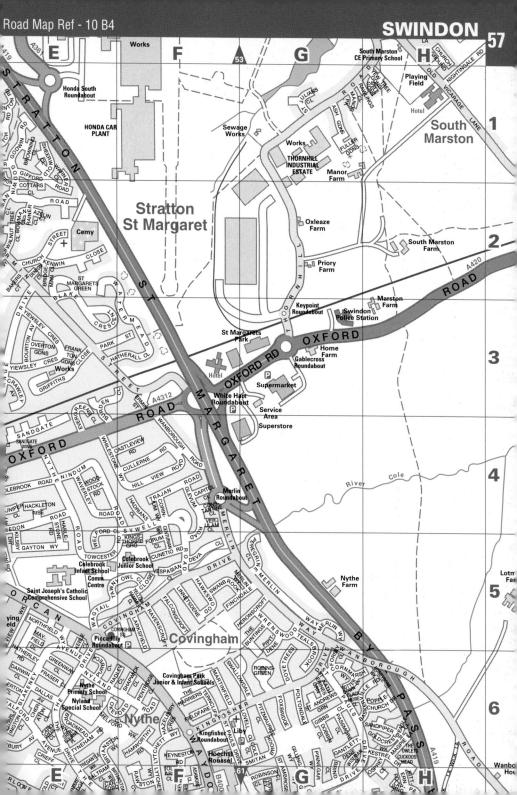

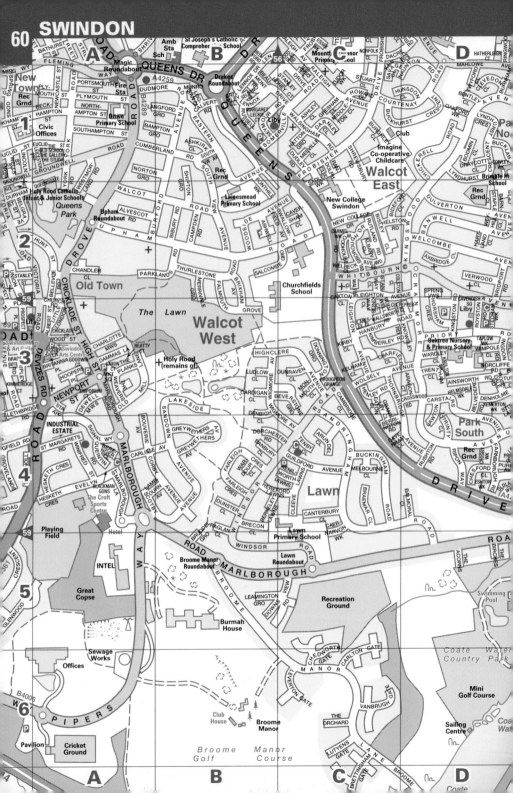

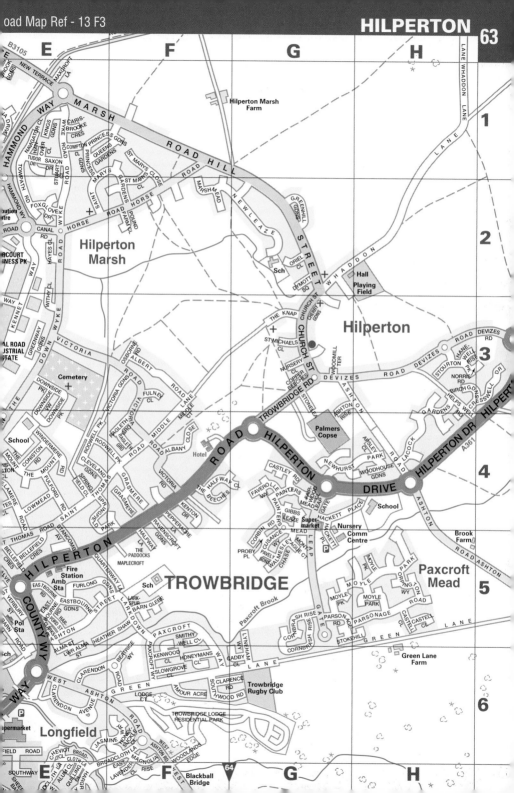

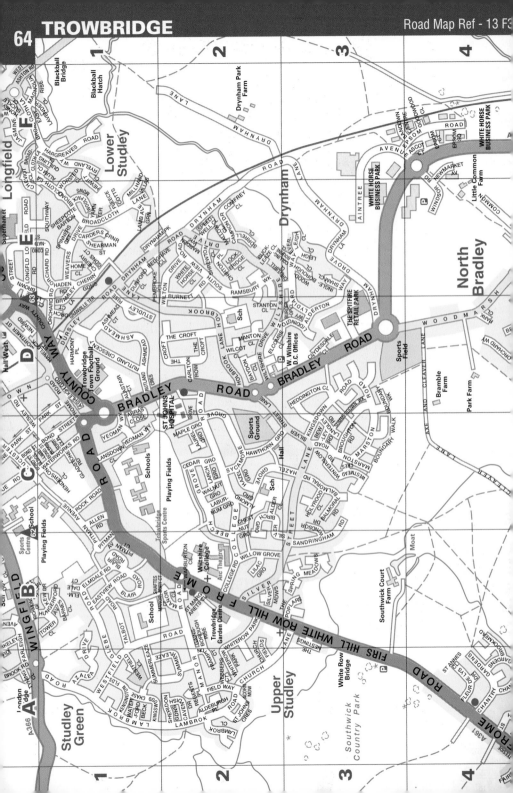

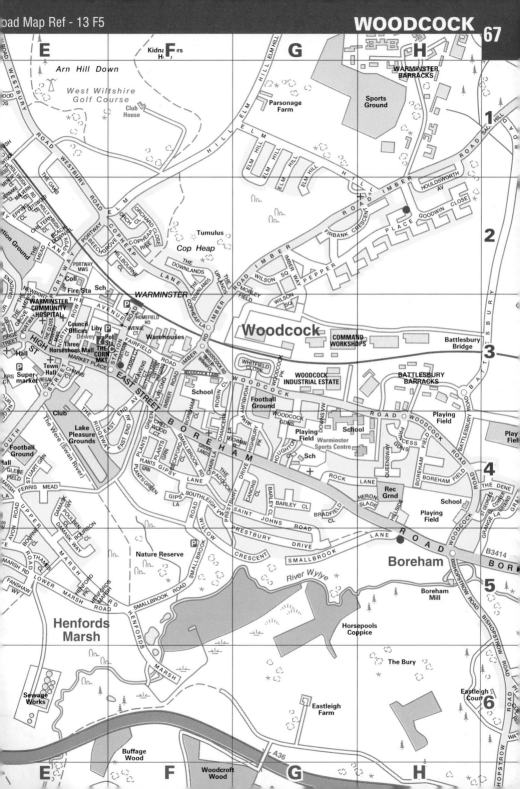

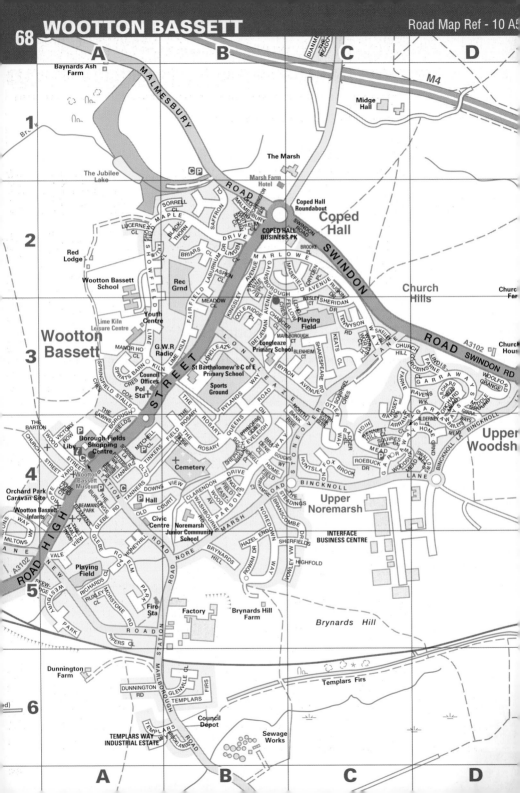

THE INDEX EXPLAINED

To ease the use of this index certain types of entries, which are additional to the street names, are shown using different colours as explained below:-

Bold Text - Place name on the road maps at the front of the atlas.
Red Text - Tourist Attractions.
Red Bold Text - Hospitals.
Blue Text - Industrial & Retail Areas / Buildings.

The Index includes some names for which there is insufficient space on the maps. These names are indicated by an * and are followed by the nearest adjoining thoroughfare.

A

Abbas Combe	**16 C3**
Abbatt Cl SP11	35 F3
Abberd House Fm SN11	25 D3
Abberd La SN11	25 D3
Abberd Way SN11	25 C4
Abbess Cl SP4	21 C3
Abbey Cl SN15	27 H6
Abbey House SN16	37 C4
Abbey La SP4	21 B2
Abbey Mill*, Church St BA15	23 F3
Abbey Row SN16	37 B4
Abbey Sq SP4	21 B2
Abbey View Rd SN25	55 E1
Abbot Rd SP1	47 F3
Abbots Gdns SN16	37 C4
Abbots Leigh	**12 A1**
Abbotsbury Way SN25	51 F3
Abbotts Ann	**15 E6**
Abbotts Cl SP9	41 C2
Abbotts Ct BA13	65 B3
Abbotts Rd SP9	41 C2
Abbottswood	**19 E3**
Abingdon	**11 G3**
Abingdon Court La SN6	29 C2
Abington Way SN2	52 A6
Ablington	**10 A1**
Abney Moor SN3	61 G5
Acacia Cl SN14	26 B1
Acacia Cres BA14	62 B5
Acacia Gro SN2	55 H2
Academy Dr SN13	28 C2
Acorn Cl SN3	61 E2
Acorn Mdw BA14	64 A2
Acril Ct SN1	59 H2
Acton Turville	**9 E6**
Adampur Rd SP9	41 A4
Adber	**16 B3**
Adcroft Dr BA14	62 D4
Adcroft St BA14	62 D4
Addington Cl SN10	31 E6
Addinsell Rd SN25	50 D3
Addison Cres SN2	56 C1
Addison Rd SN12	40 A1
Addison Sq SP4	24 C1
Adelphi Cl SP2	44 D3
Aden Ct SN25	51 E5
Adwalton Cl SN5	58 A3
Affleck Cl SN5	58 C2
Agra Rd SP9	41 A4
Aiken Rd SN25	50 B6
Ainsworth Rd SN3	60 D3
Aintree Av BA14	64 E3
Aintree Dr SN14	26 A5
Akenfield Cl SN25	51 F5
Akers Way SN2	54 C2
Alanbrooke Cl SP4	21 C1
Alanbrooke Cres SN2	55 F3
Alastair Ct BA14	64 D1
Albany Cl, Swindon SN3	60 C2
Albany Cl, Trowbridge BA14	63 F4
Albany Rd SP1	46 D6
Albany Ter SP2	44 D3
Albert Rd BA14	63 F3
Albert Ter*, Bridewell St SN10	31 E5
Albion Dr BA14	62 B5
Albion St SN1	59 F2
Alcock Crest BA12	66 D4

Aldborough Cl SN5	54 B6
Aldbourne	**10 D6**
Aldbourne Cl SN2	51 H5
Aldeburgh Pl BA14	64 A2
Alder Cl, Swindon SN2	50 C6
Alder Cl, Trowbridge BA14	64 C2
Alder Way SN12	40 A4
Alderley	**18 B2**
Alderholt	**18 B5**
Alderley	**9 E4**
Aldermaston	**15 H2**
Alderney Cl SN4	68 D4
Alderton	**9 F5**
Aldsworth	**10 B1**
Aldworth	**11 H6**
Aldworth Dr SP1	47 F3
Alexander Ho SP9	41 D1
Alexander Keiller Museum SN8	20 C4
Alexander Rd SN16	37 A3
Alexander Ter SN13	28 E2
Alexandra Cl SP2	46 A5
Alexandra Dr SP2	46 A5
Alexandra Ter SN8	39 E3
Alford	**16 B1**
Alfred St BA13	65 C2
Alhampton	**16 B1**
All Cannings	**14 A3**
All Saints Cres BA13	65 C2
Allen Rd, Corsham SN13	28 B3
Allen Rd, Trowbridge BA14	64 C1
Allington Rd SN2	51 G5
Allington Way, Chippenham SN14	26 B2
Allington Way, Salisbury SP4	21 E3
Allington, Wiltshire, SN10	**14 C6**
Allington, Wiltshire, SP4	**14 A2**
Allison Ct SN2	55 F3
Alma Pl SN8	39 E4
Alma Rd SN8	20 C1
Alma St SN11	25 B4
Alma Ter SN8	63 E6
Almond Gro BA14	64 C2
Almondsbury	**8 B5**
Alnwick Cl SN5	58 B3
Alpine Cl SN5	54 A6
Alton Barnes	**14 A3**
Alton Cl SN2	51 H5
Alton Pancras	**16 C6**
Alum Ct SP4	64 F1
Alvediston	**17 H3**
Alvescot Cl SN3	10 D2
Alvescot Rd SN3	60 A2
Alveston	**8 B4**
Alveston Cl SN5	58 C1
Alvington	**8 B2**
Alweston	**16 C4**
Amberley	**9 E2**
Amberley Cl, Calne SN11	25 A2
Amberley Cl, Swindon SN25	55 H1
Amberley Ct SN16	37 A5
Ambrose Rd SN1	59 H5
Amersham Rd SN13	61 E4
Amesbury	**14 B6**
Amesbury By-Pass SP4	21 C1
Amesbury Cl SN2	51 H5
Amesbury Ho SP9	41 E2
Amesbury Rd SP4	21 F3
Amesbury Ind Est SP4	21 D1
Amesbury Sports & Community Centre SP4	21 D2
Amour Acre BA14	63 F6
Ampfield	**19 F3**
Ampney Crucis	**10 A2**

Ampney St Mary	**10 A2**
Ampney St Peter	**10 A2**
Amport	**14 D5**
Ancaster Cl BA14	62 B5
Anchor Rd SN11	25 C4
Ancient Way SP2	49 E4
Ancliff Sq BA15	22 B5
Ancona Cl SN3	54 A6
Anderson Cl SN3	61 G3
Anderson Rd SP1	47 F4
Andover	**15 E5**
Andover Down	**15 F5**
Andover Rd SP11	35 C3
Andover St SN1	59 F2
Andrew Cl SP4	24 B1
Andrews Cl SN14	26 B6
Andrews Way SP2	48 D5
Angel Cl SN11	25 D4
Angel La BA12	36 B5
Angel Yd SN8	39 E4
Angelica Cl SN2	54 D1
Angler Rd, Salisbury SP2	45 H1
Angler Rd, Swindon SN5	58 B1
Anglesey Cl SN5	54 A6
Angus Cl SN5	54 A5
Anise Cl SN2	54 C1
Ann Cres SP4	24 C2
Anna Valley	**15 E5**
Annetts Cl SP4	21 D2
Ansford	**16 C1**
Anson Gro SN12	40 D6
Anstie Cl SN10	31 F3
Ansty	**16 D6**
Ansty Rd SP3	43 B3
Ansty Walk SN2	51 G5
Anthony Rd SN4	43 B5
Antony Rd SN25	51 E3
Antrobus Rd SP4	21 C2
Anzac Ho SN10	31 F2
Apollo Cl SN25	50 A3
Apostles Way SP1	47 F3
Apple Tree Cl SP5	33 F3
Appleford	**11 H4**
Appleshaw	**14 D5**
Appleshaw Way SP1	47 G3
Appleton	**11 F2**
Appletree Rd SP5	33 F4
Applewood Cl SN14	26 C3
Applewood Ct SN5	58 C2
Apsley Cl BA14	63 H4
Aquarius Cl SN25	50 B4
Aragon Cl SP4	21 D2
Aragon Ct SN3	60 D3
Aragon Cl SN14	26 C3
Arbury Banks SN4	68 B3
Ardington	**11 F4**
Argosy Rd SN15	36 D2
Argyle St SN2	56 A4
Ariadne Rd SN25	50 A3
Arkwright Rd SN25	52 A4
Arley Cl SN25	51 F5
Arlington	**8 D1**
Arlington	**10 A1**
Arlington Cl SN3	57 E6
Arliss Cl SN25	51 F4
Arn Vw BA12	66 D1
Arney Cl SN13	28 D3
Arnfield Moor SN3	61 H5
Arnham Cross SN15	36 C2
Arnold St SN25	50 D3
Arnolds Mead SN13	28 E2
Arran Cl SN4	68 C4
Arran Way SN6	34 B2
Arras Cl BA14	64 C1
Arthur Bennett Ct SN1	59 F2
Artis Av SN4	43 C4
Artus Ct SN4	50 D4
Arun Rd SN25	55 E1

Arundel Cl, Chippenham SN14	26 B4
Arundel Cl, Swindon SN3	60 C4
Arundell Cl BA13	65 D2
Ascham Rd SN5	58 A1
Ascot Cl SN14	26 B6
Ascot Ct BA14	64 F4
Ash Cl, Chippenham SN15	36 D2
Ash Cl, Tidworth SP9	41 E2
Ash Cres, Andover SP11	35 F3
Ash Cres, Salisbury SP1	47 F3
Ash Gdns SN3	57 G1
Ash Gro, Melksham SN12	40 A5
Ash Gro, Swindon SN2	55 H3
Ash Gro, Warminster BA12	36 C6
Ash Gro, Westbury BA13	65 A3
Ash Walk, Devizes SN10	31 G2
Ash Walk, Warminster BA12	66 D2
Ashampstead	**11 H6**
Ashbury	**10 D5**
Ashbury Av SN3	56 D6
Ashdown Dr SN10	40 D1
Ashdown Ter SP9	41 D4
Ashdown Way SN25	50 B6
Ashe Cres SN25	27 E1
Ashencope Rd SN4	43 A5
Ashfield Rd, Chippenham SN15	27 E2
Ashfield Rd, Salisbury SP2	48 B1
Ashford Hill	**15 H2**
Ashie Cl SN5	54 B3
Ashington Way SN5	58 B2
Ashkirk Cl SN3	60 B1
Ashlands SP4	47 G2
Ashleigh Gro BA14	64 D1
Ashleworth Rd SN25	51 E4
Ashley Cl, Bradford-on-Avon BA15	23 E1
Ashley Cl, Swindon SN3	60 C1
Ashley Coombe BA12	66 D5
Ashley Heath	**18 A6**
Ashley La BA15	22 C2
Ashley Pl BA12	66 D5
Ashley Rd, Bradford-on-Avon BA15	23 E1
Ashley Rd, Salisbury SP2	46 C6
Ashley Walk SP4	21 E3
Ashley, Gloucestershire	**9 G3**
Ashley, Hampshire	**19 F2**
Ashmansworth	**15 F3**
Ashmead Rd SN4	64 D1
Ashmead Ct BA14	64 D1
Ashmore	**17 F4**
Ashmore Cl SN3	61 F1
Ashridge Ct SN25	50 D4
Ashton Cl SN25	50 B3
Ashton Keynes	**10 A3**
Ashton Rd BA14	63 G3
Ashton Rise BA14	63 G4
Ashton St BA14	63 E5
Ashtree Cl SN3	52 D6
Ashurst	**19 E5**
Ashwell Cl SN3	60 B2
Ashworth Rd SN5	58 D1
Aspen Cl SN4	68 B2
Assisi Rd SP1	46 D3
Asthall	**10 D1**
Astley Cl SN9	42 C1
Aston	**11 E2**

Aston Cl SN9	42 B2
Aston Mead SP1	47 F5
Aston Tirrold	**11 H5**
Aston Upthorpe	**11 H5**
Astor Cres SP11	35 C3
Atbara Cl SN8	55 F2
Athelstan Ct SN16	37 B3
Athelstan Museum SN16	37 C4
Athelstan Rd SN16	37 B3
Athena Av SN2	56 A3
Attlee Cres SN2	56 B2
Attwood Rd SP1	47 E5
Atwell Wilson Motor Museum SN11	13 H1
Atworth	**13 F2**
Atworth Cl SN2	51 G5
Aubrey Cl SN8	38 B4
Aubrey Rise SN16	37 C2
Auchinleck Ho SP9	41 C1
Auden Cl SN25	51 E5
Audley Gate BA13	65 A3
Audley Rd SN14	26 D4
Augusta Cl SN25	50 C4
Aukland Cl SP9	41 E2
Aust	**8 B4**
Austen Cres SN3	61 F3
Australian Av SP2	46 A6
Avebury	**14 A1**
Avebury Cl, Calne SN11	25 B4
Avebury Cl, Westbury BA13	65 B1
Avebury Manor & Garden SN8	20 C4
Avebury Rd, Chippenham SN14	26 B5
Avebury Rd, Swindon SN2	51 G5
Avebury Stone Circle SN8	20 D4
Avening	**9 F3**
Avening St SN2	56 A4
Avens Cl SN4	54 D1
Avenue Cl BA12	67 F3
Avenue La Fleche SN15	27 E4
Avenue Rd SN1	59 H3
Avington	**15 E2**
Avocet Cl SN3	61 G1
Avon App SP1	48 D1
Avon Blds SP4	21 C2
Avon Castle	**18 B6**
Avon Cl, Bradford-on-Avon BA15	23 G4
Avon Cl, Calne SN11	25 B2
Avon Cl SN12	40 D2
Avon Edge SN16	37 B4
Avon Mdw SP5	32 C4
Avon Mills SN16	37 C5
Avon Pl, Melksham SN12	40 B3
Avon Pl, Pewsey SN9	42 B2
Avon Rd, Devizes SN10	30 A5
Avon Rd, Malmesbury SN16	37 A3
Avon Rd, Melksham SN12	40 B1
Avon Rd, Tidworth SP9	41 C3
Avon Rd, Warminster BA12	67 E5
Avon Reach SN15	27 E3
Avon Stoke Cl SN21	21 C3
Avon Ter, Salisbury SP2	46 C6
Avon Way BA14	63 E3
Avondown Rd SP4	24 C1
Avondyke SP5	32 B4
Avonfield Av BA15	23 G4
Avonlea Cl BA14	29 C5
Avonleaze Rd SN9	42 B1
Avonmead, Chippenham SN15	27 F3

Avonmead, Swindon SN25 54 D1
Avonvale Rd BA14 62 D3
Awbridge 19 E3
Awdry Av SN12 40 C1
Awdry CI SN14 26 A4
Awkley 8 B5
Awre 8 D1
Axbridge CI SN3 60 D2
Axe And Cleaver La BA14 64 C4
Axford 14 C1
Axis Bsns Centre SN5 54 C6
Aylburton 8 B2
Ayleswade Rd, Salisbury SP1 48 D3
Ayleswade Rd, Salisbury SP2 48 D3
Aymer PI SN3 61 E2
Ayr SN14 26 A6
Ayrshire CI, Salisbury SP2 45 H1
Ayrshire CI, Swindon SN5 54 A6
Azalea CI SN11 25 C6
Azalea Dr, Trowbridge BA14 64 A1
Azalea Dr, Warminster BA12 66 C3
Azelin Ct SN3 57 E2

B

Babcary 16 A2
Back Cut Rd SN13 28 B3
Back Hill SN16 37 C4
Back La, Aldbourne SN8 20 B2
Back La, Marlborough SN8 38 D4
Back Rd SN11 25 C5
Bacon CI SN1 59 F3
Badbury 10 C6
Badger CI SN4 68 C4
Badgers Brook SN4 43 B6
Badgers CI SN10 31 E5
Badminton 9 E5
Bagendon 9 H1
Bagshot 14 D2
Bailey CI, Devizes SN10 31 H1
Bailey CI, Pewsey SN9 42 A1
Baileys Barn BA15 23 F4
Baileys Fld SN14 26 A1
Baileys Mead SN4 68 D4
Baileys Way SN4 43 C5
Bailiffs Piece SN6 29 B1
Bainbridge SN2 58 A2
Bainton CI BA15 23 G2
Baird CI SN5 54 A5
Bakehouse CI SN15 27 F5
Bakers Ct SN3 57 E2
Bakers Fld SN15 36 B1
Bakers Rd SN4 43 C6
Ball Hill 15 F2
Ball Rd SN9 42 C2
Balmerlawn 18 D6
Balmoral CI, Chippenham SN14 26 A4
Balmoral CI, Swindon SN3 60 D4
Balmoral Rd, Salisbury SP1 47 E3
Balmoral Rd, Trowbridge BA14 64 C3
Baltonsborough 16 A1
Bampton 11 E2
Bampton Gro SN3 60 A1
Banbury CI SN3 60 B4
Bancroft BA15 23 G1
Banda Ind Est SN10 31 F6
Bank 18 D6
Bank St SN12 40 B3
Bankfoot CI SN5 54 B6
Bankside SN1 59 E3
Banwell Av SN3 60 D2
Barbel CI SN11 25 B2
Barbury Castle & Country Park SN4 10 B6
Barbury CI SN25 55 F1
Barcelona Cres SN4 43 B4
Barcote CI SN5 50 C4
Bardsey CI SN4 68 C4
Barford La SP5 32 C3
Barford St Martin 18 A2
Barken Rd SN14 26 B2
Barkstead CI SN5 58 A3
Barley La, Malmesbury SN16 37 C5
Barley La, Warminster BA12 67 G4
Barley Leaze SN14 26 A1
Barlow CI SN25 51 F3

Barn CI, Chippenham SN14 26 B3
Barn CI, Corsham SN13 28 C2
Barn Glebe BA14 63 F5
Barn Moor CI SN3 61 H3
Barn Owl Rd SN14 26 C1
Barn Piece BA15 23 G5
Barn St SN8 39 E3
Barnaby CI SP5 32 A3
Barnack CI BA14 62 B5
Barnard CI SN3 57 E6
Barnard Gate 11 F1
Barnard St SN1 49 E2
Barnards Hill Dr SP2 45 H2
Barnes CI SN14 64 B1
Barnes PI BA12 36 B5
Barnes Rd SN14 26 C1
Barnes Wallis CI SN4 21 F3
Barnfield CI SN2 55 E5
Barnfield Rd SN2 54 D5
Barnfield SN8 39 G4
Barnsley 10 A2
Barnstaple CI SN3 60 D2
Barnum Ct SN2 55 F6
Barnwell Rd SN12 40 C2
Baroda Rd SP9 41 A4
Baron CI SN3 57 E1
Barons Mead SN14 26 B3
Barra CI SN6 34 B2
Barrett Way SN4 43 B5
Barrington CI SN3 61 G4
Barrington Rd SP1 47 F4
Barrow CI SN8 39 F3
Barrow Grn SN15 27 F1
Barrow Gurney 12 A2
Barrow Street 17 F2
Barrowby Gate SN3 56 D1
Barry Glen CI SN2 56 B3
Bartlett SP1 47 E4
Bartley 18 D5
Barton Farm Country Park SN13 22 C4
Barton La BA12 36 B5
Barton Orchard BA15 23 F3
Barton Rd SN25 54 D1
Barton St David 16 A1
Barton Stacey 15 F6
Barwick 16 A4
Bashkir Rd BA13 63 A5
Basil CI SN2 54 C1
Basil Hill Rd SN13 28 A4
Basingstoke 15 H4
Baskerville Hill SN16 37 C4
Baskerville Rd SN3 57 G6
Bassett 19 F4
Bassetts Pasture BA15 23 F5
Batcombe, Dorset 16 B6
Batcombe, Somerset 12 C6
Bath 12 D2
Bath Ct SN6 29 B2
Bath Rd Bsns Centre SN10 30 A4
Bath Rd Ind Est SN13 26 C5
Bath Rd, Bradford-on-Avon BA15 23 F1
Bath Rd, Chippenham SN14 26 A6
Bath Rd, Corsham SN13 28 A2
Bath Rd, Cricklade SN6 29 A2
Bath Rd, Devizes SN10 30 A4
Bath Rd, Marlborough SN8 38 A4
Bath Rd, Melksham SN12 40 A2
Bath Rd, Primrose Hill SN10 26 D5
Bath Rd, Swindon SN1 59 G3
Bath Rd, Warminster BA12 66 C1
Bath Stone Cres SN13 28 B3
Bathampton 13 E2
Bathampton St SN1 59 F1
Batheaston 13 E2
Bathford 13 E2
Batten Rd SP5 32 A2
Battle of Beranburgh 556 10 B6
Battle of Roundway Down 1643 13 H2
Battlesbury Camp BA12 13 G5
Battlesbury Rd BA12 67 H4
Baughurst 15 H3
Baulking 10 D4
Baunton 9 H2
Baverstock 17 H1
Bawdsey Rd SP4 21 E4
Baxter CI SN25 51 F4
Bay Tree Ct SN2 55 H3
Baybridge SN8 39 F3
Baydon 10 D6
Baydon CI, Swindon SN25 55 E1

Baydon CI, Trowbridge BA14 64 D2
Baydon Gro SN11 25 C2
Baydons La SN15 27 F4
Bayleaf Av SN2 50 C6
Baylie Acre SN8 39 E2
Bayliffes CI SN15 27 G3
Baywater SN8 39 E2
Bazaar Rd SP9 41 A4
Beach Ter SN11 25 C4
Beachley 8 A4
Beacon CI, Salisbury SP4 21 D1
Beacon CI, Swindon SN5 59 E2
Beacon Vw BA12 66 B4
Beagle CI SN25 50 A4
Beale CI SN14 26 B4
Beales Barton BA14 29 C4
Beamans La SN4 68 A4
Beamont Way SP4 21 E3
Beanacre 13 G2
Beanacre Rd SN12 40 A2
Bear CI BA15 23 E2
Bearfield Bldgs BA15 23 F1
Beatrice Rd SP1 46 D4
Beatrice St SN2 55 H5
Beatrice Way BA14 63 F6
Beau Clerc St SN10 30 B4
Beauchamp CI SN25 55 E1
Beauchamp Dr SP4 21 E2
Beaufort CI SN2 61 E2
Beaufort Rd SN4 43 B4
Beaulieu 19 E6
Beaulieu CI SN5 58 C3
Beaulieu Rd SP4 21 D3
Beaumaris Rd SN5 58 A2
Beaumont Rd SN3 60 B1
Beauworth 19 H2
Beavens Ct BA12 67 F3
Beckerley La SN14 29 C4
Becket St SP3 43 B2
Becket Way SN4 49 F1
Beckford CI BA14 67 E4
Beckhampton 14 A2
Beckhampton Rd SN8 20 A6
Beckington 13 E4
Beckitt PI BA13 63 A5
Beckley 11 H1
Beddington CI SN3 50 B6
Beddoe CI BA15 23 G5
Bedford Rd, Salisbury SP2 46 C6
Bedford Rd, Swindon SN3 56 B6
Bedminster 12 A1
Bedwin St SP1 49 E1
Bedwyn CI SN2 55 H2
Bedwyn Stone Museum SN8 14 D2
Beech Av, Melksham SN12 40 A4
Beech Av, Swindon SN6 55 F3
Beech Av, Warminster BA12 66 D4
Beech Gro, Swindon SN6 34 B3
Beech Gro, Trowbridge BA14 64 B2
Beech Gro, Westbury BA13 65 A3
Beech Hill Rd SP9 41 E2
Beech Lea SN26 51 H1
Beechcroft Rd, Salisbury SP1 49 G1
Beechcroft Rd, Swindon SN3 31 G2
Beechfield Dr SN10 31 G2
Beechfield Ho SN13 28 C1
Beechfield Rd SN13 28 D2
Beechgrove BA12 67 F2
Beechingstoke 14 A3
Beechwood Dr SN10 31 G2
Beechwood Rd SN14 26 C3
Beedon 11 G6
Beer Hackett 16 B5
Beeson CI SP2 48 C5
Belcombe PI BA15 23 E3
Belcombe Rd BA15 22 D3
Belfast Mead SN15 36 D2
Bell CI BA12 66 D5
Bell Gdns SN3 57 H1
Bell Heather CI BA14 62 D1
Bell La SP2 44 C4
Bell Orchard BA13 65 C2
Bell St SP11 35 E3
Bellamy La SP1 49 F1
Belle Vue Rd SP1 46 D6
Bellefield Cres BA14 63 E5
Bellevue Rd SN10 30 C3
Bellott Dr SN13 28 D3
Bellver SN5 58 B2
Belmont CI SN3 56 D1

Belmont Cres SN1 59 G4
Belsay SN5 58 B3
Belvedere Rd SN3 60 D3
Bembridge CI SN3 61 E2
Bemerton Heath 18 B1
Bences La SN13 28 E1
Benedict Mews SN23 50 B3
Bennett CI SP5 33 F4
Bennett Hill CI SN4 68 C4
Benson CI SN8 38 C4
Bentley CI SN3 60 D1
Bentley Gro SN3 25 C5
Bentley La SN11 25 C6
Benwell CI SN5 58 C1
Berenger CI SN3 60 A4
Beresford CI SN3 61 F3
Bergamot CI SN8 38 A5
Bergham CI SN25 51 G5
Berinsfield 11 H3
Berkeley 8 C3
Berkeley Lawns SN3 60 B4
Berkeley Rd, Swindon SN4 43 C4
Berkeley Rd, Trowbridge BA14 62 A6
Berkley 13 E5
Berkley CI, Chippenham SN14 26 A4
Berkley CI, Melksham SN12 40 B5
Berkshire Dr SN5 54 A6
Berkshire Grn SN12 40 C4
Berkshire Rd SP2 48 B3
Berrington Rd SN3 60 C4
Berryfield CI SN12 40 A6
Berryfield La SN12 40 A6
Berryfield Pk SN12 40 A6
Berryfield Rd BA15 23 F2
Berton CI SN26 51 H1
Berwick Bassett 14 A1
Berwick St James 14 A6
Berwick St John 17 G3
Berwick St Leonard 17 G1
Besomers Dro SP5 33 H6
Bessels Leigh 11 F2
Bessemer CI SN2 55 F4
Bessemer Rd East SN2 55 F4
Bessemer Rd West SN2 55 F4
Betcheman Ho SN15 27 F4
Bethel Ct BA15 23 E2
Bethel Rd BA13 28 C2
Betjeman Av SN4 68 B3
Betjeman Rd SN8 38 B4
Betony CI SN25 50 D6
Beuttell Way SN16 37 B2
Bevan CI SN2 56 C2
Beverley SN5 58 B3
Beverley Way SN14 26 A6
Beversbrook Ind Est SN11 25 C1
Beversbrook La SN11 25 B2
Beversbrook Rd SN11 25 A2
Beverston 9 F3
Beverstone Gro SN3 60 B3
Bevington 8 C3
Bevisland SN3 61 E4
Bewley Rd BA14 64 C3
Beyer Rd SP4 21 E4
Bibury 10 B1
Bibury Rd SN3 60 B2
Bickton 18 B5
Bicton Rd SN25 51 E5
Biddel Springs SN6 34 D3
Biddesden La SP11 35 F3
Biddestone 13 F1
Bideford CI SN3 60 C2
Bill Turpin Ct SN3 60 D3
Bilsborough Dr SN3 60 C2
Bincknoll La SN4 68 C4
Binegar 12 B5
Bingham Rd SP1 47 F4
Binley 15 F4
Birch Gdns BA14 63 H3
Birch Gro, Chippenham SN15 27 E2
Birch Gro, Melksham SN12 40 D6
Birch St SN1 59 F2
Birchwood Dr SP4 24 C1
Birchwood Rd SN3 56 D3
Birdbrook Rd SN2 52 B6
Birdcombe Rd SN5 58 B1
Birds Marsh Vw SN15 27 E1
Birkdale CI SN25 50 C3
Bishop Rd SN11 25 B3
Bishop Sutton 12 B3
Bishop's Caundle 16 C4
Bishop's Waltham 19 H4
Bishopdown Rd SP1 47 E5
Bishops Cannings 14 A2
Bishops CI, Tidworth SP9 41 D4
Bishops CI, Warminster BA12 36 B4

Bishops Dr SP2 48 C4
Bishops Mead SP1 47 H4
Bishops Walk SP1 48 D2
Bishopsfield SN6 29 A2
Bishopstoke 19 G3
Bishopstone Rd SP2 44 B6
Bishopstone, Swindon 10 D5
Bishopstone, Wiltshire 18 A3
Bishopstrow Rd BA12 67 H5
Bishopsworth 12 A2
Bisley 9 G1
Bisley CI SN3 60 C2
Biss Mdw BA14 62 A6
Bisterne Close 18 C6
Bitham La BA13 65 C2
Bitham Pk BA13 65 C1
Bittern Rd SN3 61 H1
Bitterne 19 G4
Bitton 12 C1
Black Acre SN13 28 C3
Black Bourton 10 D2
Blackberry La SN3 26 B1
Blackberry La SN10 42 A5
Blackbridge Rd SN15 27 G3
Blackcross Rd SP4 21 D3
Blackcross SN15 21 D3
Blackdown CI BA12 67 E2
Blackfield 19 F6
Blackfriars Way SP1 49 E2
Blackman Gdns SN3 60 A4
Blackmore CI SN3 57 G6
Blackmore Ct SN12 40 D3
Blackmore Rd SN12 40 C3
Blackstone Av SN3 61 F3
Blackthorn CI SN4 68 B2
Blackthorn La SN25 55 G1
Blackthorn Mews SN15 27 G6
Blackthorn Way BA14 62 D2
Blackwell Path SN8 38 D3
Blackwellhams Rd SN15 27 F6
Blackworth CI SN6 34 C1
Blackworth Ind Est SN6 34 C1
Bladen CI SN4 43 A5
Blagdon 12 A3
Blair Par SN25 55 F2
Blair Rd BA14 64 B1
Blake Cres SN3 57 E3
Blakeney 8 C1
Blakeney Av SN3 57 E6
Blakesley CI SN3 60 C3
Blakey Rd SP1 49 F2
Blandford Alley SN6 34 C2
Blandford Camp 17 G5
Blandford CI SN3 56 D6
Blandford Forum 17 F6
Blandford St Mary 17 F6
Blashford 18 B5
Blenheim CI BA12 66 C3
Blenheim CI SN4 68 C3
Blenheim Rd SN4 43 B5
Bletchley CI SN3 61 F3
Blewbury 11 H5
Blicks Hill SN16 37 C3
Blissford 18 C4
Blockley Rise SN3 52 C6
Bloomsbury CI SN5 58 A3
Blounts CI SN10 42 A6
Blowhorn St SN8 39 E3
Blue Boar Row SP1 48 D1
Bluebell Gro SN11 25 C2
Bluebell Mead SN13 28 C3
Blunsdon Hill SN26 51 F1
Blunsdon Rd SN25 51 E5
Blunsdon St Andrew 10 B4
Blyth Way SP1 47 F4
Boar St BA12 36 B5
Boars Hill 11 G2
Boatman CI SN25 50 A3
Bobbin La BA15 22 B5
Bobbin Pk BA15 22 B6
Bodenham 18 B2
Bodiam Dr North SN5 58 C2
Bodiam Dr SN5 58 C3
Bodiam Dr South SN5 58 C3
Bodmin CI SN3 61 F3
Boldrewood SN3 61 F3
Bolingbroke Rd SN25 55 E3
Bolts Cft SN5 27 F5
Bond St BA14 64 C1
Bond St Bldgs BA14 64 C1
Boness Rd SN4 43 B4
Bonners CI SN16 37 C2
Bonnewe Rise SP4 21 E3
Bonny Mead SP4 21 B3
Boot Hill BA12 66 D4
Boothmead SN14 26 C3
Borage CI SN2 50 C6
Bore Hill BA12 66 D6

Boreham Cl BA12 67 F4
Boreham Fld BA12 67 H4
Boreham Rd BA12 67 F4
Borough Flds
Shopping Centre SN4 68 A4
Borough Flds SN4 68 A4
Boscombe **14 C6**
Boscombe Down **14 B6**
Boscombe Down
Bsns Pk SP4 21 E1
Boscombe Down Rd
SP4 21 F4
Boscombe Down SP4 21 F4
Boscombe Rd SN2 54 D1
Bosham Cl SN5 58 B3
Boswell Rd BA15 22 B6
Bosworth Rd SN5 58 A1
Botany SN6 34 B4
Bothwell Rd SN3 56 C6
Botley Copse SN5 54 A3
Botley, Hampshire **19 G4**
Botley, Oxfordshire **11 G2**
Bouchers Way SP2 48 D5
Boughspring **8 A3**
Boulton Cl BA13 65 A4
Boundary Cl SN2 52 B5
Boundary Rd,
Chippenham SN15 27 G3
Boundary Rd,
Salisbury SP1 47 H6
Boundary Walk BA14 64 C3
Bourbon Cl BA12 67 E5
Bourne Av SP1 49 F1
Bourne, Cl,
Salisbury SP1 49 G2
Bourne Cl,
Warminster BA12 67 E5
Bourne Hill SP1 49 E1
Bourne Cl,
Swindon SN2 55 E2
Bourne Rd,
Tidworth SP9 41 E3
Bourne Way SP5 49 G3
Bournes Green **9 F2**
Bourton Av SN3 57 E3
Bourton, Dorset **16 D2**
Bourton,
Oxfordshire **10 C5**
Bouverie Av South SP2 48 C5
Bouverie Av,
Salisbury SP2 48 D4
Bouverie Av,
Swindon SN3 60 A4
Bouverie Cl SP2 48 C4
Bowden Cres SN12 40 C1
Bowden Hill **13 G2**
Bower Gdns SP1 49 F2
Bower Hill Rd SP1 47 F6
Bowerchalke **17 H3**
Bowers Hill SP5 33 G3
Bowers Rd SN25 51 F6
Bowleymead SN3 61 F1
Bowling Green La SN1 59 H4
Bowman Cl SN3 57 E2
Bowmans Ct SN12 40 C2
Bowood House SN11 13 H1
Bowood Rd SN1 59 F3
Box, Gloucestershire **9 F3**
Box, Wiltshire **13 E2**
Boxford **15 F1**
Boydell Cl SN5 54 B5
Boyton **13 G6**
Brabant Way BA13 65 A5
Bradbury Cl SN15 27 H6
Bradene Cl SN4 68 B4
Bradenstoke **9 H6**
Bradfield Cl BA12 67 G4
Bradford Abbas **16 B4**
Bradford Leigh **13 E2**
Bradford Rd,
Bradford-on-Avon
BA15 22 A3
Bradford Rd,
Corsham SN13 28 A3
Bradford Rd,
Melksham SN12 40 A3
Bradford Rd,
Swindon SN1 59 H3
Bradford Wood La
BA15 23 H3
Bradford-on-Avon **13 E3**
Bradford-on-Avon
Community Hospital
BA15 23 F1
Bradford-on-Avon
Museum BA15 23 F3
Bradford-on-Avon
Tithe Barn BA15 23 F4
Bradley Rd,
Trowbridge BA14 29 C5
Bradley Cl,
Warminster BA12 66 C5
Bradley La BA14 29 C5

Bradley Rd,
Swindon SN2 56 A1
Bradley Rd,
Trowbridge BA14 64 D1
Warminster BA12 66 B6
Bradshaw Ct SN25 50 C5
Bradwell Grove **10 C1**
Bradwell Moor SN3 61 G5
Braemar Cl SN3 60 C4
Braemar Rise SP1 47 E4
Braemor Rd SN11 25 A3
Braishfield **19 E2**
Brake Mead SN15 27 F4
Brakspear Dr SN13 28 D3
Bramble Cl SN2 56 B4
Bramble Dr BA13 65 B1
Bramble Ho SN25 50 B5
Bramble Rd SN2 56 B3
Bramdean Cl SN25 51 E5
Bramley Cl,
Pewsey SN9 42 C1
Bramley Cl,
Warminster BA12 66 D2
Bramley Furlong*,
Castle St BA12 36 B5
Bramley Hill BA12 36 A5
Bramley La BA14 64 D1
Bramley Mews SN13 65 B2
Bramley Way SP4 21 D2
Bramshaw **18 D4**
Bramwell Cl SN2 52 B5
Branders SN6 29 B2
Brandon Cl SN5 58 A2
Branksome Rd SN25 54 D2
Branscombe Dr SN4 68 B3
Bratton **13 G4**
Bratton Av SN10 52 C4
Bratton Castle BA13 13 F4
Bratton Cl SN2 51 G6
Bratton Rd BA13 65 C3
Bratton Seymour **16 C2**
Bray St SN8 20 A4
Braydon Ct SN2 51 H6
Bread St BA12 66 D5
Breadstone **8 D2**
Bream **8 B2**
Bream Cl, Calne SN11 25 B2
Bream Cl,
Melksham SN12 40 D2
Breamore **18 B4**
Breamore Rd SP5 32 A5
Brecon Cl,
Melksham SN12 40 D3
Brecon Cl,
Swindon SN3 60 B4
Bremeridge Rd BA13 65 D2
Bremhill **13 H1**
Bremhill Cl SN2 51 H6
Bremhill Vw SN11 25 B3
Bremilham Rd SN16 37 B3
Bremilham Rise SN16 37 A4
Brendon Walk SN3 61 E1
Breton Rd BA13 65 A4
Brewer Mead SN15 27 G6
Brewers La SN11 25 C6
Brewery St SN6 34 C4
Brewham **16 D1**
Briar Cl BA13 65 B2
Briar Flds SN1 56 B5
Briars Cl SN4 68 B2
Briarswood Ct SN3 61 G4
Brick La SP2 46 A6
Brickham Rd SN10 31 F3
Brickley La SN10 31 E4
Bricksteed Av SN10 31 E4
Bridewell St,
Devizes SN10 30 D5
Bridewell St,
Marlborough SN8 38 A4
Bridge Av BA14 62 A6
Bridge Chapel BA15 23 F3
Bridge Ct BA13 65 A2
Bridge End Rd SN2 56 C4
Bridge St*,
Taylors Row BA15 23 F3
Bridge St,
Marlborough SN8 38 A4
Bridge St,
Salisbury SP1 48 D1
Bridge Yate **12 C1**
Bridgeman Cl SN3 57 E2
Bridgemary **19 H6**
Bridgemead Cl SN5 54 C6
Bridgewater Cl SN2 55 F5
Bridport Rd SN3 60 D2
Briery Cl SN13 56 C1
Bright Cl SN15 27 G6
Bright St SN2 56 A5
Brighthampton **11 E2**
Brighton Way SN14 26 A5
Brightwalton **11 F6**
Brimble Hill SN4 43 D6
Brimpsfield **9 G1**

Brimpton **15 H2**
Brind Cl SN3 57 G6
Brindley Cl SN2 54 D4
Brington Rd SN3 57 E5
Brinkworth **9 H5**
Brinkworth Cl SN14 26 A1
Brislington **12 B1**
Bristol **12 B1**
Bristol Rd SN14 26 A1
Bristol St,
Malmesbury SN16 37 B4
Bristol St,
Swindon SN1 59 F1
Britannia Cres SN15 36 C2
Britannia Pl SN1 60 A3
Britannia Trade Pk SN3 56 C2
Britford **18 B2**
Britford La SP2 49 E4
Britford La West SP2 48 D4
British Row BA14 62 D5
Brittain Cl SN14 26 A4
Britten Rd SN25 50 D3
Brixham Av SN3 60 B2
Brixton Deverill **13 F6**
Brize Norton **10 D1**
Broad Blunsdon **10 B4**
Broad Chalke **17 H2**
Broad Hinton **10 A6**
Broad Layings **15 F2**
Broad Oak **10 A6**
Broad Town **10 A6**
Broad Walk SP1 48 D2
Broadcloth La BA14 64 E1
Broadcloth La East
BA14 64 F1
Broadfields SN9 42 A2
Broadlands Cl SP1 47 E4
Broadleas Cl SN10 30 D6
Broadleas Cres SN10 30 D6
Broadleas Gdns SN10 30 C6
Broadleas Rd SN10 30 D6
Broadley Pk BA14 64 D4
Broadmead Walk SN3 57 E6
Broadmead,
Corsham SN13 28 F4
Broadmead,
Trowbridge BA14 62 A4
Broadmoor Rd SN3 53 F4
Broadway,
Swindon SN25 55 F2
Broadway,
Warminster BA12 66 C4
Broadwell,
Gloucestershire **8 B1**
Broadwell,
Oxfordshire **10 D2**
Broadwood Cl BA12 66 D2
Brockenhurst **18 D6**
Brockweir **8 A2**
Brockwood BA15 22 B2
Broken Cross SN11 25 C4
Brokenborough **9 G4**
Bromham **13 H2**
Bromley Cl SN3 60 B1
Bronte Cl SN3 61 F3
Brook Cl, Salisbury SP3 43 B3
Brook Cl,
Warminster BA12 66 D5
Brook Dr SN13 28 F4
Brook Rd BA14 62 A6
Brook St,
Chippenham SN14 26 C3
Brook St,
Warminster BA12 66 C4
Brook,
Hampshire, SO20 **19 E2**
Brook,
Hampshire, SO43 **18 D4**
Brookdene SN25 50 B6
Brooke Cres SN25 50 B6
Brooke Pl SN4 68 C2
Brookfield SN6 34 C2
Brooklands Av SN3 55 F3
Brooklands SN4 68 B6
Brooklime Cl SN2 50 C6
Brookmead BA14 64 A4
Brooks Cl SN2 52 B6
Brooksby Way SN3 57 E4
Brookside,
Melksham SN12 40 C3
Brookside,
Swindon SN3 55 H3
Brookway SN11 25 D4
Brookwell Cl SN14 26 D1
Broom Hill **17 H6**
Broomcroft Rd SN9 42 B1
Broome Manor
Golf Complex SN3 60 B6
Broome Manor La SN3 60 B5
Broomfield SN15 27 E1
Broomground BA15 22 B2
Brotherton CI SN15 27 G6
Broughton **19 E1**
Broughton Gifford **13 F2**

Broughton Grange SN3 60 C3
Broughton Poggs **10 C2**
Broughton Rd BA14 64 C3
Brown Candover **15 H6**
Brown St SP1 49 E1
Browning Cl SN3 61 E1
Brownleaze La SN10 42 A5
Broxburn Rd BA12 66 B4
Bruce St SN2 55 E6
Bruddel Gro SN3 60 B5
Bruges St SN15 27 G4
Bruton **16 C1**
Bryans Close Rd SN11 25 C4
Bryanston **17 F6**
Bryanston Way SN3 61 E1
Bryant St SN25 50 C6
Brydges Rd SP11 35 C3
Brynards Hill SN4 68 B5
Bryony Way SN2 50 C6
Buckhorn Weston **16 D2**
Buckhurst Cres SN3 60 C1
Buckingham Rd,
Chippenham SN15 27 H6
Buckingham Rd,
Swindon SN3 60 C4
Buckland **11 E3**
Buckland Cl SN3 60 D1
Buckland Ct SP4 21 C3
Buckland Dinham **12 D4**
Buckland Newton **16 C6**
Buckleaze Cl BA14 64 E2
Buckleaze La SN9 42 B1
Bucklebury **15 H1**
Bucklebury Cl SN3 56 D4
Buckthorn Dr SN25 54 D1
Buckthorn Row SN3 28 C3
Budbury Circle BA15 23 E2
Budbury Cl BA15 23 E2
Budbury Pl BA15 23 E2
Budbury Ridge BA15 23 E2
Budbury Tyning BA15 23 E2
Budd St SN11 25 B2
Bude Rd SN2 59 E1
Buie Cl SN5 54 B3
Bulbridge Rd SP2 44 B5
Bulford **14 B6**
Bulford Camp **14 B6**
Bulford Camp Kiwi SP4 14 C5
Bulford Droveway SP4 24 C2
Bulford SP4 24 C2
Bulford Rd, Bulford SP4 24 F2
Bulford Rd,
Durrington SP4 24 C1
Bulkington **13 G3**
Bull Pit BA15 23 F3
Buller St SN2 56 A4
Bullfinch Cl SN3 61 G1
Bumpers Ent Centre
SN14 26 A3
Bumpers Fm Ind Est
SN14 26 B2
Bumpers Way SN14 26 A3
Bunce Rd SN3 56 D3
Burbage **14 C3**
Burbage Rd SN2 51 H5
Burcombe **18 A2**
Burcombe La SP2 44 A4
Burcot **11 H3**
Burcot Cl SN3 50 B4
Burden Cl SN3 57 E4
Burderop Cl,
Swindon SN4 43 C4
Burderop Cl,
Trowbridge BA14 64 D3
Burford Av,
Salisbury SP2 49 E4
Burford Av,
Swindon SN3 60 A2
Burford La SP2 49 E4
Burford Rd SP2 49 E4
Burgess Cl SN3 56 D4
Burgess Grn SP1 47 F4
Burghclere **15 G3**
Burghley Cl SN3 60 C1
Burlands Rd SN15 27 F5
Burleaze SN15 26 D6
Burley **18 C6**
Burley Street **18 C6**
Burlington Pl SN13 28 B3
Burn Rd SN13 28 C2
Burnet Cl,
Melksham SN12 40 C5
Burnet Cl,
Swindon SN2 50 C6
Burnett **12 C2**

Burnett Rd BA14 64 D2
Burnett Way SP1 47 G4
Burnham Rd,
Malmesbury SN16 37 B3
Burnham Rd,
Swindon SN3 60 D1
Burniston Cl SN12 40 D2
Burnivale SN16 37 B4
Burns Way SN2 52 B6
Burridge **19 G5**
Bursledon **19 G5**
Burton **9 E6**
Burwood Cl SP4 21 F3
Burytown La SN26 51 H1
Buscot **10 C3**
Buscot Cl SN25 51 E4
Bushton **10 A6**
Butcher Row SP1 48 D1
Butcombe **12 A3**
Bute Cl SN6 34 B2
Butleigh **16 A1**
Butleigh Rd SN25 50 B3
Butleigh Wootton **16 A1**
Butler Cl SP2 49 E4
Butlers Ct BA12 66 C5
Butt Cl SP11 35 C2
Butt St SP11 35 C2
Butterfield Dr SP4 21 E2
Buttermere **15 E3**
Buttermere SN3 61 G3
Butterworth St SN1 59 F1
Buttons Yd BA12 67 F3
Butts Rd SP1 46 D5
Buzzard Rd SN11 25 B2
Bydemill Gdns SN6 34 B3
Byfield Way SN3 56 D5
Byre Cl SN6 29 B3
Byron Av SN4 68 B3
Byron Cl SP11 35 C2
Byron Ct SN3 53 H6
Byron Ho SN14 26 B3
Bythebrook SN14 26 B2
Byways SP1 49 F2

C

Cabul Rd SP9 41 B4
Cadby Cl BA14 63 G6
Caddy La BA12 36 A5
Cadley **14 C2**
Cadley Cl SN10 55 H2
Cadnam **18 D4**
Caen Cres SP4 21 F3
Caen Flight SN10 30 A4
Caen Vw SN5 59 E2
Caenhill Gdns SN10 30 A4
Caernarvon Walk SN3 60 C4
Cagney Dr SN25 51 F5
Caird Lawns SN10 31 F6
Cairndow Way SN2 52 B5
Calcutt Ct SN6 29 C2
Calcutt St SN6 29 C2
Calder Cl SN25 51 E6
Callaghan Cl SN3 56 D3
Callenders SN5 54 A3
Callington Rd SN25 50 B5
Callow Hill **9 H5**
Calmore **19 E4**
Calmsden **10 A1**
Calne **13 H1**
Calne Ho SN3 60 D2
Calne Road SN15 36 B1
Calshot **19 G6**
Calstock Rd SN25 50 C4
Calstone Wellington **13 H2**
Calvert Rd SN3 60 B1
Calypso Walk SN25 50 D4
Cam **8 D3**
Cambria Bridge Rd SN1 59 F1
Cambria Cl SN1 59 F2
Cambria Pl SN1 59 F2
Cambridge **8 D2**
Cambridge Cl SN3 60 C3
Cambridge Rd SP1 47 E5
Camelia Dr BA12 66 D3
Cameron Cl SN3 56 C4
Camerton **12 C5**
Camilla Cl SP4 24 D3
Camomile Dr SP11 35 D3
Campbell Rd SP1 47 E6
Campden Rd SN3 60 B2
Campion Cl,
Calne SN11 25 C2
Campion Cl,
Westbury BA13 65 C1
Campion Dr,
Melksham SN12 40 C5
Campion Dr,
Trowbridge BA14 64 E2
Canada **18 D4**
Canadian Av SP4 46 B6
Canal Cl SN11 25 B5
Canal Rd Ind Est BA14 62 D2

Canal Rd, Chippenham SN15 27 F6
Canal Rd, Trowbridge BA14 62 D3
Canal Way SN10 31 G2
Canbury Cl SP4 21 F3
Canford Cl SN3 61 E1
Cann 17 F3
Cann Common 17 F3
Cannimore Cl BA12 66 C5
Cannimore Rd BA12 66 A6
Canon Sq SN12 40 B3
Canons Cl, Tidworth SP9 41 D4
Canons Cl, Warminster BA12 67 G4
Canons Ct SN12 40 B3
Cantelo Cl SN25 51 E3
Canterbury Cl SN3 60 C4
Canterbury St SN14 26 D3
Capella Cres SN25 50 B4
Capesthorne Dr SN25 50 D5
Capitol Cl SN3 57 F4
Capulet Rd SP1 46 C4
Caradon Walk SN25 50 B4
Caraway Dr SN2 54 C1
Carders Cnr BA14 64 E1
Cardigan Cl SN3 60 B3
Cardigan Rd SN8 38 D3
Cardwell Cl SN3 57 E6
Carey Cl SN5 58 A2
Carisbrook Rd SN12 40 B5
Carisbrooke Cres BA14 63 E1
Carleton Cl SP4 21 E2
Carleton Pl SP4 21 C2
Carlingcott 12 C3
Carlisle Av SN3 60 A4
Carlton Gate SN3 60 C6
Carlton Row BA14 64 D2
Carman Cl SN3 57 E2
Carmel Walk SN3 60 C2
Carmelite Way SP1 49 E3
Carnarvon Cl SN14 26 B4
Carnegie Mews SN11 25 C4
Carnegie Rd SN11 25 D3
Carp Rd SN11 25 B2
Carpenter Cl SN15 27 G6
Carpenter Dr SP4 21 E2
Carpenters Cl SN11 25 A3
Carpenters La SN2 56 A5
Carrick Cl SN15 27 G3
Carrington Gdns SN4 68 B2
Carrion Pond Dro SP2 48 B4
Carroll Cl SN3 61 F3
Carronbridge Rd SN5 58 B1
Carshalton Rd SN3 61 E4
Carstairs Av SN3 60 D3
Carswell Marsh 11 E3
Carter Cl SN25 51 H4
Carter's Clay 18 D3
Carterton 10 D1
Cartwright Dr SN5 54 A5
Cashmoor 17 H4
Cassington 11 F1
Cassini Dr SN25 50 A4
Casson Rd SN3 56 D3
Castell Cl BA14 63 H5
Casterbridge Rd SN25 50 C6
Castilian Mews SN5 54 A6
Castle Cary 16 C1
Castle Combe 9 E6
Castle Combe Museum SN14 9 F6
Castle Ct, Andover SP11 35 C2
Castle Ct, Devizes SN10 30 D4
Castle Dore SN5 58 A2
Castle Eaton 10 B3
Castle Hill App BA12 36 B5
Castle Hill Cres BA12 36 B4
Castle Hill La BA12 36 B5
Castle Keep SP1 46 C4
Castle La, Devizes SN10 30 D4
Castle La, Salisbury SP2 44 D3
Castle Mdws SP5 32 C3
Castle Mt SP3 43 B3
Castle Rd, Devizes SN10 30 D4
Castle Rd, Salisbury SP1 46 D2
Castle St, Andover SP11 35 C2
Castle St, Calne SN11 25 B4
Castle St, Marlborough SN8 20 B2
Castle St, Salisbury SP1 46 D6
Castle St, Warminster BA12 36 B5
Castle Vw BA13 65 D2
Castle Walk SN11 25 B4
Castle Woods SP5 33 F4
Castlefield Cl SN5 58 B1
Castlefields SN11 25 B4
Castlegate Bsns Pk SP4 47 E1
Castlehaven Cl SN15 27 H6
Castleview Rd SN3 57 E4
Castley Rd BA14 63 G4
Catbrain 8 B6
Catherine Cres SP5 32 A3
Catherine St SP1 49 E2
Catherine Wayte Cl SN25 55 E1
Catmint Cl SN2 54 C1
Catmore 11 G6
Catterick Cl SN14 26 A6
Caulfield Rd SN2 56 A5
Causeway Cl SN15 27 F4
Cavalier Ct SN14 26 A3
Cavendish Dr BA14 64 A2
Cavendish Sq SN3 60 D3
Caversham Cl SN3 60 C2
Cawte Mews SN3 56 D1
Caxton Cl SN3 60 C3
Caxton Ct*, Caxton Cl SN3 60 C3
Cayenne Pk SN2 54 B1
Cecil Av SP2 48 D4
Cecil Rd SN3 56 D6
Cecil Ter SP2 48 A1
Cedar Cl, Melksham SN12 40 A4
Cedar Cl, Salisbury SP2 45 H2
Cedar Ct BA15 23 F1
Cedar Gro, Chippenham SN15 27 E1
Cedar Gro, Trowbridge BA14 64 C2
Cedar Gro, Westbury BA13 65 A3
Cedars Cl SN2 55 F2
Celandine Way SN14 26 B1
Cemetery La BA15 23 H2
Central St SP11 35 D3
Centurian Way SN3 57 F4
Centurion Cl, Chippenham SN15 27 H6
Centurion Cl, Salisbury SP2 46 A5
Century Cl SN10 31 G5
Cepen Bsns Pk SN14 26 A3
Cerne Abbas 16 C6
Cerney Wick 10 A3
Chaddleworth 11 F6
Chaffinch Dr BA14 62 B6
Chain Ct SN1 59 G3
Chain La BA12 67 F4
Chalbury Common 17 H6
Chalfield Cl BA12 66 D1
Chalfield Cres SN12 40 C2
Chalfont Cl BA14 62 A5
Chalford 9 F2
Chalford Av SN3 57 E6
Chalford Gdns BA13 65 B5
Chalk Down SP9 41 E2
Chalks Cl SP5 33 F3
Challeymead Bsns Pk SN12 40 A3
Challis Ct SP11 35 E3
Chalvedon Grn*, Bilborough Dr SN3 60 C2
Chamberlain Rd, Chippenham SN14 26 A3
Chamberlain Rd, Swindon SN3 56 D3
Chambers Av SP4 21 D4
Chancery Cl SP2 46 B6
Chancery La BA12 67 F4
Chandler Cl SN10 31 F4
Chandler's Ford 19 F3
Chandlers La SN8 20 C1
Chandos Cl SN5 58 A1
Chantry 12 D5
Chantry Ct SN10 30 D4
Chantry Gdns BA14 64 A4
Chantry La, Marlborough SN8 38 D4
Chantry La, Westbury BA13 65 C3
Chantry Mews BA12 67 E3
Chantry Rd, Salisbury SP2 44 C5
Chantry Rd, Swindon SN2 55 E2
Chantry Vw SP3 43 B2
Chapel Cl SN12 40 D2
Chapel Hill 8 A2
Chapel Hill SN26 51 G1
Chapel La, Chippenham SN15 27 E4
Chapel La, Ludgershall SP11 35 C3
Chapel Plaister SN13 13 F2
Chapel Rd, Salisbury SP5 33 G4
Chapel Rd, Swindon SN3 53 H6
Chapel Row 15 H1
Chapel St, Swindon SN2 56 A4
Chapel St, Warminster BA12 66 D5
Chapmanslade 13 E5
Charfield 8 D4
Charfield Cl SN3 60 C3
Charlbury Cl SN25 55 E2
Charlcombe 12 D2
Charles McPhearson Gdns SN3 61 F2
Charles Morrison Cl SN10 30 D5
Charles Rd SP4 24 B1
Charles St, Corsham SN13 28 D2
Charles St, Salisbury SP2 46 C6
Charles St, Trowbridge BA14 62 C4
Charlock Path SN25 50 C5
Charlotte Ct, Calne SN11 25 C3
Charlotte Ct, Trowbridge BA14 62 D5
Charlotte Mews SN1 60 A3
Charlotte Sq BA14 62 D4
Charlotte St BA14 62 D5
Charlton Adam 16 A2
Charlton Cl SN2 52 A6
Charlton Horethorne 16 C3
Charlton Mackrell 16 A2
Charlton Marshall 17 F6
Charlton Musgrove 16 D2
Charlton, Hampshire 15 E5
Charlton, Wiltshire, SN16 9 G4
Charlton, Wiltshire, SN9 14 A4
Charlton, Wiltshire, SP7 17 G3
Charlton-All-Saints 18 C3
Charlwood Rd SN13 28 D3
Charminster Cl SN3 61 E1
Charney Bassett 11 E3
Charnwood Rd, Salisbury SP2 48 B1
Charnwood Rd, Trowbridge BA14 62 A5
Charolais Dr SN5 54 A6
Charter Cl SN10 31 F3
Charter Rd SN15 27 E4
Charterhouse Cl SN4 43 B5
Charterville Allotments 11 E1
Chartwell Rd SN25 51 E4
Chastleton Rd SN25 50 D4
Chatham Cl SP1 46 C4
Chatham Ct BA12 67 F3
Chatsworth Rd SN25 51 E5
Chaucer Cl SN4 68 B3
Chaveywell Ct SN11 25 B5
Cheddar Rd SN25 54 D2
Chedworth Gate SN3 60 C6
Chelmsford Rd SN5 54 B6
Cheltenham Dr SN14 26 B6
Chelwood 12 B3
Chelwood Cl SN14 26 C5
Chelwood Ct BA12 67 F4
Chelworth Cl SN25 54 D2
Chelworth Rd SN6 29 A3
Cheney Manor Ind Est SN2 54 D4
Cheney Manor Rd SN2 55 F2
Cheney Pl SN2 55 E3
Chepston Pl BA14 62 A5
Chepstow Cl, Chippenham SN14 26 B6
Chepstow Cl, Swindon SN5 58 C3
Cheraton Cl SN3 57 E6
Cherhill 13 H1
Cherhill Ct SN25 55 E1
Cherington 9 G3
Cheriton 19 H2
Cherry Cl, Pewsey SN9 42 C1
Cherry Cl, Salisbury SP2 46 B6
Cherry Gdns Ct BA14 64 E1
Cherry Gdns, Hilperton BA14 63 G3
Cherry Gdns, Trowbridge BA14 64 E1
Cherry Orchard La SP2 48 A1
Cherry Orchard, Marlborough SN8 39 E5
Cherry Orchard, Swindon SN6 34 C3
Cherry Tree Av SP9 41 E2
Cherry Tree Ct SN11 25 B3
Cherry Tree Gro SN2 55 H2
Cherry Tree Rd SN6 29 A2
Cherrytree Way SP4 21 D2
Chervil Cl SN2 54 C1
Chesford Cl SN3 60 D4
Cheshire Cl SP2 46 A4
Chester St SN1 59 G1
Chester Way SN14 26 B6
Chesterblade 12 C6
Chesterfield Cl, Salisbury SP4 21 F2
Chesterfield Cl, Swindon SN5 58 B1
Chestnut Av, Swindon SN2 55 H2
Chestnut Av, Tidworth SP9 41 E2
Chestnut Cl SP1 47 G5
Chestnut Cnr BA14 29 C5
Chestnut Dr SN8 39 E4
Chestnut Grange SN13 28 C2
Chestnut Gro, Bradford-on-Avon BA15 22 B5
Chestnut Gro, Trowbridge BA14 64 C2
Chestnut Gro, Westbury BA13 65 A3
Chestnut Mews SN12 40 A4
Chestnut Rd SN14 26 C3
Chetnole 16 B5
Chettle 17 G4
Cheverell Av SP1 47 F5
Cheverell Cl BA14 64 E3
Cheviot Cl, Swindon SN5 58 A1
Cheviot Cl, Trowbridge BA14 63 E6
Chew Magna 12 A2
Chew Stoke 12 A3
Chewton Mendip 12 B4
Cheyney Walk BA13 65 D2
Chichester Cl SP2 49 E4
Chichester Pk BA13 65 B2
Chickerell Rd SN3 60 D1
Chicklade 17 F1
Chicksgrove 17 G2
Chicksgrove Rd SP3 43 D1
Chicory Cl SN2 54 B1
Chieveley 15 G1
Chilbolton 15 F6
Chilcomb 19 G2
Chilcompton 12 B4
Child Okeford 17 E4
Childrey 11 E5
Chilmark 17 G1
Chilmark Rd, Salisbury SP3 43 D1
Chilmark Rd, Trowbridge BA14 62 A5
Chiltern Cl, Melksham SN12 40 D3
Chiltern Cl, Warminster BA12 67 E2
Chilthorne Domer 16 A4
Chilton 11 G5
Chilton Cantelo 16 A3
Chilton Foliat 15 E1
Chilton Gdns SN25 55 E2
Chilvester Hill SN11 25 A4
Chilworth 19 F4
Chilworth Cl SN25 50 D5
Chimney 11 E2
Chinns Ct BA12 67 E3
Chippenham 13 G1
Chippenham Cl SN25 51 G5
Chippenham Community Hospital SN15 26 D5
Chippenham Golf Club SN15 9 F6
Chippenham Museum SN15 27 E4
Chippenham Rd SN16 37 C6
Chippenham Walk SN2 51 G5
Chipper La SP1 48 D1
Chipping Sodbury 8 D5
Chirton Pl BA14 64 E2
Chisbury 14 D2
Chisbury Chapel SN8 14 D2
Chiselbury Gro SP2 48 D4
Chiseldon 10 B6
Chiselhampton 11 H3
Chissell Brook SN11 25 C3
Chitterne 13 H5
Chittoe 13 G2
Chivers Rd SN15 27 F6
Chives Way SN2 54 C1
Chobham Cl SN3 52 D6
Cholderton 14 C6
Cholderton Rare Breeds Farm Park SP4 14 C6
Cholderton YHA SP4 14 C6
Cholsey 11 H5
Chopin Mews SN25 50 D4
Chopping Knife La SN8 39 G4
Choristers Sq SP1 48 D2
Christchurch Rd BA15 23 F1
Christchurch Ter BA12 66 D4
Christian Malford 9 G6
Christie Cl SN3 61 F3
Christie Miller Rd SP2 46 B6
Christin Ct BA14 62 A6
Christopher Cl SP2 48 C5
Chubb Cl SN16 37 B2
Chudleigh SN5 58 A3
Church Acre BA15 23 F2
Church End 9 H6
Church Farm La SN3 53 H6
Church Farm Mews SN15 36 B1
Church Flds BA14 64 A2
Church Gate SP11 35 C3
Church Ground SN3 53 H6
Church Hatch SP5 32 C3
Church Hill Cl SN4 68 C3
Church Hill, Salisbury SP5 33 H5
Church Hill, Swindon SN4 43 A6
Church La, Amesbury SP4 21 B2
Church La, Bemerton SP2 46 A6
Church La, Britford SP5 49 G5
Church La, Bulford SP4 24 D2
Church La, Chippenham SN15 36 C2
Church La, Cricklade SN6 29 B2
Church La, Ludgershall SP11 35 C3
Church La, Melksham SN12 40 C1
Church La, Tidworth SP9 41 D4
Church La, Trowbridge BA14 64 A2
Church La, Warminster BA12 36 B5
Church La, Westbury BA13 65 C2
Church La, Westbury Leigh BA13 65 A5
Church Pl SN1 59 F1
Church Rd SP1 47 G6
Church St, Amesbury SP4 21 B3
Church St, Bradford-on-Avon BA15 23 F3
Church St, Calne SN11 25 C4
Church St, Corsham SN13 28 F2
Church St, Hilperton BA14 63 G3
Church St, Lyneham BA12 36 B5
Church St, Melksham SN12 40 B3
Church St, Pewsey SN9 42 B2
Church St, Swindon SN3 57 E2
Church St, Tisbury SP3 43 B3
Church St, Trowbridge BA14 64 A4
Church St, Warminster BA12 66 D2
Church St, Westbury BA13 65 C3
Church Street Cl SP3 43 B3
Church Vw, Chippenham SN14 26 D1
Church Vw, Swindon SN6 34 C3
Church Walk North SN25 55 E1
Church Walk South SN2 55 E2
Church Walk, Devizes SN10 31 E4
Church Walk, Marlborough SN8 20 B4
Church Walk, Melksham SN12 40 B3
Church Walk, Upper Stratton SN2 56 B2
Church Way SN3 57 E2
Church Yd SN10 30 D5
Churches BA15 23 E2
Churchfield SN25 55 E1
Churchfields Rd SP2 48 B1
Churchill Av, Melksham SN12 40 D2
Churchill Av, Salisbury SP4 24 E3
Churchill Av, Swindon SN26 51 H1
Churchill Cl, Calne SN11 25 C6

Churchill Cl, Salisbury SP3 43 B2
Churchill Cl, Tidworth SP9 41 B1
Churchill Ct SP2 44 D3
Churchill Est SP3 43 B2
Churchill Way East SP1 49 E1
Churchill Way SN13 28 E1
Churchill Way South SP1 49 E3
Churchward Av SN2 55 F3
Churchward Pk SN5 58 D2
Churchway SN26 51 H1
Cineworld Cinema SN3 56 C5
Cirencester 9 H2
Cirencester Rd, Cricklade SN6 29 B1
Cirencester Rd, Malmesbury SN16 37 D2
Cirencester Way SN2 56 A3
Clandown 12 C4
Clanfield 10 D2
Clanfield Rd SN3 61 E2
Clanville 15 E5
Clapgate 17 H6
Clare Walk SN5 58 B3
Clarence Cl SP11 35 C3
Clarence Rd, Chippenham SN14 26 A4
Clarence Rd, Trowbridge BA14 63 F6
Clarendon Av BA14 63 E6
Clarendon Dr SN4 68 B4
Clarendon La SN1 59 F2
Clarendon Rd, Salisbury SP1 49 F1
Clarendon Rd, Trowbridge BA14 63 E6
Claridge Cl SN8 20 C2
Clark Av SN11 25 C2
Clarke Dr SN5 54 A5
Clary Rd SN2 50 C6
Claverton 12 D2
Claydon Rd SN25 51 E4
Claypole Mead SN15 27 F6
Clays Cl SN2 56 B1
Clayton Rd SP4 24 E3
Clearwell 8 A1
Cleasby Cl SN5 58 C1
Cleeve Lawns SN3 60 C4
Cleevedale Rd SN13 28 E4
Clementine Rd SN25 50 A4
Clements La BA12 36 C6
Clench Common 14 C2
Clevancy 10 A6
Clevedon Cl SN3 60 D1
Cleveland Gdns BA14 63 E4
Cleveland Way BA13 65 A4
Cleverton 9 H5
Cleverton Ct SN2 51 H5
Clews La BA12 36 C4
Cley Hill BA12 13 F5
Cley Vw BA12 66 C4
Cliffords SN6 29 A2
Clift Av SN15 27 F2
Clifton 12 B1
Clifton Cl SN14 26 C3
Clifton Hampden 11 H3
Clifton Rd SP2 46 C6
Clipsham Rise BA14 62 B5
Cloche Way SN2 56 B1
Cloford Cl BA14 62 B5
Cloudberry Rd SN25 50 D5
Clouts Wood SN5 54 A3
Clover Cl SN12 40 C5
Clover Dean SN14 26 B5
Clover Gdns SP11 35 D3
Clover Pk SN25 54 D1
Cloverlands SN25 50 D6
Club La SP9 41 C4
Clutton 12 B3
Clydesdale Cl, Swindon SN5 54 A6
Clydesdale Cl, Trowbridge BA14 64 D3
Clyffe Pypard 10 A6
Coach Ho Mews SP4 21 C3
Coach House Ct SN25 50 C4
Coaley 8 D2
Coalpit Heath 8 C6
Coalway 8 B1
Coate 14 A3
Coate La SN10 31 G2
Coate Water Country Park SN3 60 D6
Coates 9 H2
Coatside Way SN3 61 G6
Cobbett Cl SN25 51 F4
Cobbett Pl BA12 66 D3
Cobden Rd SN2 55 F5
Cobham Centre SN5 54 C6
Cock Hill BA14 62 B4
Cock Hill House Ct BA14 62 B5
Cocklebury La SN15 27 F1
Cocklebury Rd SN15 27 E3
Codford St Mary 13 H6
Codford St Peter 13 G6
Codrington 8 D6
Colbert Pk SN25 51 E5
Colborne Cl SN15 27 H6
Colborne St SN1 56 A5
Colchester Cl SN5 58 C3
Cold Ash 15 H1
Cold Ashton 12 D1
Cold Harbour La BA12 66 C2
Cold Harbour SP4 21 C2
Colden Common 19 G3
Coldharbour La, Marlborough SN8 39 E3
Coldharbour La, Salisbury SP2 46 C6
Cole 16 C1
Cole Cl SN3 57 G6
Colebrook Rd SN3 56 D4
Coleford, Gloucestershire 8 A1
Coleford, Somerset 12 C5
Colehill 17 H6
Colemans Cl SN11 25 C4
Coleridge Cl, Swindon SN4 68 B3
Coleridge Cl, Warminster BA12 66 B4
Coleridge Rd SN25 51 E5
Colerne 13 E1
Colerne Airport SN14 13 E1
Coleshill 10 C3
College Cl SN15 27 G3
College Flds SN8 38 B4
College Rd BA14 64 B2
College St SP1 46 D6
Collen Cl SN14 26 B4
Collett Av SN2 55 F4
Collingbourne Cl BA14 64 E3
Collingbourne Ducis 14 C4
Collingbourne Kingston 14 C4
Collingsmead SN3 61 F2
Collins Ct SP9 41 C1
Collis Ter SP11 35 D2
Colman Pk SN25 51 F5
Coln Cres SN25 51 F6
Coln Rogers 10 A1
Coln St Aldwyns 10 B1
Coln St Dennis 10 A1
Colston Cl SN3 60 C2
Colston Rd SN10 30 C3
Coltsfoot Cl SP4 21 D2
Combe 15 E3
Combe Down 12 D2
Combe Hay 12 D3
Comet Close SN15 36 C2
Comfrey Cl, Swindon SN2 54 C1
Comfrey Cl, Trowbridge BA14 64 E2
Command Workshops BA12 67 G3
Commercial Rd SN10 30 D3
Common Hill SN6 29 A2
Common Rd SN16 37 A5
Common Slip SN15 27 F4
Commonweal Rd SN1 59 G3
Compton Abbas 17 F4
Compton Bassett 13 H1
Compton Beauchamp 10 D5
Compton Chamberlayne 17 H2
Compton Cl, Swindon SN3 61 E3
Compton Cl, Trowbridge BA14 63 E1
Compton Dando 12 C2
Compton Martin 12 A3
Compton Pauncefoot 16 C2
Compton, Hampshire 19 G3
Compton, West Berkshire 11 H6
Compton, Wiltshire 14 B4
Conan Doyle Walk SN3 61 G3
Concord Walk*, Rutland Rd SN3 60 C2
Conference Cl BA12 66 D3
Conigre Cl SN12 40 B4
Conigre Hill BA15 23 F2
Conisborough SN5 58 B2
Coniston Cl SP4 21 F3
Coniston Rd, Chippenham SN14 26 A5
Coniston Rd, Trowbridge BA14 63 E4
Connelly Cl SN25 50 B6
Conrad Cl SN3 61 G3
Consciences La SN10 30 A1
Constable Rd SN2 56 B3
Constable Way SP2 48 B3
Constantine Cl SN3 57 F4
Conway Cres SN12 40 B5
Conway Rd, Chippenham SN14 26 B4
Conway Rd, Swindon SN3 61 F3
Cook Cl SN8 20 C1
Cook Rd SN8 20 C1
Cookham Rd SN25 50 B4
Cooks Cl SP2 45 H1
Coombe Bissett 18 A2
Coombe Cl SN4 43 D6
Coombe Rd, Salisbury SP2 48 B5
Coombe Rd, Swindon SN25 55 E2
Cooper Flds SN25 51 F5
Coopers Cl, Malmesbury SN16 37 C2
Coopers Cl, Salisbury SP4 21 C2
Cop Croft SN11 25 C4
Coped Hall Bsns Pk SN4 68 B2
Copes Yd SN8 39 F4
Copheap La BA12 67 F2
Copheap Rise BA12 67 F2
Coping Cl SN10 31 E5
Copper Beeches, Swindon SN6 34 C3
Copper Beeches, Trowbridge BA14 63 G3
Copperfields SN25 50 B5
Coppice Cl, Swindon SN2 54 C1
Coppice Cl, Warminster BA12 67 E3
Coppice Hill BA15 23 F2
Copse Av SN1 56 B5
Copythorne 18 D4
Corbin Rd BA14 63 G5
Corby Av SN3 60 A4
Corfe Cl SN25 55 F1
Corfe Cres SN11 25 A3
Corfe Rd, Melksham SN12 40 C5
Corfe Rd, Swindon SN5 58 A3
Coriander Way SN2 50 C6
Corinium Way SN3 57 F4
Corn Gastons SN16 37 A3
Cornbrash Pk SN14 26 B2
Cornbrash Rise BA14 63 G5
Cornfield Rd SN10 31 F4
Cornfields SN14 26 B2
Cornflower Cl SN11 25 C2
Cornflower Rd SN25 50 D6
Cornflower Way, Andover SP11 35 D3
Cornflower Way, Melksham SN12 40 C5
Cornmarsh Way SN3 57 G6
Cornwall Av SN2 55 F4
Cornwall Cres, Devizes SN10 30 D5
Cornwall Cres, Melksham SN12 40 C3
Cornwall Rd SP1 46 D5
Coronation Av BA15 23 G2
Coronation Cl SN9 42 B2
Coronation Rd, Andover SP11 35 E3
Coronation Rd, Bemerton SP2 46 A5
Coronation Rd, Durrington SP4 24 B1
Coronation Rd, Melksham SN12 40 C4
Coronation Rd, Swindon SN4 43 B5
Coronation Rd, Tidworth SP9 41 C1
Coronation Sq SP2 45 F4
Coronation St BA14 64 E1
Corsham 13 F1
Corsham Court SN13 28 F1
Corsham Ct SN13 28 F1
Corsham Rd SN2 51 H6
Corsley 13 E5
Corsley Heath 13 E5
Corston, Bath & NE Somerset 12 C2
Corston, Wiltshire 9 G5
Corton 13 G6
Corton Cres SN5 58 B1
Corton Denham 16 C3
Cothill 11 G2
Coton Down SP3 43 B2
Cotswold Cl, Calne SN11 25 D5
Cotswold Cl, Melksham SN12 40 D3
Cotswold Cl, Warminster BA12 67 E2
Cottars Cl SN3 57 E2
Cottington Cl SN5 58 A3
Cottle Mead SN13 28 D3
Cottles La BA15 22 B3
Cotton House Gdns BA12 67 F3
Couch La SN10 30 D4
Coulston 13 G4
Coulston Rd SN13 28 E1
Countess Rd, Amesbury SP4 21 B1
Countess Rd, Durrington SP4 24 A2
County Way BA14 64 D1
Court Hill SN10 42 A6
Court St SP3 43 C2
Court Street Cl SP3 43 C1
Courtenay Rd SN3 60 C1
Courtsknap Ct SN1 59 F2
Courtwood Cl SP1 49 F2
Coventry Cl SN4 43 C5
Covingham 10 B5
Covingham Dr SN3 57 E5
Covingham Sq SN3 57 E5
Cow La SP1 47 F6
Cowbridge Cres SN16 37 D6
Cowdrey Cl SN5 58 A3
Cowleaze Cres SN4 43 A5
Cowleaze Walk SN2 56 B1
Cowley 11 H2
Cowley Walk SN3 60 D1
Cowslip Bank SN13 28 C3
Cowslip Cl SN10 31 G3
Cowslip Gro SN11 25 C2
Cowslip Mews SN12 40 C5
Coxhill La SN10 42 A6
Coxley 12 A6
Coxs Hill SN11 25 B4
Coxstalls SN4 68 A3
Crab Tree Cl SN16 37 B4
Crampton Rd SN3 56 D5
Cranborne 18 A4
Cranborne Chase SN25 50 B6
Cranbury Cl SP5 32 C5
Crandon Lea BA14 29 C4
Crane Bridge Rd SP1 48 D2
Crane Furlong SN6 34 C1
Crane St SP1 48 D2
Cranesbill Rd SN10 31 F3
Cranleigh Cl SP4 21 F3
Cranmore 12 C6
Cranmore Av SN3 60 D2
Cranmore Cl BA14 62 B5
Cranwell Cl SN14 26 B5
Crawford Cl SN5 58 A3
Crawlboys La SP11 35 E2
Crawlboys Rd SP11 35 D2
Crawley 19 F1
Crawley Av SN3 57 E3
Crawley Cres BA14 62 B6
Craybourne Rd SN12 40 C2
Crescent Rd, Melksham SN12 40 D1
Crescent Rd, Salisbury SP4 24 E3
Cresswell Dr BA14 63 H3
Cresswells SN13 28 D3
Crestmount Dr SP2 46 A5
Cricketts La SN15 27 G6
Cricklade 10 A4
Cricklade Ct SN1 60 A3
Cricklade Leisure Centre SN6 29 A2
Cricklade Museum SN6 29 C2
Cricklade Rd, Highworth SN6 34 A4
Cricklade Rd, Malmesbury SN16 37 C3
Cricklade Rd, Swindon SN2 51 H3
Crieff Cl SN3 57 E6
Crispin Cl SN3 56 D2
Crockerton 13 F6
Croft Rd SN1 59 H5
Croftmead SN1 59 H5
Crofton Beam Engines SN8 14 D2
Cromhall 8 D4
Cromhall Common 8 C4
Crompton Rd SN25 52 A4
Cromwell Rd SN10 31 F5
Cromwell SN5 58 A4
Crooked Cnr SN8 20 B1
Crookham 15 H2
Croome Cl SN25 50 B3
Crosby Walk SN3 60 D4
Croscombe 12 B5
Cross Hayes La SN16 37 C4
Cross Hayes SN16 37 C4
Cross Keys Rd SN13 28 E1
Cross La SN8 38 D3
Cross St BA14 62 D5
Crossways Av SN25 55 H1
Crossways Cl SP5 32 A3
Crosswood Rd SN3 60 D3
Crow La SP2 44 C3
Crown Cl SN15 27 G6
Crown Ct, Bradford-on-Avon BA15 23 H2
Crown Ct, Salisbury SP2 46 A5
Crown La SP11 35 C2
Crudwell 9 G4
Crudwell Way SN2 51 H5
Crusader Pk Bsns Pk BA12 66 C1
Cruse Cl SN14 26 A3
Crux Easton 15 F4
Cucklington 16 D2
Cuckoos Mead SN3 57 H6
Cuckoos Nest La BA12 66 C3
Cuddesdon 11 H2
Cuffs La SP3 43 B1
Culham 11 G3
Culkerton 9 G3
Cullerne Rd SN3 57 F4
Culpepper Cl SN3 60 C3
Culver Rd BA15 23 G4
Culver St SP1 49 E2
Culvermead Cl SN8 39 E4
Culverwell Rd SN14 26 B4
Cumberland Rd SN1 60 A1
Cumner 11 F2
Cunetio Rd SN3 57 F5
Cunningham Ho SP9 41 C1
Cunningham Rd SN2 55 F3
Cunnington Cl SN10 31 F4
Curbridge, Hampshire 19 H5
Curbridge, Oxfordshire 11 E1
Curdridge 19 H4
Curie Av SN1 59 F3
Curlcroft Rd SN13 28 C4
Curlew Dr SN14 26 B1
Curtis Cl BA12 66 D4
Curzon Cl SN11 25 B4
Curzon St SN11 25 B4
Cusance Way BA14 63 G5
Cygnet Cl SN10 31 G2
Cygnet Dr SP4 24 C2
Cygnet Way BA14 62 D1
Cypress Gro SN2 55 F2

D

Dace Rd SN11 25 B2
Dacre Rd SN3 56 C6
Daglingworth 9 H2
Dairy Cl SP5 33 F5
Dairy Meadow La SP1 49 G3
Dairyhouse Bri SP1 49 G3
Daisy Cl, Melksham SN12 40 D4
Daisy Cl, Swindon SN2 54 C1
Dales Cl SN25 51 F4
Dales Rd BA13 65 A4
Dalewood Rise SP1 47 H6
Dallas Av SN3 57 E6
Dallas Rd SN14 26 D3
Dalton Cl SN3 56 C6
Dalwood Cl SN3 61 E4
Damask Way BA12 67 E4
Damerham 18 B4
Dammas La SN1 60 A3
Dando Dr SN8 38 B4
Dane Cl BA15 22 A2
Dane Rise BA15 22 A2
Danes Cl SN15 27 G6
Daniel Cl SN5 59 E3
Daniell Crest BA12 66 D4
Daniell Dr SN15 27 F5
Danvers Rd SN13 28 C2
Danvers Way BA13 65 D2
Darcy Cl SN15 27 G3
Darius Way SN25 51 F4
Dark La, Malmesbury SN16 37 B4
Dark La, Warminster BA12 36 C5
Darnley Cl SN3 60 C1
Darrell Rd SP4 21 D2
Dart Av SN25 55 F1
Dartmoor Cl SN5 59 E3
Dartmoor Rd BA13 65 A5
Darwin Cl SN3 57 E6
Dasna Rd SP9 41 B4
Daunch Cl SP9 41 B1
Dauntsey 9 H5
Dave Watkins Ct SN2 56 B2
Davenham Cl SN3 60 C4

Davenwood SN2	52	B6
David Stoddard Gdns SN2	55	G4
Davies Cl SN8	38	B4
Davies Dr SN10	31	H1
Dawbeny Dr SP4	21	E2
Dawlish Rd SN3	61	E1
Day House La SN3	61	E5
Days Cl SN3	56	C4
De Vaux Pl SP1	48	D2
Dean Cl SN12	40	D2
Dean St SN1	59	F1
Dean, Dorset	**17**	**H4**
Dean, Hampshire	**19**	**H3**
Dean, Somerset	**12**	**C5**
Deane	**15**	**H4**
Deanland	**17**	**H4**
Deans Cl SP9	41	D4
Deansfield SN6	29	B3
Deansway Ct SN15	26	D1
Deansway SN15	27	E1
Deben Cres SN25	51	E6
Deburgh St SN2	59	E1
Deerhurst Way SN5	58	C2
Delamere Dr SN3	56	D1
Delamere Rd BA14	63	E4
Delta Bsns Pk SN5	58	C1
Delta Tennis Centre SN5	58	C1
Denbeck Wood SN5	54	B6
Denbigh Cl SN3	60	B3
Denchworth	**11**	**E4**
Dene Cl BA13	65	B5
Deneb Dr SN25	50	B3
Denes Av BA12	36	B4
Denholme Rd SN3	60	D3
Denison Rise SP1	47	F4
Denton Ct SN3	57	E2
Deptford	**13**	**H6**
Derby Cl, Chippenham SN15	27	G6
Derby Cl, Swindon SN2	54	D4
Derby Ct*, Lennox SN3	60	C2
Derriads Grn SN14	26	B4
Derriads La SN14	26	A5
Derrlards Ho SN14	26	A5
Derry Hill	**13**	**G1**
Derwent Dr SN2	52	C6
Desborough SN5	58	A4
Deva Cl SN3	57	F5
Deverell Cl BA15	23	G5
Devereux Rd SP4	21	D2
Deverill Rd BA12	66	D6
Devizes	**13**	**H3**
Devizes Castle SN10	30	C4
Devizes Community Hospital SN10	30	D3
Devizes Garden Ind Est SN10	31	F2
Devizes Ho SP9	41	D2
Devizes Leisure Centre SN10	31	E5
Devizes Rd, Devizes SN10	30	A2
Devizes Rd, Melksham SN12	40	D5
Devizes Rd, Salisbury SP2	46	A3
Devizes Rd, Swindon SN1	60	A3
Devizes Rd, Trowbridge BA14	63	G3
Devizes Rd, Wroughton SN4	43	C6
Devizes Visitor Centre SN10	30	D4
Devizes Wharf Canal Centre SN10	31	H2
Devon Cl SN14	26	A5
Devon Dr BA13	65	C1
Devon Rd SN2	55	G4
Devonshire Pl SN12	40	C3
Devonshire Rd SP1	47	E5
Dew Cl SN13	28	F4
Dewberry Cl SN25	50	D6
Dewell Mews SN3	60	A3
Dewey Museum SN4	67	E3
Deweys La SP11	35	C2
Dews Rd SP2	48	C1
Dexter Cl SN5	54	A6
Dibden	**19**	**F5**
Dibden Purlieu	**19**	**F6**
Dickens Av SN13	28	D2
Dickens Cl SN3	61	F3
Dickenson Rd SN25	50	B6
Dicketts Rd SN13	28	E4
Dickson Rd SN15	36	C3
Dickson Way SN15	27	F6
Dinder	**12**	**B5**
Dinmore Rd SN25	51	F5
Dinton	**17**	**H1**
Dione Cres SN25	50	A4
Ditcheat	**16**	**B1**
Dixon Way SN11	25	B3
Dobbin Cl SN3	57	G6
Dobson Cl SN25	51	F3
Dockle Way SN2	56	B1
Doctors Pl SP3	43	B1
Dodington	**8**	**D6**
Dog Kennel La BA13	65	B5
Dolina Rd SN25	50	C5
Dolphin Trading Est SP1	49	F2
Don Cl SN25	51	F6
Donaldson Rd SP1	47	E5
Doncaster Rd SN14	26	A6
Donhead St Andrew	**17**	**G2**
Donhead St Mary	**17**	**F3**
Donnington Gro SN3	60	C3
Dorcan Bsns Village SN3	61	H1
Dorcan Ind Est SN3	61	H2
Dorcan Way SN3	56	D5
Dorchester	**11**	**H3**
Dorchester Rd SN3	60	B4
Dores Cl SN2	56	B2
Dores Rd SN2	56	A1
Doris Archer Ct SN2	55	G3
Dorney Cl BA13	65	B5
Dorney Rd SN25	50	B3
Dorothy Walk BA12	66	D2
Dorset Cl SN2	24	F2
Dorset Cres SN12	40	C3
Dorset Dr BA13	65	C1
Dorset Grn SN2	55	E2
Dorset Rd SP1	47	E5
Double Hedges SP4	24	E3
Doubledays SN6	29	B2
Doughton	**9**	**F4**
Dovecote Cl BA14	62	B6
Dovecote Dr SN13	28	D2
Dovedale SN25	51	E3
Dover St SN14	26	D4
Dovetrees SN3	57	G6
Dowlais Cl SN25	50	B4
Dowland Cl SN25	50	D3
Down Ampney	**10**	**A3**
Down View Rd SP1	47	G6
Down Vw SN2	56	B4
Downavon BA15	23	G4
Downend	**11**	**G6**
Downham Mead SN15	27	G3
Downhayes Rd BA14	62	D4
Downhead	**12**	**C5**
Downing St SN14	26	D3
Downland Rd, Calne SN11	25	B4
Downland Rd, Swindon SN2	54	C1
Downland Way SP4	24	A1
Downlands Cl SP5	32	C4
Downlands Rd SN10	31	E6
Downleaze Rd SP4	24	B1
Downs Cl BA15	23	E2
Downs View Rd SN3	60	B5
Downs Vw, Bradford-on-Avon BA15	23	E2
Downs Vw, Highworth SN6	34	C2
Downs Vw, Swindon SN4	68	A4
Downs Vw, Warminster BA12	67	G4
Downs Way SN3	61	G6
Downside Cl BA12	36	C4
Downside Pk BA14	63	E3
Downside SP2	44	B4
Downside Vw BA14	62	E3
Downsview Rd BA13	65	B2
Downsway SP1	47	E3
Downton	**18**	**C3**
Downton Hill SP5	33	F3
Downton Leisure Centre SP5	32	A3
Downton Moot SP11	32	C3
Downton Rd, Salisbury SP2	49	E4
Downton Rd, Swindon SN2	51	G6
Doyle Cl SN25	50	B6
Doynton	**12**	**D1**
Dr Behr Ct SN2	55	H3
Drake Cl SP1	47	F3
Drake Cres SN14	26	A5
Drakes Av SN10	31	E5
Drakes Way SN3	56	B6
Draycott Cl SN3	60	D1
Drayton	**11**	**G3**
Drew St SN2	55	E6
Drews Pond La SN10	30	D6
Driffield	**10**	**A3**
Drovers Vw SP11	35	C3
Druces Hill BA15	23	F2
Druids Cl SN11	25	A4
Dry Sandford	**11**	**G2**
Dryden Cl SP2	49	F5
Dryden Pl SN4	68	C2
Drynham Dro BA14	64	D3
Drynham La BA14	64	E1
Drynham Pk BA14	64	E1
Drynham Rd BA14	64	E1
Duchess Way SN2	52	A5
Duck La SP1	47	G6
Duck St, Devizes SN10	42	A6
Duck St, Salisbury SP3	43	B1
Ducklington	**11**	**E1**
Ducks Mdw SN8	39	E5
Dudley Rd SN3	60	C1
Dudmore Rd SN3	60	A1
Dukes Cl SN2	52	B6
Dukes Way SP4	24	F2
Dulcote	**12**	**A5**
Dulverton Av SN3	60	D2
Dummer Way SN15	27	G6
Dunbar Rd SN4	43	B4
Dunbeath Ct SN2	56	A4
Dunbeath Rd SN2	56	A4
Dunbeath Trading Est SN2	56	A4
Duncan St SN11	25	C2
Dunch La SN12	40	A1
Dundas Cl SN10	30	A4
Dundry	**12**	**A2**
Dunedin Cl SP9	41	E3
Dunford Cl BA14	64	E1
Dunkirk Hill SN10	30	B3
Dunley Cl SN25	50	C4
Dunley Way SP1	47	F2
Dunnet Cl SN11	25	C3
Dunnington Fm SN4	68	A6
Dunnington Rd SN4	68	A6
Dunraven Cl SN3	60	C3
Dunsford Cl SN1	59	E3
Dunster Cl SN3	60	B4
Duntisbourne Abbots	**9**	**G1**
Duntisbourne Rouse	**9**	**G1**
Duntish	**16**	**C6**
Dunvant Rd SN25	50	B3
Dunwich Dr SN5	58	C3
Dunworth Rise SP3	43	B2
Durley, Hampshire	**19**	**H4**
Durley, Wiltshire	**14**	**C2**
Durnford Rd, Salisbury SP4	46	B1
Durnford Rd, Swindon SN2	51	H6
Durrington	**14**	**B5**
Durrington Walk SN2	51	H6
Durrington Walls SP4	24	A2
Dursden La SN9	42	C1
Dursley	**8**	**D3**
Dursley Rd BA14	64	D1
Durweston	**17**	**F5**
Dussele Pl SN25	50	D3
Dyehouse La SN10	30	D3
Dyers Cl SN15	27	G5
Dymott Sq BA14	63	G2
Dyrham	**8**	**D6**
Dyrham Ct SN25	51	E3

E

East Stratton	**15**	**H6**
East Tytherley	**18**	**D2**
East Tytherton	**9**	**H6**
East Wellow	**18**	**D3**
East Woodhay	**15**	**F3**
Eastbourne Gdns BA14	63	E5
Eastbury	**11**	**E6**
Eastbury Way SN25	50	D4
Eastcombe	**9**	**F2**
Eastcott	**13**	**H4**
Eastcourt	**9**	**G4**
Easter Compton	**8**	**A5**
Eastern Av, Chippenham SN15	27	G3
Eastern Av, Swindon SN3	60	B1
Easterton	**13**	**H4**
Easterton La SN9	42	C2
Eastington	**9**	**E2**
Eastleach Martin	**10**	**C2**
Eastleach Turville	**10**	**C1**
Eastleaze Rd SN5	58	B1
Eastleigh	**19**	**F3**
Eastleigh Cl SN10	31	F5
Eastleigh Rd SN10	31	F5
Eastman Cl SP5	32	C4
Eastmere SN3	61	G3
Easton	**19**	**G2**
Easton La SN14	26	B6
Easton Grey	**9**	**F4**
Easton Royal	**14**	**C3**
Easton-in-Gordano	**8**	**A6**
Eastrop SN6	34	C3
Eastview Rd BA14	64	B1
Eastville Rd SN25	55	H1
Eastwood Av SN4	68	B4
Eaton	**11**	**F2**
Eaton Cl SN3	60	C3
Eaton Hastings	**10**	**D3**
Ebbesborne Wake	**17**	**H3**
Ebble Cl SP9	41	D2
Ebble Cres BA12	66	D4
Ebor Cl SN25	51	E4
Ecchinswell	**15**	**G3**
Eccleston Cl SN3	61	E4
Ecklington SN3	61	E2
Edale Moor SN3	61	H4
Edelweiss Cl SP11	35	D3
Eden Vale Rd BA13	65	B3
Edencroft SN3	34	D1
Edgam Pl SP2	45	F4
Edgar Row Cl SN4	43	B5
Edge	**9**	**E1**
Edgehill SN5	58	A3
Edgeworth	**9**	**G2**
Edgeworth Cl SN5	54	B5
Edinburgh St SN2	56	A4
Edinburgh Way SN13	28	D4
Edington	**13**	**G4**
Edington Cl SN5	58	B2
Edington Priory BA13	13	G4
Edison Rd, Salisbury SP2	48	B1
Edison Rd, Swindon SN3	61	G2
Edmondsham	**18**	**A5**
Edreds Ct SN11	25	C5
Edridge Cl SN15	27	G3
Edridge Pl SN13	28	D2
Edward Rd SN10	31	E5
Edward St BA13	65	C2
Edwardian Ct SN9	42	B1
Edwards Mdw SN8	38	C4
Edwards Rd SP4	21	C2
Edwin Young Gallery SN2	48	D1
Egdon Cl SN25	50	C5
Egerton Cl SN3	57	E6
Eider Av SN15	36	C3
Elane Ho SP11	35	E3
Elberton	**8**	**B4**
Elborough Rd SN2	54	C2
Elcombe	**10**	**B6**
Elcombe Av SN4	43	A5
Elcombe Cl BA14	64	D2
Elcombe Gdns SN10	30	C4
Elcot Cl SN8	39	G4
Elcot La SN8	39	F4
Elcot Orchard SN8	39	G4
Eldene	**10**	**C5**
Eldene Dr SN3	61	E3
Eldene Shopping Centre SN3	61	F2
Elder Cl, Corsham SN13	28	C3
Elder Cl, Swindon SN2	54	C1
Eleanor Cl SN3	35	C3
Elgar Cl SN25	50	D4
Elgin Dr SN2	56	A4
Elgin Ind Est SN2	56	A3
Eling	**19**	**E5**
Eliot Cl SN3	61	G4
Elizabeth Cl SP5	32	A3
Elizabeth Ct SN25	50	D4
Elizabeth Dr SP2	48	D1
Elizabeth Dr SN10	31	F4
Elizabeth Rd, Durrington SP4	24	B1
Elizabeth Rd, Wilton SP2	44	B1
Ellendune Centre SN4	43	B5
Ellingdon Rd SN4	43	A4
Elliot Pl BA14	62	A5
Elliott Pl SN12	40	A1
Ellwood	**8**	**B1**
Elm Cl, Chippenham SN15	36	D2
Elm Cl, Ludgershall SP11	35	F3
Elm Cl, Melksham SN12	40	A1
Elm Cl, Salisbury SP1	47	G5
Elm Cl, Swindon SN4	68	B2
Elm Ct SP1	49	E1
Elm Gro, Corsham SN13	28	D2
Elm Gro, Salisbury SP1	49	F1
Elm Gro, Westbury BA13	65	A3
Elm Grove Pl SP1	49	F1
Elm Grove Rd SP1	49	E1
Elm Hayes SN13	28	E4
Elm Hall BA12	67	F2
Elm Pk SN4	68	A6
Elm Rd SN2	55	F3
Elm Tree Cl SN10	31	F5
Elm Tree Gdns SN10	31	F5
Elmdale Cl BA14	64	B1
Elmdale Rd BA14	64	B1
Elmer Cl SN16	37	C2
Elmfield BA15	23	E2
Elmfield Cl SP5	33	F5
Elmore SN3	61	F2
Elms Cross BA15	22	D6
Elms Cross Dr BA15	23	F4
Elms Ct SN6	34	B3
Elmscross Bsns Pk BA15	23	F5
Elmscross Shopping Centre BA15	23	F5
Elmswood Cl SN25	52	B5
Elmwood SN15	27	E1
Elsfield	**11**	**H1**
Elsham Way SN25	51	E5
Elsie Millin Ct SN2	55	H3
Elstree Way SN25	51	E5
Ely Cl SN5	58	C2
Ely Ct SN4	43	B6
Emborough	**12**	**B4**
Emerson Cl SN25	51	G5
Emery Down	**18**	**D5**
Emery Gate Shopping Centre SN15	27	E4
Emery La SN15	27	F4
Emlyn Sq SN1	59	G1
Emmanuel Cl SN25	51	F6
Empire Ct SN1	59	H1
Empire Rd SP2	46	A6
Emporium Ct SN1	60	A3
Empress Way SP11	35	C3
Emwell St BA12	66	D3
Enborne	**15**	**F2**
Endless Cl SN15	36	C2
Endless St SP1	49	E1
Enford	**14**	**B4**
Enford Av SN1	51	H6
Engine Common	**8**	**D5**
Englefield SN4	68	B4
Englishcombe	**12**	**C2**
Enham Alamein	**15**	**E5**
Ensor Cl SN25	51	F3
Epney	**8**	**D1**
Epping Cl, Melksham SN12	40	D1
Epping Cl, Warminster BA12	67	E2
Epping Dr SN12	40	D2
Epsom Cl SN14	26	A5
Epsom Ct BA14	64	F4
Epsom Rd BA14	64	F4
Epsom Sq BA14	64	F4
Eric Long Cl SN3	61	F2
Erleigh Dr SN15	26	D4
Erlestoke	**13**	**G4**
Erlestoke Way SN2	51	H5
Ermin Mews SN3	56	D2
Ermin St, Blunsdon SN26	51	F1
Ermin St, Upper Stratton SN3	52	C6
Ernestoun Cres SN13	28	E2
Ernle Rd SN11	25	C3
Eshton Walk SN3	60	D4
Esmead SN15	27	F3
Espringham Pl SN2	52	B6
Essex Sq SP2	48	B4
Essex Walk SN3	56	C6
Estcourt Cres SN10	31	E4
Estcourt Hill SN10	30	D5

Estcourt Rd SP1 49 E1
Estcourt St SN10 31 E4
Estelle CI SN25 50 C5
Etchilhampton 14 A3
Ethelred PI SN13 28 D2
Europa Ind Pk SN3 56 C1
Evans CI SN15 27 F1
Eveleigh Rd SN4 68 B4
Evelyn St SN3 60 A4
Eveque CI SP2 45 F4
Evercreech 12 B6
Evergreen Way SP4 21 D3
Evergreens CI SN3 57 E4
Everleigh 14 C4
Everleigh CI BA14 64 E3
Everleigh Rd,
  Pewsey SN9 42 B3
Everleigh Rd,
  Swindon SN2 51 H6
Eversglade SP2 16 A6
Evershot 9 H6
Ewen 19 F6
Exbury CI SN25 51 F4
Exe CI SN25 51 F6
Exeter CI SN14 26 A6
Exeter St SN1 59 G1
Exmoor CI SN25 50 B6
Exmoor Rd BA13 65 A5
Exmouth St SN1 59 F2
Exton SN16 37 A3
Eynsham 11 F1
Eyres Way SP1 49 E2

F

Faccombe 15 E3
Factory La BA12 66 B4
Failand 12 A1
Fair Oak 19 G4
Fair View Rd,
  Salisbury SP1 49 F1
Fair View Rd,
  Salisbury SP2 45 E3
Fairdown Av BA13 65 D3
Fairfax CI,
  Salisbury SP4 21 B2
Fairfax CI,
  Swindon SN3 56 C6
Fairfield Cotts SP2 44 D2
Fairfield Rd,
  Salisbury SP1 46 D4
Fairfield Rd,
  Warminster BA12 67 F3
Fairfield, Cricklade SN6 29 B2
Fairfield, Swindon SN3 68 B3
Fairfoot CI SN14 26 B4
Fairford 10 B2
Fairford Cres SN25 55 H1
Fairholm Way SN2 56 C1
Fairlawn SN3 61 F4
Fairleigh Vw BA15 22 B6
Fairview,
  Cricklade SN6 29 C2
Fairview,
  Highworth SN6 34 C3
Fairway SN12 40 D2
Fairwood CI BA14 63 G4
Falcon CI SP9 41 E2
Falcon Rd SN11 25 D4
Falcon Way SN12 40 D6
Falconer Mews SN25 51 G5
Falcons Way SP2 48 D5
Falconscroft SN3 57 F3
Falfield 8 C4
Falkirk Rd SN4 43 B4
Falkner CI SN8 38 C4
Fallow Field CI SN14 26 C1
Falmouth Gro SN3 60 B2
Falstaff Ct SN1 25 C3
Fanshaw Way BA12 67 E5
Fanstones Rd SN3 61 E3
Faraday Pk SN3 61 H1
Faraday Rd,
  Salisbury SP2 48 B1
Faraday Rd,
  Swindon SN3 61 G2
Fareham 19 H5
Fareham CI SN3 60 D2
Faringdon 10 D3
Faringdon Rd SN1 59 F1
Farleigh Av,
  Melksham SN12 40 B5
Farleigh Av,
  Trowbridge BA14 62 A6
Farleigh CI,
  Chippenham SN14 26 A4
Farleigh CI,
  Westbury BA13 65 B1
Farleigh Cres SN3 60 B4
Farleigh Hungerford 13 E3
Farley 18 C2
Farley Rd SP1 49 F2

Farm CI BA14 62 B4
Farm La,
  Marlborough SN8 20 C3
Farm La,
  Salisbury SP2 48 B1
Farman CI SN3 61 E3
Farmborough 12 B3
Farmer CI SN15 27 F1
Farmer Cres SN25 51 H4
Farmer Giles
  Farmstead SP3 17 G1
Farmhouse La SN1 56 B6
Farmoor 11 G1
Farnborough 11 F5
Farnborough Rd SN3 60 D4
Farne Way SN4 68 C3
Farnham 17 G4
Farrar Dr SN8 38 B4
Farrfield SN2 56 B1
Farriers CI SN1 56 B5
Farrington Gurney 12 B4
Farthinghale Cotts SN13 28 C1
Faulkland 12 D4
Faverolle Way BA14 63 G4
Fawley CI SN25 50 B3
Fawley, Hampshire 19 F6
Fawley,
  West Berkshire 11 F5
Feather Wood SN5 58 C2
Fell Rd BA13 65 A3
Felton 12 A2
Fennel CI SN2 54 C1
Fenton Av SN25 50 D4
Ferguson Rd SN10 31 F6
Ferndale Rd SN2 55 E5
Fernham 10 D4
Fernham Rd SN25 55 E2
Ferozeshah Rd SN10 31 H1
Ferris Gro SN12 40 C3
Ferris Mead BA12 67 E4
Festival Av SP2 45 H4
Feversham Rd SP1 47 E4
Fiddle Fm SN6 29 A3
Fiddleford 17 E4
Field CI BA13 65 C1
Field Rise SN1 59 F4
Field Vw SN15 27 E4
Field Way BA14 64 A2
Fieldfare SN3 57 F6
Fieldins BA15 22 B2
Fifehead Magdalen 16 D3
Fifehead Neville 16 D5
Figgins La SN8 38 D4
Figheldean 14 B5
Figsbury CI SN25 50 C5
Figsbury Ring SP2 18 C1
Filands SN16 37 B1
Filsham Rd SN25 50 B4
Filton 8 B6
Finchdale SN3 57 F5
Finchley Rd SP2 46 B6
Finnis Rd SP4 21 D2
Fir Tree CI SN2 55 F2
Firbank Cres BA12 67 G2
Firecrest Vw SN3 61 G1
Firs Hill SN14 64 A3
Firs Hill Way SN10 42 B5
Firsdown 18 C1
Firth CI SN3 55 F1
Fish Row SP1 49 E1
Fisher's Pond 19 G3
Fison Walk SP1 47 G3
Fitkin Ct SN25 50 D3
Fittleton 14 B5
Fitwell Rd SN5 50 B4
Fitzmaurice CI,
  Bradford-on-Avon
  BA15 23 G5
Fitzmaurice CI,
  Swindon SN3 57 G6
Fitzmaurice PI BA15 23 F4
Fitzmaurice Sq SN11 25 C4
Fitzroy Rd SN1 59 H5
Five Stiles Rd SN8 39 F4
Flax Bourton 12 A1
Fleece Cotts BA14 64 E1
Fleet Rd SN15 27 E3
Fleetwood Ct SN5 58 A4
Fleming CI SP11 35 D3
Flers Ct BA12 67 E3
Fleur De Lys Dr BA14 64 A4
Flint Hill SN5 58 B3
Flitcroft SN3 21 D3
Florence St SN2 55 H4
Florey Ct SN1 59 F3
Flower La SP4 21 B2
Flowers Yd SN15 27 E5
Foghamshire SN15 27 E4
Folke 16 C4
Folkestone CI SN14 26 B5
Folkestone Rd SP2 48 C4
Folly CI, Salisbury SP2 48 C4
Folly CI, Swindon SN6 34 C2
Folly Cres SN6 34 C2

Folly Dr SN6 34 C2
Folly La, Salisbury SP2 46 A5
Folly La,
  Warminster BA12 66 A4/5
Folly Rd SN10 31 F1
Folly Vw SP2 45 H2
Folly Way SN6 34 C2
Follyfield BA15 23 G5
Fonthill Bishop 17 G1
Fonthill Gifford 17 G2
Fonthill Walk SN3 60 B2
Fontmell Magna 17 F4
Foots Hill SP2 45 G4
Ford 9 F6
Ford La SP4 47 H2
Ford St SN1 59 F1
Forders CI SN5 33 F6
Fordingbridge 18 B4
Fordson Rd SN10 31 F6
Fore Brooke
  Bsns Pk SN11 25 D1
Fore St,
  Warminster BA12 66 D4
Fore St, Westbury BA13 65 C2
Foreman St SN11 25 C4
Forest Ct SP9 41 E2
Forest Dale Rd SN8 39 G4
Forest Dr SP9 41 E2
Forest La SN15 27 G6
Forest Rd,
  Fordingbridge SP6 33 F6
Forest Rd,
  Melksham SN12 40 C2
Forester CI SN3 61 G3
Foresters Park Rd
  SN12 40 D3
Forrester PI SN16 37 C2
Forsey CI SN3 57 G6
Fortune Way SN5 58 A6
Forty Acres Rd SN10 31 F4
Forum CI SN3 57 F5
Fosbury 14 D3
Fosse CI SN2 59 E1
Fossebridge 10 A1
Fosters Bushes SP4 21 E3
Fotherby Cres SP1 47 F4
Foundry La SN15 27 E3
Foundry Rd SN16 37 B3
Fountain Ct BA13 65 C2
Fovant 17 H2
Fovant CI SN5 54 A4
Fowlers Hill SP1 49 F2
Fowlers Rd SP1 49 F2
Fox Brook SN4 68 C4
Fox CI SN14 26 C1
Fox Wood SN5 58 C2
Foxbridge SN3 57 G6
Foxglove CI SN12 40 D4
Foxglove Dr BA14 63 E2
Foxglove Rd SN25 50 D6
Foxglove Way SN11 25 C2
Foxgrove SN14 26 B1
Foxham 9 H6
Foxhill CI SN25 55 E1
Foxleaze SN6 29 A1
Foxley 9 F5
Foxley CI,
  Swindon SN2 56 A1
Foxley CI,
  Warminster BA12 66 D2
Foxley Rd SN16 37 A5
Foxtail Gdns SP11 35 D3
Frampton CI SN5 58 D3
Frampton Cotterell 8 C5
Frampton Ct BA14 64 A2
Frampton Mansell 9 G2
Frampton on Severn 8 D1
Francis St BA14 62 C4
Francis Way SP2 48 D5
Francklyn Acre SN8 39 E2
Francomes SN25 50 D6
Frank Warman Ct SN3 50 C3
Frankel Av SN25 50 C3
Frankela Pk SN12 40 D2
Frankton Gdns SN3 57 E3
Fraser CI SN3 57 E6
Frederick Taylor Ct
  BA12 66 D5
Fredericks Av SN16 26 A4
Frees Av SN13 38 B1
Freesia CI BA12 66 C3
Freestone Way SN13 28 B3
Frenchay 8 C6
Frenchgrass BA15 23 F3
Frensham Way SN4 43 A5
Freshbrook Way SN5 58 A3
Freshford 13 E3
Fretherne 8 D1
Friary CI BA15 22 B5
Friary La SP1 49 E3

Friesland CI SN5 54 A6
Frilford Dr SN3 56 D3
Frilsham 15 H1
Frith Copse SN5 54 A3
Fritham 18 C4
Frobisher Dr SN3 60 C1
Frocester 8 D2
Frog La SN8 20 B5
Frogmore Rd BA13 65 B1
Frogwell Pk SN4 26 B3
Frogwell SN14 26 B3
Frome 13 E5
Frome Rd,
  Bradford-on-Avon
  BA15 23 F3
Frome Rd,
  Southwick BA14 64 A4
Frome Rd,
  Swindon SN25 55 E1
Frome Rd,
  Trowbridge BA14 64 B2
Frome St Quintin 11 B6
Froxfield 14 D2
Fry CI SN5 59 E2
Fugglestone SP2 45 E3
Fulford Rd BA14 63 E4
Fuller Av SN13 28 D3
Fuller CI,
  Chippenham SN15 27 C5
Fuller CI, Swindon SN2 52 C5
Fuller Gdns SN3 57 G1
Fullers Av SN6 29 B2
Fullers CI SN12 40 C2
Fullerton 15 E6
Fullerton Walk SN5 59 E2
Fulmar CI SN12 40 D6
Fulney CI BA14 63 F3
Funtley 19 H5
Furlong BA12 66 H5
Furlong CI SN25 51 E6
Furlong Gdns BA14 63 E5
Furnax La BA12 66 D1
Furse Hill Rd SP9 41 D4
Furze CI SN5 54 A3
Furze Hill SP9 41 E4
Furze PI SN5 54 A3
Furzehill SN13 28 D3
Fyfield Av SN2 51 H6
Fyfield CI SP1 47 G3
Fyfield Down NNR SN8 14 B1
Fyfield,
  Gloucestershire 10 C2
Fyfield, Hampshire 14 D5
Fyfield, Oxfordshire 11 F3
Fyfield, Wiltshire 14 B1
Fynamore Gdns SN11 25 B6
Fynamore PI SN11 25 C3
Fyne CI SN5 54 B3

G

Gable CI SN25 51 G4
Gables CI SN10 31 F6
Gabriel Cres SN25 50 B3
Gains La SN10 31 E4
Gainsborough Av SN4 68 B2
Gainsborough CI SP2 45 H3
Gainsborough
  Rise BA14 64 B2
Gainsborough
  Way SN5 58 A2
Gairlock CI SN5 54 B3
Gales CI SN15 27 G3
Gales Ground SN8 39 F4
Galhampton 16 C2
Gallen Vw SN1 59 F4
Galley Orchard SN6 29 C2
Galloway CI SN5 54 A6
Galloway Rd SN25 50 B6
Galsworthy CI SN3 61 F2
Galton Way SN2 54 C4
Gamekeepers CI SN25 51 E4
Gantlettdene SN3 57 G6
Ganton CI SN2 56 B3
Ganton Way SN2 56 B4
Garden Ct SN11 25 B3
Gare Hill 13 E6
Garfield CI SN3 57 E1
Garford 11 F3
Garrard Way,
  Swindon SN3 56 C4
Garrard Way,
  Swindon SN3 56 C5
Garraways SN4 68 C4
Garsdon 9 G4
Garside Grn SN2 52 B6
Garsington 11 H2
Garsington Dr SN25 50 B4
Garson Rd SN25 51 G4
Gas Ct SN16 37 B3
Gas La, Cricklade SN6 29 B2
Gas La, Salisbury SP2 46 C6
Gascelyn CI SN14 26 B4

Gascelyn PI SN14 26 B4
Gason Hill Rd SP9 41 C1
Gastard 13 F2
Gastons Rd,
  Chippenham SN16 26 D3
Gastons Rd,
  Malmesbury SN16 37 B4
Gaunt's Common 17 H6
Gauntlet Rd SP4 21 C2
Gaveller Rd SN25 50 C4
Gawthorne Dr SP2 48 C4
Gaynor CI SN25 51 F4
Gays PI SN2 52 B6
Gayton Way SN3 57 E5
Geneville Rise SP4 21 E3
George CI SN11 25 D4
George La SN8 38 D4
George St South SP1 48 D1
George St,
  Swindon SN1 59 F1
George St,
  Trowbridge BA14 62 D5
George St,
  Warminster BA12 67 E3
George Street PI BA12 67 E3
George Tweed Gdns
  SN5 54 A5
George VI Rd SP9 41 C1
Gerard Walk SN5 58 A1
Gibbs CI, Salisbury SP1 47 F2
Gibbs CI,
  Swindon SN3 57 G6
Gibbs CI,
  Westbury BA13 65 C2
Gibbs Leaze BA14 63 G4
Gifford Rd SN3 57 E1
Gigant St SP1 49 E2
Gilbert Way SP1 47 F4
Giles Av SN6 29 B3
Gilling Way SN3 57 G6
Gillingham 17 E2
Gilman CI SN25 51 F3
Giotto CI SN25 50 B3
Gipsy La,
  Chippenham SN15 26 D4
Gipsy La,
  Salisbury SP5 49 H2
Gipsy La,
  Swindon SN2 56 B4
Gipsy La,
  Trowbridge BA14 29 C4
Gipsy La,
  Warminster BA12 67 F4
Gisborne CI SP9 41 E3
Gladstone Rd,
  Chippenham SN15 27 E4
Gladstone Rd,
  Trowbridge BA14 64 C1
Gladys Plumley Gdns
  SN2 56 A5
Glanvilles Wootton 16 C5
Glebe CI SN8 20 C2
Glebe Fld BA12 67 E4
Glebe PI SN6 34 C3
Glebe Rd,
  Salisbury SP4 24 B1
Glebe Rd,
  Swindon SN4 68 A4
Glebe Rd,
  Trowbridge BA14 64 A1
Glebe Way SN13 28 C3
Glendale Cres SP1 49 G1
Glendale Dr SN15 27 F5
Glendale Rd SP4 24 C1
Gleneagles CI SN15 27 G4
Glenmore Rd,
  Salisbury SP1 47 F5
Glenmore Rd,
  Swindon SN25 50 B6
Glenside SN12 40 C1
Glenville CI SN4 68 B6
Glenwood CI SN1 59 H5
Glevum Rd SN3 60 A4
Globe Ct SN11 25 B3
Gloucester CI SN14 26 B5
Gloucester Rd Ind Est
  SN16 37 C3
Gloucester Sq SN12 40 C3
Gloucester St SN1 59 F1
Gloucester St SN16 37 C4
Gloucester Walk BA13 65 C1
Glovers Ct SN16 37 B4
Glyndebourne CI SP2 45 H3
Goatacre 9 H6
Goathill 16 C4
Goddard Av SN1 59 G3
Goddard Rd SN9 42 B2
Goddards La SN8 20 B2
Godley Rd SP2 48 D1
Godshill 18 C4
Godwin Rd SN3 57 E1
Goggs La SP5 33 H4
Gold Vw SN5 59 E3

Goldcrest Walk SN3 57 H6
Golding Av SN8 38 B4
Goldney Av SN14 26 D3
Goldney Ho SN13 28 E2
Goldsborough Cl SN5 58 B1
Gomeldon 18 C1
Goodhall Ho SN11 25 C3
Goodwin Cl BA12 67 H2
Goodwin Ct SN1 60 A3
Goodwood Cl BA14 64 F4
Goodwood Way SN14 26 A6
Goodworth Clatford 15 E6
Goose Cl SN8 39 E5
Gooselands BA13 65 A4
Goosey 11 E4
Gore Cl SN25 51 E5
Gorringe Rd SP2 48 B1
Gorse Pl SN13 28 C3
Gosport 19 H6
Goughs Way SN4 68 B4
Gould Cl SP11 35 C3
Goulding Cl SN3 56 D3
Gower Cl SN2 56 B2
Grace Cl SP2 45 H1
Grafton 10 D2
Grafton Rd SN2 51 H5
Grailey Cl SN3 61 F3
Gramshaw Rd SP2 46 A6
Granary Cl SN10 31 F4
Granary Rd SN10 31 F4
Grancia Cl SN25 50 C4
Grand Trunk Rd SP9 41 A4
Grange Cl SN6 34 D4
Grange Dr SN3 56 D4
Grange Gdns SP1 47 F6
Grange Vw BA15 23 G2
Granham Cl SN8 38 D5
Granham Hill SN8 38 D6
Grantham Cl SN5 58 A4
Grantley Cl SN3 60 C3
Granville Rd SN12 40 A1
Granville Ter BA14 64 D1
Grasmere Cl SP2 48 D4
Grasmere,
  Swindon SN3 61 G3
Grasmere,
  Trowbridge BA14 63 F4
Graspan Rd SP11 35 F3
Grasshills La SN8 20 B1
Grateley 14 D6
Gravel Cl SP5 32 B2
Grayling Cl SN11 25 B2
Graythwaite Cl SN25 51 E5
Great Bedwyn 14 D2
Great Chalfield Manor (NT)
  SN12 13 F2
Great Cheverell 13 G4
Great Coxwell 10 D4
Great Durnford 14 B6
Great Elm 12 D5
Great Hinton 13 G3
Great Orchard BA15 22 B5
Great Pks BA14 29 D4
Great Roc Rd BA13 65 A2
Great Shefford 11 F6
Great Somerford 9 G5
Great Western Cl SN4 30 D4
Great Western Designer
  Village SN2 59 F1
Great Wishford 18 A1
Green Cl BA14 29 C5
Green Dro SN9 42 B3
Green Hill 10 A5
Green La,
  Bradford-on-Avon
  BA15 22 B3
Green La,
  Devizes SN10 31 E6
Green La, Downton SP5 32 B3
Green La, Ford SP4 47 G1
Green La,
  Trowbridge BA14 63 F6
Green La,
  Westbury BA13 65 B4
Green Lane Cl SP4 47 G1
Green Meadow Av
  SN25 55 E1
Green Ore 12 A4
Green Rd SN2 56 B1
Green St SN8 20 D4
Green Ter BA14 62 D4
Green Valley Av SN5 55 E1
Greenacres SP5 32 A3
Greenacres Way SN11 25 A3
Greenbridge Ind Est
  SN3 56 C5
Greenbridge Rd SN3 56 D6
Greenbridge
  Retail Pk SN3 56 C5
Greencroft St SP1 49 E1
Greenfield Rd SN10 31 E6
Greenfields SN3 53 G6
Greenham 15 G2
Greenhill Gdns BA14 63 G2

Greenhill Rd SN2 55 E2
Greenland Mills BA15 23 G3
Greenland Vw BA15 23 G3
Greenlands Cl SP4 24 C1
Greenlands Rd SN2 55 E2
Greens La SN4 43 C6
Greens Meade SP5 33 F5
Greensand Cl SN25 51 E4
Greenway Av SN15 27 E2
Greenway Cl SN3 57 E6
Greenway Ct SN15 27 E1
Greenway Dr SN15 36 B3
Greenway Gdns,
  Chippenham SN15 27 E2
Greenway Gdns,
  Trowbridge BA14 63 E3
Greenway La SN15 27 E1
Greenway Pk SN15 27 E2
Greenwich SN25 51 F5
Greenwood Av SP1 49 G1
Greenwood Ho SN25 50 C5
Greenwood Rd SN12 40 A5
Grenadier Cl BA12 66 D3
Gresham Cl SN3 60 C1
Greyfriars Cl SP1 49 E3
Greyhound La SP2 44 D3
Greywethers Av SN3 60 B4
Grierson Cl SN11 25 C4
Griffin Alley*,
  High St SN16 37 C4
Griffiths Cl SN3 57 E3
Grittenham 9 H5
Grittleton 9 F6
Grosmont Dr SN5 58 A2
Grosvenor Rd SN1 59 F2
Ground Cnr BA14 29 B5
Groundwell Ind Pk
  SN2 51 H4
Grouse Rd SN11 25 C2
Grove 11 F4
Grove Ct BA14 64 C2
Grove Hill SN6 34 C2
Grove La SP5 33 G3
Grove Leaze BA15 23 E3
Grove Orchard SN6 34 B2
Grove Rd SN13 28 E3
Grovelands Av SN1 59 H4
Grovelands BA12 67 F4
Grovelands Way BA12 66 C6
Grovely Cl SN5 54 A3
Grovely Vw SP2 44 B5
Groves St SN2 59 E1
Grundys SN3 61 G4
Gryphon Cl BA13 65 A2
Guensey Cl SN25 50 C5
Guilder La SP1 49 E1
Guildford Av SN3 60 C4
Gundry Cl,
  Chippenham SN15 27 G6
Gundry Cl,
  Devizes SN10 31 F4
Guppy St SN2 55 E6
Gurney Slade 12 B2
Gussage All Saints 17 H5
Gussage St Michael 17 H4
Guthrie Cl SN11 25 C3
Guy's Marsh 17 F3
Guyers La SN13 28 B2

H

Habrels Cl SN15 27 G5
Hackett Cl SN2 52 B6
Hackett Pl BA14 63 G4
Hackleton Rise SN3 57 E4
Hackney Way BA13 65 A3
Hackpen Cl SN4 43 C4
Haddons Cl SN16 37 A5
Haden Rd BA14 64 E1
Hadleigh Cl SN5 58 C1
Hadleigh Rise SN3 52 C6
Hadrians Cl,
  Salisbury SP2 46 A6
Hadrians Cl,
  Swindon SN3 57 F4
Haig Cl SN2 56 A1
Haines Ter SN9 42 B2
Hale 18 C4
Half Way Fm SN13 28 A2
Halfway 15 F2
Halfway Cl BA14 63 F4
Halfway Rd BA14 63 F5
Halifax Cl SN4 43 B4
Halifax Rd SN12 40 C6
Hall Cl SN4 43 B6
Hallam Moor SN3 61 G5
Hallatrow 12 C3
Hallen 8 A6
Hallsfield SN6 29 A2
Hallum Cl SP1 47 G4
Halmore 8 C2
Halstock 16 A5
Ham Cl BA14 29 B5

Ham Grn BA14 29 B5
Ham Rd BA13 65 A1
Ham Street 16 A1
Ham,
  Gloucestershire 8 C3
Ham, Wiltshire 15 E2
Hamble Cl SP1 47 E4
Hamble Rd SN25 55 H1
Hamble-le-Rice 19 G5
Hambleton Av SN10 31 G1
Hamilton Cl,
  Salisbury SP4 21 F3
Hamilton Cl,
  Swindon SN3 56 C6
Hamilton Dr SN14 26 A5
Hamilton Pk SP5 32 C2
Hamilton Rd SP1 46 D6
Hamlet Ct SN15 27 E2
Hammond Way BA14 63 E1
Hammonds SN6 29 C2
Hammoon 17 E4
Hampshire Cl,
  Salisbury SP4 24 F2
Hampshire Cl,
  Swindon SN5 54 A6
Hampshire Gdns BA13 65 C1
Hampshire Pl SN12 40 C3
Hampstead Norreys 11 G6
Hampstead Way SN25 51 E4
Hampton Cl SP2 45 F4
Hampton La BA12 66 D4
Hampton Mews BA13 65 B4
Hamptworth,
  Golf Club SP5 18 C3
Hamptworth Lodge SP5 18 C3
Hamstead Marshall 15 F2
Hamworthy Rd SN3 57 F6
Hanbury Rd SN3 60 C3
Hancock Cl SN15 27 H6
Handel St SN2 55 H5
Hanewell Rise BA14 63 F3
Hanging Langford 17 H1
Hanham 12 B1
Hankerton 9 H4
Hanks Cl SN16 37 B2
Hannington Cl SN2 51 G5
Hannington Wick 10 B3
Hannington,
  Hampshire 15 H4
Hannington,
  Swindon 10 B4
Hanover Cl BA14 63 E1
Hanson Cl SN5 54 B5
Harbour Cl SN5 55 E1
Harbour Vw SN25 55 E1
Harcourt Bsns Pk BA14 63 E2
Harcourt Rd SN2 55 F5
Harcourt Ter SP1 48 D1
Hardenhuish Av SN15 26 D3
Hardenhuish Brook
  SN14 26 A1
Hardenhuish La SN14 26 C2
Hardenhuish Pk SN14 26 C2
Hardens Cl SN15 27 G6
Hardens Mead SN15 27 H5
Hardhams Rise SN13 28 D3
Hardie Cl SN3 56 D3
Hardie Walk SN12 40 B4
Hardington 12 D4
Hardington
  Mandeville 16 A5
Hardington Marsh 16 A5
Hardley 19 F6
Hardway 16 D1
Hardwick 11 E1
Hardwick Cl SN25 51 F6
Hardwicke 9 E1
Hardy Cl SN25 50 C5
Hare & Hounds St
  SN10 31 E4
Hare Cl SN2 52 B5
Hare Knapp BA15 23 E3
Hare Warren Cl SP2 44 B5
Harebell Cl SN25 50 D6
Harebell Way SN10 31 G3
Harescombe 9 E1
Haresfield 9 E1
Harford Cl SN15 27 G6
Hargreaves Rd,
  Swindon SN25 52 A5
Hargreaves Rd,
  Trowbridge BA14 64 F1
Harlech Cl SN5 58 B3
Harlestone Rd SN3 57 E4
Harmony Pl BA14 64 F1
Harnham 18 B2
Harnham Rd SP2 48 B3
Harnham Trading Est
  SP2 48 A3
Harnhill 10 A2
Harnish Way SN14 26 C1
Harnwood Rd SP2 48 C5
Harper Rd SP2 46 B6
Harpers La SN16 37 B4

Harrier Cl SN11 25 A2
Harrier Ct SN12 40 C6
Harrington Way SN3 56 C6
Harris Ct SN11 25 C2
Harris Rd, Calne SN11 25 C2
Harris Rd, Swindon SN2 55 F3
Harrow Cl SN3 56 C3
Harrow Grove SN15 36 C2
Hartfield SN10 30 C6
Hartham La SN13 28 D1
Harthill Drove SP5 33 G5
Hartington Rd,
  Salisbury SP2 46 C6
Hartington Rd,
  Swindon SN25 50 B4
Hartland Cl SN3 60 D2
Hartley Way SP1 47 F2
Hartmoor Cl SN10 30 C5
Hartmoor Rd SN10 30 C6
Hartsthorn Cl SN2 54 C1
Harvard Cl SN2 48 D5
Harvard Way SP4 21 E3
Harvey Gro SN2 55 F3
Harwell 11 G4
Hastings Ct SN4 43 B6
Hastings Ct*,
  Devizes Rd SP2 46 C6
Hastings Drive SN15 36 C2
Hastings Rd SN13 28 E3
Hatch 17 G2
Hatch Rd SN3 56 D1
Hatchers Cres SN26 51 G1
Hatches La SP1 49 G3
Hatfield Cl SN25 50 D5
Hatford 11 E3
Hathaway Cl SN3 46 C4
Hathaway Rd SN2 52 B6
Hathaway Retail Pk
  SN15 27 E3
Hatherall Cl SN3 57 E3
Hatherden 15 E4
Hatherleigh Ct SN3 56 D6
Hatherley Rd SN3 57 E6
Hatherop 10 B2
Hathersage Moor SN3 61 G5
Hatton Gro SN3 60 C1
Hatton Way SN13 28 C3
Havelock St BA14 64 D1
Haven Cl SN3 56 D4
Havisham Dr SN25 50 C5
Hawcroft BA14 29 C4
Hawker Rd SN3 61 E3
Hawkeridge 13 F4
Hawkesbury 8 D5
Hawkesbury Upton 9 E4
Hawkfinch Cl SN3 61 G1
Hawkins Cl SN15 27 F6
Hawkins Mdw SN8 38 B4
Hawkins Rd SN8 20 B2
Hawkins St SN2 55 F6
Hawks Ridge SP2 48 D5
Hawkswood SN3 57 F5
Hawksworth Ind Est
  SN2 55 F6
Hawksworth Way SN2 55 F6
Hawthorn Av SN2 55 H3
Hawthorn Cl,
  Pewsey SN9 42 C1
Hawthorn Cl,
  Salisbury SP2 48 C1
Hawthorn Gro,
  Trowbridge BA14 64 C2
Hawthorn Gro,
  Westbury BA13 65 A3
Hawthorn Rd,
  Chippenham SN15 27 F2
Hawthorn Rd,
  Tidworth SP9 41 E2
Hayburn Rd SN25 51 E3
Haydock Cl SN14 26 A6
Haydon 16 C4
Haydon Court Dr SN25 50 D4
Haydon Ct SN25 50 D6
Haydon End La SN25 50 C5
Haydon View Rd SN25 51 H1
Haydon Wick 10 B4
Haydonleigh Dr SN25 50 D6
Hayes Cl BA14 63 E2
Haygrove Cl BA12 66 B4
Hayle Rd SN2 59 E1
Haynes Cl SN3 60 C4
Haynes Rd BA13 65 C3
Haywain Cl SN25 51 H4
Haywain SP4 21 D3
Hayward Cl,
  Chippenham SN15 27 G6
Hayward Cl,
  Swindon SN25 51 F5
Hayward Pl BA13 65 A4
Hazel Cl,
  Marlborough SP9 39 G4
Hazel Cl, Salisbury SP2 45 G3
Hazel Copse SN14 26 A5
Hazel End SN4 68 B5

Hazel Gro, Calne SN11 25 C6
Hazel Gro,
  Swindon SN25 55 H2
Hazel Gro,
  Trowbridge BA14 64 C3
Hazel Gro,
  Westbury BA13 65 A3
Hazel Way SN13 28 C3
Hazelbury Bryan 16 D5
Hazelbury Cres SN3 57 H4
Hazelmere Cl SN3 61 E3
Hazelwood Rd SN12 40 A4
Hazzards Hill BA12 36 C5
Headbourne Worthy 15 H1
Headington 11 H1
Headlands Gro SN2 56 A2
Headlands Ind Est SN2 56 B2
Headley 15 H3
Heath End 15 H3
Heath Rd SP2 46 A4
Heath Way SN3 56 D4
Heathcote Cl SN5 54 A5
Heathcote Rd SN12 40 C4
Heather Av SN12 40 C4
Heather Cl BA13 65 B2
Heather Shaw BA14 63 E5
Heather Way SN11 25 C6
Heathfield SN15 27 F1
Heaton Cl SN25 51 F5
Hebden Cl SN25 50 D4
Hebden Rd BA15 22 B6
Hector Rd SN25 50 B4
Heddington 13 H2
Heddington Cl,
  Swindon SN2 51 H6
Heddington Cl,
  Trowbridge BA14 64 D3
Hedge End 19 G5
Hedgerow Cl SN3 61 E2
Hedges Cl SN3 56 D2
Hedley Davis Ct SP2 48 B1
Hei-Lin Way SP11 35 C3
Helena Rd SN25 50 B3
Helmdon Rd BA14 62 A5
Helmsdale SN25 55 E1
Helmsdale Walk SN3 60 D3
Helps Well Rd BA14 63 H3
Helston Rd SN3 60 C2
Hemington 12 D4
Henbury 8 A6
Henderson Cl BA14 64 C1
Henford Pk BA12 67 E5
Henfords Marsh BA12 67 F5
Henley Dr SN6 34 C2
Henley Rd SN3 60 C3
Henman Ct SN25 51 F6
Henstridge 16 D3
Hepworth Rd SN25 51 E5
Herbert Rd,
  Redlynch SP5 33 F4
Herbert Rd,
  Salisbury SP2 46 A5
Herd St SN8 39 E3
Hereford Cl SN14 26 B6
Hereford Lawns SN3 60 B4
Herman Miller
  Ind Est SN14 26 C6
Hermitage La SN2 56 B2
Hermitage, Dorset 16 B5
Hermitage,
  West Berkshire 15 G1
Heron Cl SN11 25 D4
Heron Walk SP4 24 D2
Heron Way SN14 26 A4
Heronbridge Cl SN5 58 B2
Heronscroft SN3 57 F5
Heronslade BA12 67 H4
Heronswood SP2 48 D5
Herschel Cl SN5 50 A3
Hertford Cl SN3 60 C1
Hesketh Cres SN3 60 A4
Hewelsfield 8 A2
Hewitt Cl,
  Swindon SN3 61 F3
Hewitt Cl,
  Trowbridge BA14 64 E1
Hewlett Cl SN15 27 H6
Hexham Cl,
  Chippenham SN14 26 A5
Hexham Cl,
  Swindon SN5 58 A2
Heyford Cl SP4 21 F3
Heytesbury 13 G6
Heywood 13 F4
Heywood Cl SN12 51 G6
Hicks Cl SN4 43 B5
Hidcot Ct SN25 51 E4
High Cogges 11 F1
High Lawn SN10 30 B4
High Littleton 12 B3
High Mead SN4 68 C4
High Post
  Golf Club SP4 18 B1
High Rd, Salisbury SP5 49 F5

High Rd,
Swindon SN26 51 H1
High St, Amesbury SP4 21 B2
High St, Avebury SN8 20 C4
High St,
Blunsdon SN26 51 G1
High St, Bulford SP4 24 D3
High St, Calne SN11 25 B4
High St,
Chippenham SN15 27 E4
High St,
Corsham SN13 27 E4
High St, Cricklade SN6 29 B3
High St, Devizes SN10 30 D4
High St, Downton SP5 32 C3
High St,
Durrington SP4 24 B1
High St,
Haydon Wick SN25 51 E6
High St,
Highworth SN6 34 C3
High St,
Ludgershall SP11 35 C3
High St,
Malmesbury SN16 37 C4
High St, Manton SN8 38 A5
High St,
Marlborough SN8 38 D4
High St,
Melksham SN12 40 B4
High St, Pewsey SN9 42 B2
High St, Potterne SN10 42 A6
High St, Salisbury SP1 48 D2
High St, Swindon SN1 60 A3
High St, Tisbury SP3 43 B2
High St,
Warminster BA12 67 E3
High St,
Westbury BA13 65 C3
High St,
Wootton Bassett SN4 68 A5
High St,
Wroughton SN4 43 B6
High View Cl SP3 43 B3
Highbury Av SP2 46 B6
Highbury Cl SP2 46 B6
Highbury Pk BA12 67 G3
Highclere 15 F3
Highclere Av SN3 60 B3
Highdown Way SN25 51 F3
Highfield La SP5 33 F5
Highfield Rd,
Amesbury SP4 21 C3
Highfield Rd,
Bradford-on-Avon
BA15 23 G2
Highfield Rd,
Salisbury SP2 46 B6
Highfold SN4 68 C5
Highgrove Cl SN11 54 A6
Highland Cl SN5 54 A6
Highlands Rd SP2 46 B6
Highlands SN10 42 B5
Highnam Cl SN3 56 D3
Highway 14 A1
Highwood Cl SN2 54 C1
Highworth 10 B3
Highworth Community
Golf Centre SN6 34 A4
Highworth Rd,
South Marston SN3 53 G3
Highworth Rd,
Swindon SN3 56 D1
Highworth Recreation
Centre SN6 34 B4
Hill 8 C3
Hill Cl SP3 43 C1
Hill Corner Rd SN15 26 D1
Hill Grn SN15 27 E1
Hill Head 19 H6
Hill Rd SP1 47 G6
Hill Rise SN15 27 E1
Hill St BA14 63 F1
Hill Top 19 F6
Hill Top Av SP9 41 C1
Hill View Cl SP4 21 C2
Hill View Rd SN3 57 F4
Hill Vw SN10 30 C6
Hillary Cl SN25 55 H1
Hillbourne Cl BA12 67 F2
Hillcrest Cl SN1 59 F3
Hillcrest SN16 37 D5
Hillcroft SN1 25 C5
Hillesley 8 D4
Hilliers Yd SN8 39 E4
Hillingdon Rd SN3 60 D3
Hillmead Dr SN5 54 A4
Hillmead Employment
Area SN5 54 A4
Hillside Av SN1 59 F3
Hillside BA12 67 H4
Hillside Pk BA13 65 D3
Hillside Way SN26 51 F1
Hilltop Way SP1 46 D3

Hillview Rd SP1 49 E1
Hillwood Cl BA12 66 D5
Hillwood La BA12 66 D5
Hillwood Rd SN8 20 B3
Hillworth Gdns SN10 30 D5
Hillworth Rd SN10 30 C5
Hilly Flds SN13 28 C3
Hilmarton 9 H6
Hilmarton Av SN2 51 H5
Hilmarton Rd SN15 36 B1
Hilperton 13 F3
Hilperton Dr BA14 63 G4
Hilperton Rd BA14 63 E5
Hilton 17 E6
Hindle Way SN3 61 F2
Hindon 17 F1
Hindon La SP3 43 B1
Hinkson Cl SN25 13 F3
Hinton 8 D6
Hinton Blewett 12 B3
Hinton
Charterhouse 12 D3
Hinton Martell 17 H5
Hinton Parva 10 C5
Hinton St Mary 17 B3
Hinton St SN14 26 B3
Hinton Waldrist 11 E3
Hither Cl SN14 26 B3
Hitherspring SN13 28 D3
Hoadley Grn SP1 47 G4
Hobbes Cl SN16 37 B3
Hobbs Row SN3 56 D1
Hobbs Walk SN13 28 E2
Hobhouse Cl BA15 23 G5
Hobley Dr SN3 56 D2
Hocketts Cl SN15 36 B1
Hodds Hill SN5 54 A3
Hodge Cl SN10 31 F4
Hodge La SN16 37 B3
Hodson 10 B6
Holbrook La BA14 64 D2
Holbury 19 F6
Holcombe 12 C4
Holdcroft Cl SN26 51 H1
Holden Cres SN25 51 G4
Holders Rd SP4 21 D1
Holford Rise SN16 37 B4
Holliday Cl SN25 51 F5
Hollins Moor SN3 61 G5
Holloway SN16 37 C4
Hollows Cl SP2 48 C4
Holly Cl, Calne SN11 25 C6
Holly Cl, Pewsey SN9 42 C1
Holly Cl, Swindon SN2 55 F3
Holly Cres SN3 28 D3
Holly Tree Walk SN9 42 B2
Hollybush Cl,
Bradford-on-Avon
BA15 22 B2
Hollybush Cl,
Chippenham SN14 26 B1
Hollybush La SN9 42 C1
Hollybush Rd BA12 67 E1
Holmleigh SN25 54 D1
Holnest 16 C5
Holt Rd BA15 23 G3
Holt, Dorset 17 H6
Holt, Wiltshire 13 F3
Holton 16 C2
Holwell, Dorset 16 D5
Holwell, Oxfordshire 10 C1
Holyrood Cl BA14 64 C3
Holywell 16 B6
Home Cl BA14 64 E1
Home Fld BA12 36 A5
Home Fm SN6 34 B2
Home Grnd SN6 29 A1
Home Ground SN4 68 D4
Home Mead SN13 28 C3
Homefield Ho BA12 67 F3
Homefield SN4 68 B4
Homefields SN8 39 F5
Homington 18 B2
Homington Rd SN5 48 B6
Honda Car Plant SN3 53 E6
Honey Garston SN11 25 C4
Honeybone Walk SN3 57 H6
Honeybrook Cl SN14 26 C3
Honeyhill SN4 68 A5
Honeylight Vw SN25 51 F5
Honeymans Cl BA14 63 F6
Honeymead SN11 25 C4
Honeysuckle Cl,
Calne SN11 25 A3
Honeysuckle Cl,
Swindon SN25 50 D6
Honeysuckle Cl,
Trowbridge BA14 63 F6
Honiton Rd SN3 61 E2
Hook 10 A3
Hook Cl SN5 54 A3
Hooke 16 A6
Hoopers Pl SN1 60 A3
Hopgood Cl SN10 31 H1

Hopkins Orchard SN6 29 B3
Hopkins Rd SN10 31 G5
Hopton Cl SN5 58 B4
Hopton Ind Est SN10 31 G1
Hopton Rd SN10 31 G1
Horace St SN2 55 E6
Horcott Rd SN5 54 A3
Hornbeam Cres SN12 40 A4
Hornbeam Ct SN2 55 D3
Hornblotton Green 16 B1
Hornes Mead SN13 28 B2
Horningsham 13 E6
Hornsey Gdns SN3 52 D6
Horse Fair La SN6 29 C2
Horse Fair SN16 37 B3
Horse Rd BA14 63 E2
Horsebridge 19 E2
Horsebrook Pk SN11 25 C5
Horsebrook SN11 25 C5
Horsell Cl SN4 68 B4
Horsham Cres SN3 60 D3
Horsington 16 D3
Horsley 9 E3
Horspath 11 H2
Horton Av SN10 31 G1
Horton Cl BA15 23 G5
Horton Heath 19 G4
Horton Rd,
Devizes SN10 31 H1
Horton Rd,
Swindon SN2 52 B5
Horton, Dorset 17 H5
Horton,
South Gloucestershire
8 D5
Hospital Rd BA13 65 C4
Houghton 19 E1
Houghton Cl BA12 67 G4
Houldsworth Av BA14 67 H2
Howard Cl SN1 60 C1
Hubble Vw SN25 50 A4
Huddleston Cl SN2 56 A5
Hudson Rd,
Amesbury SP4 21 D2
Hudson Rd,
Malmesbury SN16 37 B3
Hudson Rd,
Salisbury SP1 46 C4
Hudson Way SN2 51 F5
Hudswell La SN13 28 A3
Hughenden Yd SN8 38 D4
Hughes Cl SN3 28 B4
Hughes St SN2 55 E6
Hugo Dr SN25 51 F4
Huish 14 B2
Hulbert Cl SN13 28 C3
Hullavington 9 F5
Hulse Rd SP1 46 D5
Humber La SP9 41 C4
Humbolts Hold SN5 27 F6
Hungerdown La SN14 26 B6
Hungerford 15 E1
Hungerford Av BA14 64 B1
Hungerford
Newtown 15 E1
Hungerford Rd,
Calne SN11 25 C3
Hungerford Rd,
Chippenham SN15 26 D2
Hunstrete 12 C2
Hunters Chase BA13 65 A4
Hunters Gro SN3 55 G4
Huntingdon Pl BA15 23 F2
Huntingdon Rise BA15 23 E1
Huntingdon St BA15 23 F1
Huntingdon Way SN14 26 B5
Huntley Cl SN3 56 C6
Hunts Hill SN26 51 G1
Hunts Rise SN3 53 E4
Huntsland SN4 68 C4
Hurley Cl SP4 21 F3
Hursley 19 F3
Hurst Cres SN2 55 H2
Hurstbourne Priors 15 F5
Hurstbourne Tarrant 15 F4
Hyde La,
Marlborough SN8 38 D3
Hyde La, Salisbury SP3 32 A3
Hyde Rd, Swindon SN2 52 A5
Hyde Rd,
Trowbridge BA14 62 D4
Hyde,
Gloucestershire 9 F2
Hyde, Hampshire 18 B5
Hylder Cl SN2 54 C1
Hyson Cres SP11 35 E3
Hysopp Cl SN2 54 B1
Hythe 19 F5
Hythe Mews SN1 59 G3

Ibberton 17 E5
Ibsley 18 B5
Ibthorpe 15 E4
Ibworth 15 H4
Icomb Cl SN5 58 B3
Idmiston 18 C1
Idovers Dr SN5 58 B2
Idstone 10 D5
Iffley Rd SN2 55 F5
Iford La BA15 22 A6
Iford Manor BA15 22 A6
Ilchester 16 A3
Ilkeston Rd SN25 50 B4
Imber 13 G5
Imber Av SP4 21 E3
Imber Rd BA12 67 F3
Imber Walk SN2 51 G5
Imber Way BA12 67 G2
Imberwood Cl BA12 67 F3
India Av SP2 46 B6
Indigo Gdns BA13 65 B3
Inglesbatch 12 C3
Inglesham 10 C3
Inglesham Rd BA14 64 E3
Inglesham Rd SN2 51 H6
Ingram Cl BA13 65 B3
Ingram Rd SN12 40 D3
Ingram St SN16 37 C4
Ingst 8 B4
Inkpen 15 E2
Inlands Cl SN9 42 B1
Intercity Ind Est SN12 40 A2
Interface Bsns Centre
SN4 68 C5
International Business
Centre 11 G5
Inverary Rd SN4 43 B4
Ipswich St SN2 55 H5
Iron Acton 8 C5
Ironmonger Cl SN3 38 D3
Ironstone Cl SN25 50 D4
Irston Way SN5 58 A3
Irving Way SN8 38 C4
Isbury La SN8 39 E5
Isbury Rd SN8 39 E5
Isis Cl, Calne SN11 25 B2
Isis Cl, Swindon SN25 55 G1
Isis Trading Est SN1 56 C4
Islandmead SN3 61 F2
Islay Cres SN6 34 B2
Islington BA14 62 D4
Itchen Abbas 19 H1
Itchen Stoke 19 H1
Itchington 8 C5
Ivy Field Cl SN15 27 E4
Ivy Fld SN13 28 E1
Ivy La SN15 27 E4
Ivy Mead BA12 36 C5
Ivy Rd SN15 27 E4
Ivy St SP1 49 E2
Ivy Ter SP1 23 F2
Iwerne Courtney or
Shroton 17 F5
Iwerne Minster 17 F4
Ixworth Cl SN5 54 A6

Jack Paul Cl BA12 36 B4
Jack Thorne Cl SN5 54 A3
Jackson Cl SN10 31 F5
Jacobs Walk SN3 61 G3
Jaggard Vw SP4 21 D3
James Rd SP4 21 D1
James St,
Salisbury SP2 46 C6
James St,
Trowbridge BA14 62 D4
James Watt Cl SN2 55 F6
Jamrud Rd SP9 41 B3
Jargeau St SN3 28 E3
Jasmine Cl, Calne SN11 25 C6
Jasmine Cl,
Chippenham SN14 26 B2
Jasmine Cl,
Swindon SN25 54 D1
Jasmine Way BA14 63 E6
Javelin Cl SP4 21 E3
Jefferies Av SN2 56 A2
Jefferies Cl SN8 38 C4
Jenkins St BA14 62 C4
Jennings St SN2 55 E6
Jersey Pk SN5 54 A5
Jewell Cl SP1 47 G4
Joanna Cl SP5 32 A3
Jogoda Cl SN25 50 C5
John Betjeman Cl
SN16 37 C2
John French Way SP4 24 E3
John Gay Rd SP4 21 D2
John Herring Cres SN3 56 D4

John Rennie Cl,
Bradford-on-Avon
BA15 23 G5
John Rennie Cl,
Devizes SN10 30 C5
John Rumble Ct SN10 31 E4
Johnson Way SP11 35 C3
Joiner La SN1 60 A3
Jole Cl SN2 52 B5
Jolliffe St SN1 59 F1
Jones Hill BA15 23 E5
Jordon Cl SN15 27 G6
Joseph St SN1 59 F2
Joyce Cl SN25 51 F4
Jubilee Cl BA13 65 C3
Jubilee Gdns SN16 37 B3
Jubilee Rd SN2 54 D2
Jump Farm Rd SN10 31 F4
Junction Rd BA15 23 F3
Juniper Cl SN3 57 E4
Juniper Ct SP9 41 E2
Juniper Dr SP1 46 D3
Juno Way SN5 59 E3

Kandahar SN8 20 C1
Karachi SP9 41 C1
Karslake Cl SN3 61 E3
Katifer La SN16 37 B4
Keates Cl BA14 63 E4
Keates Cl SN4 68 C3
Keats Cres SN11 56 C1
Keble Cl SN3 57 E6
Keevil 13 G3
Keevil Av SN11 25 A4
Keinton Mandeville 16 A2
Kelham Cl SN3 60 C3
Kelham Gdns SN8 39 E4
Kellsboro Rd SN4 43 A4
Kelly Gdns SN25 51 F5
Kelmscott Rd SN25 55 H1
Kelmscott 10 D3
Kelsey Rd SP1 49 E1
Kelso Cl SN4 26
Kelston 12 D2
Kelvin Rd SN3 56 D5
Kemble 9 G3
Kemble Dr SN2 55 F6
Kembles Cl SN16 37 D5
Kembrey Bsns Pk SN2 52 A3
Kembrey St SN2 56 A3
Kemerton Walk SN3 60 D3
Kemp Cl SN10 31 F4
Kempsford 10 D2
Kempton Park Ct SN14 26 A5
Ken Savage Cl SN3 60 C1
Kencot Cl SN2 51 H5
Kencot 10 D2
Kendal SN5 58 B3
Kendrick Cl BA13 65 C3
Kendrick Ind Est SN2 24 D5
Kenilworth Gdns SN12 40 B5
Kenilworth Lawns SN3 60 C4
Kennedy Dr SN3 61 F2
Kennet & Avon
Canal Museum SN10 30 D5
Kennet Av SN25 55 G1
Kennet Cl,
Melksham SN12 40 A1
Kennet Cl,
Warminster BA12 66 D5
Kennet Gdns BA15 23 F4
Kennet Mews SN8 39 E4
Kennet Pl SN8 39 E4
Kennet Rd,
Devizes SN10 31 E6
Kennet Rd,
Swindon SN4 43 B4
Kennet Rd,
Tidworth SP9 41 E2
Kennet Way BA14 63 E3
Kennington 11 G2
Kensington Cl BA14 63 E4
Kensington Flds BA14 64 A1
Kensington Rd SP2 46 C6
Kensington Way SN14 26 A5
Kent Cl SN14 26 B5
Kent Rd SP2 48 B4
Kent's Oak 19 E3
Kenton Cl SN3 61 E1
Kenton Dr BA14 63 F4
Kenwin Cl SN3 57 E2
Kenwood Cl BA14 63 F6
Kerrs Way SN4 43 B5
Kerry Cl SN5 54 A6
Kerry Cres SN11 25 C5
Kershaw Rd SN3 61 F3
Kestrel Cl, Calne SN11 25 B2
Kestrel Cl,
Tidworth SP9 41 E2
Kestrel Dr SN3 57 H6
Keswick Rd SN3 61 E3

Ketton Cl BA14 62 A4
Kew Dr BA14 64 B1
Keyneston Rd SN3 57 F6
Keynsham 12 B2
Keynsham Walk SN3 61 E3
Kickdom Cl SP4 21 E3
Kilda Rd SN6 34 B2
Kilmersdon 12 C4
Kilmington 17 E1
Kiln Cl SN10 31 G5
Kiln La SN2 55 E4
Kiln Rd SP5 33 G3
Kilsby Dr SN3 57 E5
Kilsyth Cl SN5 58 A2
Kilverts Cl SN14 26 B5
Kimberley Rd SN3 60 C3
Kimmeridge Cl SN3 60 C3
Kimmeridge Ct SN1 59 H3
Kimpton 14 D5
Kimpton Av SP1 47 G3
King Alfred Dr SN9 42 B1
King Alfred St SN15 26 D2
King Alfred Way BA15 22 A2
King Charles Ho SN14 26 A3
King Charles Rd SN5 58 A3
King Edward Cl SN11 25 B3
King La BA12 66 C4
King St,
  Melksham SN12 40 B4
King St, Salisbury SP2 44 D3
King St,
  Warminster BA12 66 C5
King's Somborne 19 E2
King's Stag 16 D5
King's Stanley 9 E2
Kingfisher Cl SP2 48 D5
Kingfisher Ct SN11 25 B2
Kingfisher Dr,
  Devizes SN10 31 G2
Kingfisher Dr,
  Salisbury SP4 24 C1
Kingfisher Dr,
  Swindon SN3 57 F6
Kingfisher Dr,
  Westbury BA13 65 C2
Kingham Cl SN14 26 D4
Kings Av,
  Chippenham SN14 26 A4
Kings Av,
  Corsham SN13 28 D1
Kings Av,
  Swindon SN6 34 C3
King's Cnr SN9 42 C2
Kings Ct, Salisbury SP2 44 D3
Kings Ct,
  Swindon SN5 58 B3
Kings Ct,
  Warminster BA12 66 C5
Kings Gdns BA14 63 E1
Kings Rd SP1 46 D6
Kings Rise BA12 66 C4
Kings Walk SN16 37 C4
Kings Wall SN16 37 C4
Kings Worthy 19 G1
Kingsbury Sq,
  Melksham SN12 40 B4
Kingsbury Sq,
  Salisbury SP2 44 D4
Kingsbury St,
  Calne SN11 25 C5
Kingsbury St,
  Marlborough SN8 38 D3
Kingsclere 15 G3
Kingscote 9 E3
Kingsdon 16 A2
Kingsdown Golf Club
  SN13 13 E2
Kingsdown Ind Est
  SN25 52 D5
Kingsdown La SN2 51 H3
Kingsdown Orchard
  SN2 52 B6
Kingsdown Rd,
  Swindon SN2 52 C6
Kingsdown Rd,
  Trowbridge BA14 64 C3
Kingsfield BA15 23 G2
Kingsfield Cl BA15 23 G2
Kingsfield Grange Rd
  BA15 23 G2
Kingsford Cl SP5 33 F5
Kingshill Ct*,
  Kingshill Rd SN1 59 F2
Kingsland Rd SP2 46 C6
Kingsley Av SN4 68 B3
Kingsley Gdns SN10 31 F5
Kingsley Pl BA14 62 A5
Kingsley Rd,
  Chippenham SN14 26 C4
Kingsley Rd,
  Devizes SN10 31 F4
Kingsley Way SN2 52 A6
Kingsmanor Wharf
  SN10 31 G2

Kingsmere Pad BA12 36 A5
Kingsthorpe Gro SN3 57 F5
Kingston Av BA15 23 G4
Kingston Bagpuize 11 F3
Kingston Deverill 17 E1
Kingston Lisle 10 D4
Kingston Rd,
  Bradford-on-Avon
  BA15 23 F3
Kingston Rd,
  Swindon SN3 60 D3
Kingston, Dorset 16 D5
Kingston,
  Hampshire 18 B6
Kingsway Cl SN3 60 C3
Kingsway Trading Est
  SP2 44 D2
Kingswood Av BA15 60 D2
Kingswood Chase
  BA14 64 A1
Kingswood SN4 43 B6
Kingswood,
  Gloucestershire 8 D4
Kingswood,
  South Gloucestershire
  12 C1
Kington Langley 9 G6
Kington Magna 16 D3
Kington St Michael 9 F6
Kingweston 16 A2
Kinneir Cl SN13 28 F3
Kintbury 15 E2
Kipling Cl SP3 45 E2
Kipling Gdns SN2 52 B6
Kirby Cl, Devizes SN10 31 F3
Kirby Cl, Swindon SN3 60 C2
Kirby Rd SN13 28 D2
Kirkee Rd SP9 41 C3
Kirkstall Cl SN5 58 B2
Kirktonhill Rd SN5 58 C1
Kishorn Cl SN5 54 B3
Kitchener Rd SP4 21 C2
Kitchener St SN2 55 H4
Kitefield SN6 29 B2
Kivel Ct SP2 46 D6
Knapp Cl SN2 55 F3
Knapp Hill SN8 14 B2
Knole Cl SN25 51 E3
Knolton Walk SN3 60 D3
Knook 13 G6
Knowlands SN6 34 D1
Knowle 12 B1
Knowsley Rd SN3 60 D3
Kohat Cl SP9 41 B2
Kohat Rd SP9 41 C4
Kopernik Rd SN2 50 C4

L

Laburnum Dr,
  Melksham SN12 40 A5
Laburnum Dr,
  Swindon SN4 68 B2
Laburnum Gro BA14 64 C2
Laburnum Rd SN2 55 H2
Lacemakers Rd SN16 37 C2
Lackham Circus SN14 26 C5
Lackham Country Park
  SN15 13 G1
Lacock 13 F2
Lacock Abbey (NT)
  SN15 13 G2
Lacock Dr BA14 63 H4
Lacock Gdns BA14 63 H4
Lacock Rd,
  Corsham SN13 28 F2
Lacock Rd,
  Swindon SN2 51 H6
Ladds La SN15 15 E5
Lady Coventry Rd
  SN15 27 G4
Lady Diana Ct SP11 35 D2
Lady Down Vw SP3 43 C1
Lady Godley Rd SP9 41 C1
Lady Jane Walk SP11 35 D2
Lady La SN25 51 E5
Lady Mead SN6 29 B2
Ladydown, Calne SN11 25 C3
Ladydown,
  Trowbridge BA14 62 D3
Ladyfield Brook SN14 26 C3
Ladyfield Rd SN14 26 C4
Ladysmith Rd SP2 46 A5
Lahore Cl SP9 41 C1
Lahore Rd SP9 41 D3
Laines Head SN14 26 D1
Laineys Cl SN8 39 E3
Lake 14 B6
Lakeside SN3 60 B3
Lamb Ale Grn BA14 64 E1
Lambdown Ter SP11 41 F2
Lambert Cl SN5 58 A4
Lamberts SN14 26 B3

Lambourn 11 E6
Lambourn Av SN3 60 A4
Lambourne Cres SN12 40 C3
Lambrok Cl BA14 64 A2
Lambrok Rd BA14 64 A1
Lampard Ter SP2 44 B4
Lampeter Rd SN25 50 B4
Lamyatt 16 C1
Lanac Rd SN3 56 D4
Lancaster Mews SN3 53 F4
Lancaster Pl SN3 53 F4
Lancaster Rd,
  Melksham SN12 40 C6
Lancaster Rd,
  Swindon SN4 43 B5
Lancaster Sq SN15 36 C1
Landford 18 C4
Landford Manor 18 D3
Landor Rd SN25 51 E3
Lanes Cl SP4 21 D2
Lanfear Cl SP4 21 D2
Langdale Dr SN5 58 A4
Langford 10 D2
Langford Gro SN3 60 A1
Langford La SP5 33 F3
Langford Rd BA14 62 C4
Langholm Av BA12 66 B4
Langholm Cl BA12 66 B4
Langley 19 G6
Langley Burrell 9 G6
Langley Ct SN15 27 E3
Langley Rd,
  Chippenham SN15 27 E3
Langley Rd,
  Swindon SN5 54 A4
Langley Rd,
  Trowbridge BA14 64 C3
Langley Wood NNR
  SP5 18 C3
Langport Cl SN5 58 A2
Langridge 12 D1
Langstone Way SN5 58 B1
Lanhams Cl BA13 65 C3
Lanhill Vw SN14 26 C1
Lanhydrock Cl SN5 58 A3
Lansbury Dr SN3 56 B1
Lansdown Cl,
  Melksham SN12 40 D2
Lansdown Cl,
  Trowbridge BA14 64 C1
Lansdown Gro SN15 27 E2
Lansdown Pl SN8 39 E3
Lansdowne Cl SN11 25 B3
Lansdowne Ct
  Bsns Pk SN14 26 B3
Lansdowne Grn*,
  Sheep St SN14 31 E4
Lansdowne Ter*,
  Sheep St SN14 31 E4
Lapwing Cl SN3 61 H1
Lapwing Cres SN14 26 C1
Larch Cl SN12 40 A4
Larch Gro BA14 64 C2
Larchmore Cl SN25 55 F2
Lark Cl SP9 41 E2
Larkdown BA14 63 F5
Larkhall 12 D2
Larkham Rise SN15 27 H2
Larkhill 14 B6
Larkhill Rd SP4 24 A2
Larkin Cl SP11 35 D3
Larksfield SN3 57 F5
Larkspur BA14 63 F5
Late Broads BA15 22 A2
Latteridge 8 C5
Lattiford 16 C2
Latton 10 A3
Latton Cl SN2 51 G5
Laughton Way SN25 51 F5
Laurel Cl SN2 56 B2
Laurel Dr,
  Chippenham SN15 26 D5
Laurel Dr,
  Marlborough SN8 39 G4
Laurel Gro BA14 64 C2
Laurence Ct SP11 35 C3
Lavender Cl,
  Melksham SN12 40 C5
Lavender Cl,
  Trowbridge BA14 64 F1
Lavender Dr SN11 25 C6
Laverstock 18 B2
Laverstock Pk SP1 47 G6
Laverstock Pk West SP1 47 G6
Laverstock Rd SP1 49 F1
Laverstoke 15 G5
Laverton 13 E4
Laverton Cl BA13 65 C2
Laverton Grn BA13 65 B5
Laverton Rd BA13 65 B5
Lawrence Acre SN8 39 E2
Lawrence Cl,
  Devizes SN10 31 E6

Lawrence Cl,
  Salisbury SP4 21 D3
Lawrence Cl,
  Swindon SN3 61 E3
Lawton Cl SN3 60 D4
Le Marchant Cl SN10 31 G2
Lea 9 G5
Lea Cl SN25 51 F3
Leaf Cl SN8 39 E3
Leafield Pl BA14 62 A5
Leafield Way SN13 28 C4
Leamington Gro SN3 60 B5
Leap Gate BA14 63 G4
Leaze Rd,
  Marlborough SN8 38 D3
Leaze Rd,
  Melksham SN12 40 D1
Lechlade 10 C2
Lechlade Rd SN6 34 C3
Leckford 19 F1
Leckhampstead 11 F6
Ledger Hill Cl SP4 24 D3
Lee 19 E4
Lees Ct SP2 46 C6
Legate Cl SN15 27 H6
Leigh Cl,
  Trowbridge BA14 64 E3
Leigh Cl,
  Westbury BA13 65 A5
Leigh Common 16 D2
Leigh Delamere 9 F6
Leigh Park Rd BA15 23 F1
Leigh Park Way BA13 63 A4
Leigh Rd,
  Bradford-on-Avon
  BA15 23 G1
Leigh Rd,
  Swindon SN2 51 H6
Leigh Rd,
  Trowbridge BA14 29 A4
Leigh Rd,
  Westbury BA13 65 B4
Leigh upon Mendip 12 C5
Leigh Woods 12 A1
Leigh, Dorset 16 B5
Leigh, Wiltshire 10 A4
Leighterton 9 E4
Leighton 12 D6
Leighton Av SN3 60 C3
Leighton Grn BA13 65 C4
Leighton Home
  Farm Ct BA13 65 C4
Leighton La BA13 65 B4
Leighton Park Rd BA13 65 B5
Leighton Pk North
  BA13 65 B5
Leighton Pk West BA13 65 A5
Leighton Recreation
  Centre BA13 65 C4
Leland Cl SN16 37 C2
Lena Cl SP11 35 C3
Lennox Dr SN3 60 B1
Lenton Cl SN14 26 A4
Leonard Cheshire Cl
  SP4 21 E3
Leonard Stanley 9 E2
Leslie Cl SN5 58 A3
Leslie Rise BA15 22 C6
Letcombe Bassett 11 E5
Letcombe Regis 11 E5
Lethbridge Rd SN1 59 H4
Letterage Rd SN5 54 A3
Levell Ct SP11 35 C3
Leven SN5 58 A4
Leverton Gate SN3 60 C6
Lew 11 E1
Lewis Cl SN13 28 C3
Lewis Cl*,
  Hepworth Rd SN25 51 E5
Lewisham Cl SN25 55 E2
Lewis's Ct SN10 30 D4
Ley Rd BA13 65 A4
Lichen Cl SN2 54 C1
Lickhill Rd SN11 25 B2
Lidbrook SN11 25 C3
Liddington 10 C5
Liddington St SN2 55 H2
Liddington Way BA14 64 F3
Liden Dr SN3 61 F4
Light Cl SN13 28 E1
Lightning Rd SP4 21 E3
Lilac Cl SN2 55 G3
Lilac Gro,
  Trowbridge BA14 64 B2
Lilac Gro,
  Westbury BA13 65 A3
Lilac Way SN11 25 C6
Lillian Lock Gdns SN2 51 H6
Lillington 16 B5
Lily Walk SP4 24 D2
Lime Av SN12 40 A4
Lime Cl SN15 36 D2
Lime Kiln
  Leisure Centre SN4 68 A3

Lime Kiln SN4 68 A3
Lime Kiln Way SP2 48 D5
Lime Tree Cl SN11 25 A4
Limes Av SN25 55 G2
Limestone Dr SN13 28 C3
Limington 16 A3
Limpley Stoke 12 D3
Lincoln Grn SN12 40 C1
Linden Av SN25 55 H2
Linden Cl,
  Andover SP11 35 E3
Linden Cl, Calne SN11 25 C5
Linden Cl,
  Salisbury SP1 49 G1
Linden Cl,
  Swindon SN4 68 B2
Linden Cres BA15 22 C6
Linden Gro SN12 40 B5
Linden Ter SN10 31 E4
Lindisfarne Cl BA15 22 B2
Lindisfarne SN4 68 B3
Lindley Cl SP9 41 E3
Linford 18 B5
Linford Rd SP1 47 G3
Lingfield SN14 26 A6
Link Av SN5 58 A1
Link Centre SN5 58 B1
Link Way SP1 47 F3
Linkenholt 15 E3
Linley Cl SN1 59 H5
Linley Rd SN26 51 H1
Linnet Rd SN14 25 C2
Linnetsdene,
  Salisbury SP2 48 D5
Linnetsdene,
  Swindon SN3 57 F5
Linslade St SN2 59 E1
Linwood 18 C5
Liskeard Way SN5 58 A4
Lismore Rd SN6 34 B2
Lister Gro BA15 22 C6
Lister Rd SN4 43 C4
Litchfield 15 G4
Little Av SN2 55 F3
Little Badminton 9 E5
Little Bedwyn 15 D2
Little Brittox SN10 30 D4
Little Cheverell 13 H4
Little Clarendon SP3 17 H1
Little Common BA14 64 E4
Little Coxwell 10 D4
Little Down SN14 26 C4
Little Englands SN15 27 F5
Little Faringdon 10 C2
Little Island SN9 42 A1
Little Langford 17 H1
Little London 15 F4
Little Orchard BA14 66 D3
Little Park Cl SN15 36 B3
Little Parks SN14 29 C4
Little Sodbury 8 D5
Little Somborne 19 F1
Little Somerford 9 H5
Little Wittenham 11 H4
Little Woodfalls Dr SP5 33 F6
Littlecote Cl SN5 58 C2
Littlecote Rd SN25 26 B5
Littlejohn Av SN12 40 C1
Littlemore 11 H2
Littleton 11 H2
Littleton Drew 9 E6
Littleton Panell 13 H4
Littleton-upon-
  Severn 8 B4
Littleworth 10 D3
Litton 12 B4
Llandogo 8 A2
Lockeridge 14 B2
Lockeridge Cl BA14 64 E2
Lockerley 18 D2
Locks Heath 19 G5
Locks La SP2 45 F4
Locksgreen Cres SN25 54 D1
Lockside SN15 27 F6
Loddon Way BA15 23 G4
Lode Hill SP5 32 D3
Lodge Cl SN15 25 A4
Lodge Ct BA14 63 F6
Lodge Dro SP5 33 F6
Lodge Rd SN15 27 G6
Logan Cl SN3 60 B1
Lombard St SN5 58 B3
Lomond Cl SN5 54 B3
London Rd, Calne SN11 25 C5
London Rd,
  Chippenham SN15 27 F5
London Rd,
  Devizes SN10 31 E4
London Rd,
  Marlborough SN8 39 E4
London Rd,
  Salisbury SP4 21 C2
London St SN1 59 G1
Long Ashton 12 A1

Long Cl,
Chippenham SN15 27 G5
Long Cl, Salisbury SP5 32 A3
Long Common 19 G4
Long Crichel 17 G5
Long Hill BA12 36 A5
Long Newnton 9 G4
Long Ridings SN14 26 D1
Long St SN10 30 D4
Long Wittenham 11 H3
Longbarrow Rd SN11 25 A4
Longbridge Deverill 13 F6
Longburton 16 C5
Longcot 10 D4
Longcroft Av SN10 31 F4
Longcroft Cres SN10 31 F5
Longcroft Rd SN10 31 F4
Longfellow Cl SN25 51 F2
Longfellow Cres SN8 68 C3
Longfield Cl SP4 24 B1
Longfield SN8 20 B5
Longfields Walk SN10 31 E6
Longford Rd SN12 40 B5
Longhill Dr SP2 49 E5
Longland SP2 48 B1
Longleat Gdn SN2 51 H6
Longleat House
& Safari Park BA12 13 E5
Longleaze La,
Melksham SN12 40 C5
Longleaze La,
Melksham SN12 40 D5
Longleaze SN4 68 B3
Longparish 15 F5
Longs Yd BA15 23 F3
Longstock 19 E1
Longstock Ct SN5 58 B1
Longstone SN14 26 B2
Longthorpe Cl SN5 58 C3
Longworth 11 F3
Longworth Dr SN25 50 B4
Lonsdale Cl SN26 51 H1
Lonsdale Gdns SN25 40 B5
Loosehanger SP5 33 H6
Lopcombe Corner 18 C1
Lopes Way BA13 65 B1
Lord Wilmot Ho SN14 26 A3
Lords Cft SP4 21 C1
Lords Mead SN14 26 B3
Lordsmead Rd BA12 36 C6
Lorne St SN1 59 G1
Lottage Rd SN8 20 C2
Lottage Way SN8 20 C1
Louise Rayner Pl SN15 27 F4
Louviers Way SN1 59 H5
Love La SP1 49 E2
Loveage Cl SN2 54 C1
Lovell Cl SN3 57 G6
Lover 18 C3
Loveridge Cl SN2 52 B5
Lovers Walk SN15 27 E5
Lovett Grn SP1 47 F4
Lovington 16 B2
Low Ct SN25 51 F3
Low La SN11 25 D5
Lowa Cl SP9 41 C3
Lowa Rd SP9 41 B3
Lowbourne SN12 40 B3
Lowden Av SN14 26 D3
Lowden Hill SN15 26 D4
Lowden SN15 26 D5
Lower Alma St BA14 63 E6
Lower Bond St Bldgs
BA14 64 C1
Lower Cam 8 D2
Lower Church Flds
SN8 39 E5
Lower Chute 15 E4
Lower Cl BA14 62 D4
Lower Field SN14 26 B2
Lower Folly SP2 44 B6
Lower Green 15 E2
Lower Marsh Rd BA12 67 E5
Lower Prospect Pl SN8 39 E3
Lower Rd, Britford SP5 49 F5
Lower Rd,
Quidhampton SP2 45 F4
Lower Rd,
Salisbury SP2 46 A6
Lower St SP2 48 C3
**Lower Stanton
St Quintin** 9 G5
Lower Swanwick 19 G5
Lower Upham 19 H3
Lower Wharf SN10 30 C4
Lower Woodford 18 B1
Lowes Cl SN5 54 A3
Lowmead BA14 63 E4
Loxley Cl SN12 40 C1
Loxley Walk SN3 60 D4
Loyalty St SN14 26 C4
Luccombe Quarry
BA15 23 G2
Lucerne Cl SN4 68 A2

Luckett Way SN11 25 C3
Luckington 9 E5
Luddesdown Rd SN5 58 B3
Ludgershall 14 D4
Ludgershall
Bsns Pk SN16 35 C4
Ludgershall
Castle SP11 35 C2
Ludgershall Rd,
Swindon SN5 59 E3
Ludgershall Rd,
Tidworth SP9 41 D2
Ludlow Cl,
Chippenham SN15 27 G6
Ludlow Cl,
Swindon SN3 60 B3
Ludlow Cl,
Warminster BA12 66 D5
Ludlow Cl,
Westbury BA13 65 B1
Ludmead Rd SN13 28 F3
Ludwell 17 G3
Lukas SN25 51 E3
Lullington 12 D4
Lulsgate Bottom 12 A2
Lulworth Rd SN25 54 D1
Lumley Cl SP2 45 H2
Lumley Walk SP4 21 E3
Luna Ct SN25 50 A4
Lupin Ct SN2 56 B1
Lutyens Gate SN3 60 C6
Luxfield Rd BA12 66 C3
Lyall Cl SN25 51 E3
Lyddieth Ct BA15 22 A2
Lyddon Way SN25 55 E1
Lydiard House
& Park SN5 10 A5
Lydiard Millicent 10 A5
Lydiard SN14 26 B5
Lydiard Way BA14 64 D3
Lydlinch 16 D4
Lydney 8 B2
Lyford 11 F3
Lyme Av BA12 66 D4
Lyme Way SN25 51 F6
Lynch Cl BA12 36 C5
Lynch Field Rd SP4 21 C3
Lynchets Rd SP4 21 C3
Lyndhurst 19 E5
Lyndhurst Cres SN3 60 D1
Lyndhurst Rd SP4 21 C3
Lyneham 9 H6
Lyneham Cl SN2 51 G5
Lyneham Way BA14 63 G5
Lynes Vw SN8 38 C4
Lynmouth Rd SN2 59 E1
Lynton Rd SN2 55 E3
Lynwood Dr BA14 62 A5
Lynwood Gro SN2 54 C1
Lyon's Gate 16 C6
Lypiatt Mead SN13 28 E4
Lypiatt Rd SN13 28 E4
Lysander Rd SN12 40 C6
Lysley Cl SN15 27 G4
Lytchett Way SN3 57 F6
Lytham Cl SN15 27 G4

M

Macaulay Sq SN11 25 C4
Macie Dr SN13 28 C3
Mackensie Cl SN3 61 G4
Macklin Rd SP2 46 B5
MacNeice Dr SN8 38 B4
Maddocks Hill BA12 66 C5
Magistrates Ct SN15 27 F5
Magnolia Cl SN2 55 G3
Magnolia Ct SN2
Magnolia Rise,
Calne SN11 25 C6
Magnolia Rise,
Trowbridge BA14 63 F6
Magnon Rd BA15 23 E2
Magpie La SN3 57 H6
Magpie Mews*,
Bridewell St SN10 31 E5
Maida Vale SN25 50 C4
Maiden Bradley 13 E6
Main Rd SP4 21 F3
Maitland Cl SN15 27 G6
Maitland Rd SN3 56 C6
Majoram Cl SN2 50 C6
Mall Mews SN1 59 G3
Mallard Av SN15 36 C2
Mallard Cl, Calne SN11 25 D5
Mallard Cl,
Salisbury SP2 48 C3
Mallard Cl,
Swindon SN3 61 G1
Mallard Cl,
Westbury BA13 65 C2
Mallow Cl,
Swindon SN2 54 C1

Mallow Cl,
Trowbridge BA14 64 E2
Malmesbury 9 F5
Malmesbury
Bsns Pk SN16 37 B1
Malmesbury
By-Pass SN16 37 C5
**Malmesbury Community
Hospital SN16** 37 C5
Malmesbury Ho SP9 41 E2
Malmesbury
House SN2 48 D2
Malmesbury Rd,
Chippenham SN15 26 D1
Malmesbury Rd,
Cricklade SN6 29 B2
Malmesbury Rd,
Swindon SN2 68 A1
Malthouse Cl SN26 51 H1
Malthouse Farm Cl
SN12 40 D2
Malthouse La SP1 48 D1
Malvern Cl,
Melksham SN12 40 D3
Malvern Cl,
Warminster BA12 67 E2
Malvern Rd SN2 55 H4
Mangotsfield 8 C6
Manley Cl BA14 62 C5
Manning Cl SP1 47 F3
**Manningford
Bohune** 14 B3
Manningford Bruce 14 B3
Mannington 18 A6
Mannington Employment
Area SN5 58 D2
Mannington La SN5 58 C2
Mannington Pk SN2 55 E6
Manor Bridge Ct SP9 41 D1
Manor Cl,
Blunsdon SN26 51 H1
Manor Cl,
Swindon SN4 43 C6
Manor Cl,
Trowbridge BA14 64 B2
Manor Cres SN2 55 E3
Manor Ct, Pewsey SN9 42 B3
Manor Ct,
Salisbury SP1 47 F6
Manor Ct,
Trowbridge BA14 64 B2
Manor Farm Cl,
Ford SP4 47 G1
Manor Farm Rd,
Salisbury SP1 49 F1
Manor Gdns,
Swindon SN2 55 E3
Manor Gdns,
Warminster BA12 67 E3
Manor Ho SN6 34 C3
Manor House Cl SN4 68 A3
Manor Orchard SN6 29 C2
Manor Pk SN3 57 G1
Manor Rd,
Chippenham SN14 26 B3
Manor Rd,
Corsham SN13 28 D1
Manor Rd,
Salisbury SP1 49 F1
Manor Rd,
Swindon SN1 59 F2
Manor Rd,
Trowbridge BA14 64 A2
Manor Rd,
Warminster BA12 36 B4
Mansion House Mews
SN13 28 E2
Manston 17 E4
Manswood 17 G5
Manton 14 B2
Manton Cl,
Marlborough SN8 38 A5
Manton Cl,
Trowbridge BA14 64 D2
Manton Dro SN8 38 A4
Manton Hollow SN8 38 A4
Manton Rd SN8 38 A5
Manton St SN2 55 E5
Maple Cl, Calne SN11 25 C6
Maple Cl,
Melksham SN12 40 D2
Maple Cl, Pewsey SN9 42 C1
Maple Cres,
Andover SP11 35 E3
Maple Cres,
Salisbury SP2 45 E3
Maple Dr SN2 68 A2
Maple Gro,
Swindon SN2 55 H3
Maple Gro,
Trowbridge BA14 64 C2
Maple Ter SP9 41 E2
Maple Way,
Amesbury SP4 21 E2

Maple Way,
Chippenham SN15 27 E1
Maple Way,
Durrington SP4 24 A1
Maplecroft,
Salisbury SP2 48 D5
Maplecroft,
Trowbridge BA14 63 F5
Mappowder 16 D6
Marbeck Cl SN25 50 D4
March Cl SN25 51 F4
Marcham 11 G3
Marchwood 19 F5
Marden 14 A3
Marden Walk BA14 64 E2
Marden Way SN11 25 B5
Margaret Leckie Ct
SN3 60 B1
Margaret Marsh 17 E4
Margaret St SN12 40 B2
Margha Rd SP9 41 C3
Marie Av SP5 32 A3
Marigold Cl,
Melksham SN12 40 C4
Marigold Cl,
Swindon SN2 54 C1
Marina Cl,
Devizes SN10 31 H1
Marina Cl,
Salisbury SP4 24 B2
Marina Cres SP4 24 B2
Marina Dr BA14 62 D1
Marina Rd,
Salisbury SP1 49 F2
Marina Rd,
Swindon SN2 24 B2
Marine Cl SN4 43 C4
Mariner Rd SN25 50 B3
Maristow St BA13 65 C2
Markenfield SN3 58 C2
Market Cross SN16 37 C4
Market Hill SN11 25 B4
Market La SN16 37 C4
Market Lavington 13 H4
Market Lavington
Museum SN10 13 H4
Market Pl,
Chippenham SN15 27 F4
Market Pl,
Devizes SN10 31 H4
Market Pl,
Lyneham BA12 36 B5
Market Pl,
Melksham SN12 40 B4
Market Pl, Pewsey SN9 42 B2
Market Pl,
Salisbury SP2 44 D3
Market Pl,
Swindon SN6 34 C3
Market Pl,
Warminster BA12 67 E3
Market Pl,
Westbury BA13 65 C2
Market Sq SN1 60 A3
Market St BA15 23 F2
Marksbury 12 C3
Marlborough 14 B1
Marlborough Ct,
Chippenham SN15 26 C4
Marlborough Ct,
Swindon SN3 68 B3
Marlborough
Golf Club SN8 38 D2
Marlborough La SN3 60 A4
Marlborough
Leisure Centre SN8 38 C4
Marlborough Rd,
Marlborough SN8 20 B2
Marlborough Rd,
Pewsey SN9 42 A1
Marlborough Rd,
Salisbury SP1 47 E6
Marlborough Rd,
Swindon SN3 60 A3
Marlborough Rd,
Wootton Bassett SN4 68 A6
Marlborough Rd,
Wroughton SN4 43 C6
Marlborough St SN1 59 F2
Marlowe Av SN3 56 C6
Marlowe Way SN4 68 B2
Marney Rd SN5 58 A1
Marnhull 17 E4
Marsh Baldon 11 H3
Marsh Farm La SN1 56 B6
Marsh La SP2 46 C6
Marsh Rd BA14 63 E1
Marsh St BA12 66 D5
Marshall St SN5 54 B4
Marshall St SN14 26 D3
Marshfield 13 E1

Marshfield Rd SN15 26 D3
Marshfield Way SN3 56 D3
Marshgate Ind Est SN1 56 C5
Marshgate SN1 56 C5
Marshmead BA14 63 F2
Marsland Rd SN2 56 A2
Marston Av SN2 52 A6
Marston Gate SN3 56 B3
Marston Magna 16 B3
Marston Meysey 10 B3
Marston Rd SN4 64 C3
Marston, Oxfordshire 11 H1
Marston, Wiltshire 13 G3
Marten 14 D3
Marti Cl SN12 40 B3
Martigny Ct SN12 40 C4
Martigny Rd SN12 40 C4
Martin 18 A3
Martin Cl SP9 41 E2
Martin Crest BA12 66 C5
Martin Drove End 18 A3
Martin Way SN10 25 D4
Martinfield SN3 57 F6
Martins Cl,
Chippenham SN15 27 G3
Martins Cl,
Salisbury SP2 48 D5
Martinsell Grn SN9 42 B1
Martlesham Rd SP4 21 E4
Martlet Cl SN12 40 D6
Maryland Ct SP2 45 H2
Maryport St SN10 30 D4
Masefield Av SN2 56 A2
Masefield Rd BA12 66 B3
Masefield SN4 68 C2
Maskeleyne Way SN4 43 B5
Maslen Cl SN10 31 G4
Maslin Row SN3 56 D1
Mason Rd SN25 51 G4
Masons La BA15 23 F2
Masons Way SN13 28 C2
Massey Cl SN15 27 F6
Massey Rd SN10 31 F6
Matford Hill SN15 27 G3
Mathern 8 A4
Matilda Way SN10 31 F3
Matley Moor SN3 61 G5
Matravers Cl BA13 65 B3
Matthew Ley Cl BA13 65 B4
Mattock Cl SN10 31 F4
Maud Cl SN10 31 F3
Maude Heath Cl SN15 27 E2
Maulton Cl BA14 29 B5
Maunders Dr SN2 62 D1
Maundrell Rd SN11 25 C2
Maunsell Way SN4 43 A4
Maur Cl SN15 27 G4
Maxcroft La BA14 63 E1
Maxey Cl SN5 54 A5
Maxwell St SN1 59 G1
May Cl SN2 55 H3
Maybold Cres SN25 50 C6
Mayenne Pl SN10 30 A4
Mayfair Rd SP1 49 G1
Mayfield Cl SN3 57 E5
Mayfield SN8 39 F4
Mayfly Rd SN25 50 A3
Mayo Cl SN13 28 D2
Mazurek Way SN25 50 D4
Mckie Rd SP4 21 E3
Mead Way SN5 54 A3
Meade Rd SP11 35 E3
Meadland SN13 28 D2
Meadow Cl,
Chippenham SN14 26 B4
Meadow Cl,
Swindon SN4 68 B3
Meadow Cl,
Westbury BA13 65 B2
Meadow Dr SN10 31 F4
Meadow La BA13 65 C3
Meadow Rd South SP1 48 D1
Meadow Rd,
Bulford SP4 24 E3
Meadow Rd,
Melksham SN12 40 C1
Meadow Rd,
Salisbury SP2 46 C6
Meadow Rd,
Swindon SN2 55 E6
Meadowcroft SN2 52 A6
Meadowfield BA15 22 D3
Meadowsweet Cl SN25 50 D5
Meadowsweet Dr SN13 25 A3
Meads Pl SN10 31 E4
Meads Rd SP4 24 B1
Meadway BA14 62 A6
Meares Dr SN5 54 A5
Medina Way SN2 52 D1
Medlar Cl SN2 55 G3
Medway Rd SN25 55 E1
Meerut Rd SP9 41 D3
Melbourne Cl SN3 60 C4

Melbury Abbas 17 F3
Melbury Bubb 16 B6
Melbury Osmond 16 A5
Melbury Sampford 16 A6
Melcombe Bingham 16 D6
Melford Walk SN3 57 E6
Melfort Cl SN5 54 A3
Melksham 13 G2
Melksham Cl SN2 51 G5
Melksham Community
  Hospital SN12 40 C5
Melksham Ho SP9 41 D2
Melksham Rd SN15 26 C6
Melksham Trading Est
  SN12 40 A1
Mellow Ground SN25 50 D6
Mells 12 D5
Melor Vw SP4 21 D3
Melrose Av BA12 66 C4
Melrose Cl,
  Swindon SN5 54 B6
Melrose Cl,
  Warminster BA12 66 C4
Melsome Rd SN5 36 B3
Melton Rd BA14 62 D4
Melville Cl SN3 60 C1
Melvin Cl SP1 49 G1
Melvyn Webb Pl SN2 56 A5
Mendip Cl,
  Melksham SN12 40 D3
Mendip Cl,
  Swindon SN25 55 H1
Mendip Cl,
  Warminster BA12 67 E2
Mere 17 E1
Mere By-Pass BA12 36 A4
Mere Museum BA12 36 B5
Meriden Walk SN3 61 E3
Meridian Walk BA14 62 B6
Meriton Av SN13 28 E2
Merlin Ct BA13 65 B2
Merlin Rd SN11 25 C2
Merlin Way,
  Melksham SN12 40 C6
Merlin Way,
  Swindon SN3 57 F4
Merrifield Rd SP4 47 F2
Merrivale Gro SN3 60 B2
Merton Av SN2 56 A1
Mervin Webb Pl SN2 56 A5
Methuen Av SN12 40 C1
Methuen Cl BA15 23 G5
Methuen Dr SP1 49 F2
Methuen Pk SN14 26 B6
Methuen Sth SN14 26 B6
Methuen Way SN13 28 E1
Metis Cl SN25 50 A3
Meynell Cl SN25 51 F3
Meyrick Av SP2 48 D4
Meysey Hampton 10 B3
Michael Pyms Rd SN16 37 C2
Micheldever 15 G6
Michelmersh 19 E2
Middi Haynes Ct SN6 34 C2
Middle Ct BA14 63 F4
Middle Grnd SN6 29 A2
Middle Ground SN4 68 D3
Middle La BA14 63 F4
Middle Leaze SN14 26 B2
Middle Rank BA15 23 F3
Middle St SP2 48 B2
Middle Wallop 14 D6
Middle Winterslow 18 C3
Middle Woodford 18 A1
Middlefield Cl SN10 31 F4
Middlefield Rd SN14 26 B2
Middlemarsh 16 C5
Middlemass Grn SN9 42 C1
Middleton 15 F6
Middleton Cl,
  Swindon SN3 60 C1
Middleton Cl,
  Warminster BA12 66 C4
Middlewick La SN13 28 C1
Midgham 15 H2
Midhurst Av SN3 61 E1
Midlands Ind Est BA14 29 A4
Midsomer Norton 12 C4
Midwinter Cl SN5 54 A3
Midwinter Gdns SN3 56 D3
Milborne Port 16 C3
Milborne Wick 16 C3
Milbourn Cl BA15 22 A2
Milbourne La SN16 37 D2
Milbury Heath 8 A5
Mildenhall 14 C1
Mildenhall Way SN2 51 H3
Mile Elm 13 H2
Miles Ct SN2 56 B1
Milestone Way SN15 26 D1
Milford Hill SP1 49 E2
Milford Hollow SP1 49 F2
Milford Manor Gdns
  SP1 49 G2

Milford Mill Rd SP1 49 G2
Milford Pk SP1 49 G2
Milford St SP1 49 E1
Milford Trading Est SP1 49 F2
Milkwall 8 B1
Mill Cl, Devizes SN10 31 F6
Mill Cl, Swindon SN4 43 C5
Mill Green Rd SP4 21 D3
Mill Hill Av SP9 41 C1
Mill La, Bradford-on-Avon
  BA15 23 F3
Mill La,
  Malmesbury SN16 37 C4
Mill La, Salisbury SP1 46 B3
Mill La, Swindon SN1 58 D6
Mill La,
  Warminster BA12 36 C6
Mill Rd, Nursteed SN10 31 F6
Mill Rd, Potterne SN10 42 A5
Mill St SN11 25 C4
Mill Stream App SP1 46 D6
Milland Cl SN25 51 G5
Millbrook 19 F4
Millbrook SP1 49 F1
Millbuck Cl SN2 56 B3
Millennium Cl,
  Devizes SN10 31 G5
Millennium Cl,
  Salisbury SP2 49 E5
Millennium Ct SN9 42 B2
Millers Cl SP1 46 B3
Millgrove St SN25 50 C3
Millhand Villas BA14 64 E1
Millington Dr BA14 62 B6
Mills Rd SN12 40 D3
Mills Way SP4 21 E1
Milston 14 B5
Milston Av SN2 51 H6
Milston Rd SP4 24 D1
Milston Vw SP4 24 C1
Milton 11 G4
Milton Abbas 17 E6
Milton Abbas SN12 40 C4
Milton Clevedon 16 C1
Milton Hill 11 G4
Milton Lilbourne 14 B3
Milton on Stour 17 E2
Milton Rd,
  Amesbury SP4 21 F3
Milton Rd, Pewsey SN9 42 C2
Milton Rd,
  Salisbury SP2 49 E4
Minchinhampton 9 F2
Minety 9 H4
Minety Rd SN2 51 H3
Minnow Cl, Calne SN11 25 C2
Minnow Cl,
  Swindon SN25 50 A3
Minot Cl SN16 37 B2
Minstead 18 D5
Minster Cl SN25 51 E4
Minster Lovell 10 D1
Minster St,
  Salisbury SP1 48 D1
Minster St,
  Salisbury SP2 44 D4
Minster Vw BA12 66 C3
Minster Way SN14 26 B6
Mint Cl SN2 54 C1
Minterne Magna 16 C6
Mir Cres SN25 50 A4
Miserden 9 G1
Mitchell Cl SN4 68 A4
Mitchell Rd SP2 48 B1
Mitchells Cl SP5 33 F4
Moat Walk SN4 43 C6
Moberly Rd SP1 46 B5
Mockbeggar 18 B5
Moffatt Rise SN16 37 C2
Mompesson House (NT)
  SP1 48 D2
Monday Market St
  SN10 30 D4
Monet Cl SN25 51 E4
Monks Cl SP9 41 C2
Monkton Cl SN3 61 E3
Monkton Combe 12 D3
Monkton Deverill 13 F6
Monkton Farleigh 13 E2
Monkton Hill SN15 27 E3
Monkton Up Wimborne
  17 H4
Monmouth Cl SN3 60 C3
Monmouth Rd SP3 43 A3
Montagu St SN2 55 E6
Montague Cl SN15 27 G3
Montague Ct BA14 63 G5
Montague Pl SN12 40 D2
Montague Rd SP2 48 A3
Montgomery Av SN3 55 G3
Montgomery Gdns SP2 46 B6
Montgomery Ho SP9 41 C1
Montrose Cl SN2 55 E6
Monxton 15 E5

Monxton Cl SP1 47 G3
Moonrakers SN10 31 F2
Moorhem Cl SN3 62 D1
Moorhen Cl SN3 61 G1
Moorlands SN15 27 F1
Moormead Rd SN4 43 C5
Moot Cl SP5 32 C4
Moot Gdns SP5 32 B4
Moot La SP5 32 B5
Moray Rd SN2 56 B4
More Crichel 17 H5
Moredon Pk SN2 54 D1
Moredon Rd SN25 54 D2
Moresby Cl SN5 58 C1
Morestead 19 G2
Moreton Valence 8 B3
Morgan Walk BA13 65 A4
Morgan's Vale 18 C3
Morgans Rise Rd SP5 33 F3
Morgans Vale Rd SP5 33 F4
Morie Cl SN5 54 B3
Morley Fld BA12 67 G2
Morris La SN10 30 D4
Morris Rd SN8 38 B4
Morris St SN2 55 E6
Morrison St SN2 55 E6
Morse Cl SN16 37 C3
Morstone Rd SN4 68 A5
Mortimer Cl SN5 54 B5
Morton 8 B4
Moss Mead SN3 26 A3
Motcombe 17 E2
Mottisfont 18 D2
Mouldon Hill
  Country Park SN2 54 A1
Moulsford 11 H5
Moulton Dr BA15 23 F5
Mount La BA12 66 D5
Mount Pleasant,
  Bradford-on-Avon
  BA15 23 F2
Mount Pleasant,
  Chippenham SN14 26 B1
Mount Pleasant,
  Salisbury SP3 43 A3
Mounton 8 A4
Moyle Pk BA14 63 G5
Moyne Cl SN10 30 C4
Moyne Gdns SP4 21 F3
Muddyford La SP5 33 F3
Mudford 16 A3
Muirfield SN25 50 C4
Mulberry Cl SN4 26 B2
Mulberry Gro SN2 55 F2
Mundy Av SN3 61 E2
Munks Cl SP2 48 B3
Munro Cl SN3 60 B1
Murdock Rd SN3 61 H1
Murray Rd BA14 62 D4
Murray Walk SN12 40 C2
Murrayfield SN15 27 E2
Muscovey Cl SN15 36 C2
Mycroft Rd SN25 50 C4
Myrfield Rd SP1 47 G3
Myrtle Av BA12 66 D4
Myrtle Gdns SN2 55 H2
Mythern Mdw BA15 23 G4

N

Nadder Cl SP3 43 C2
Nadder La SP2 45 F4
Nadder Rd SP9 41 D2
Nadder Ter,
  Bulbridge SP2 44 B4
Nadder Ter,
  Salisbury SP2 48 B1
Nailsworth 9 E3
Naini Tal Rd SP9 41 C2
Nantwich SN5 58 A4
Napier Cl,
  Swindon SN5 55 F6
Napier Cl,
  Tidworth SP9 41 C2
Napier Cres SP1 49 G1
Nash Cl SN25 50 C4
Nash La SN8 20 A6
Naughton Av SN10 31 G2
Naunton Rd SN3 60 D1
Navigator Cl BA14 63 E1
Neal Cl SP1 47 F2
Neale Ct SN13 28 C2
Neate Rd SN10 31 F3
Neeld Cres SN14 26 C3
Nelson Rd SP1 46 D6
Nelson St SN1 59 F2
Nempnett Thrubwell 12 A3
Nepaul Rd SP9 41 C2
Neptune Ho SP1 50 A3
Ness Cl SN5 54 A2
Nestleton Cl SN11 25 C6
Neston 13 F2
Nether Compton 16 B4

Nether Leaze SN9 42 A1
Nether Wallop 18 D1
Netheravon 14 B5
Netheravon Cl SP1 47 E5
Netheravon
  Dovecote SP4 14 B5
Netheravon Rd,
  Durrington SP4 24 A2
Netheravon Rd,
  Salisbury SP2 47 E5
Netherend 8 B2
Netherhampton 18 A2
Netherhampton Rd
  SP2 45 E6
Netherton Cl SN3 61 E3
Netley 19 F5
Netley Marsh 19 E5
Nettlebridge 12 C5
Nettleton 9 E6
Neville Cl SP1 47 F4
Nevis Cl SN5 54 B3
New Alresford 19 H1
New Bridge Rd SP1 49 E3
New Broughton Rd
  SN12 40 B3
New Canal SP1 48 D2
New College Dr SN3 60 C2
New College Walk*,
  Bilborough Dr SN3 60 C2
New Cut BA12 36 C5
New Dro SP11 35 C4
New Grounds 8 D2
New Harnham Rd SP2 48 D4
New Hinksey 11 G2
New Lawns SN12 40 B4
New Mills 8 A1
New Park Rd SN10 30 D4
New Park St SN10 30 D4
New Rd, Bradford-on-Avon
  BA15 23 G2
New Rd, Calne SN11 25 C5
New Rd,
  Chippenham SN15 27 E3
New Rd,
  Marlborough SN8 39 E4
New Rd, Salisbury SP4 24 C2
New Rd, Swindon SN8 68 A5
New St SP1 48 D2
New Zealand Av SP2 46 A6
Newall Tuck Rd SN15 27 G4
Newark Cl SN5 58 A4
Newbridge 18 D4
Newburgh Pl SN6 34 B2
Newburn Cres SN1 59 E2
Newbury 15 G1
Newbury Av SN11 25 G3
Newbury Dr,
  Chippenham SN14 26 B6
Newbury Dr,
  Swindon SN5 58 A4
Newby Acre SN8 39 E2
Newcombe Dr SN2 55 F5
Newcroft Cl SN11 25 B2
Newcroft Rd SN11 25 B3
Newhurst Pk BA14 63 G4
Newland 8 A1
Newland Rd SN25 55 F2
Newlands Rd SN13 28 E2
Newleaze BA14 63 G2
Newmans Way SP4 24 E3
Newmarket Av BA14 64 E4
Newmarket Cl SN14 26 A5
Newmarket St*,
  Ipswich St SN1 55 H5
Newnham 8 C1
Newnton Gro SN16 37 A3
Newopaul Way BA12 66 D1
Newport 8 D3
Newport BA12 67 E2
Newport St SN1 60 A3
Newstead Cl*,
  Bicton Rd SN25 51 E5
Newton Abbot Cl SN14 26 A5
Newton Rd SP2 48 A1
Newton St Loe 12 C2
Newton Stacey 15 F6
Newton Tony 14 C6
Newton Way SN1 55 H1
Newtown, Bradford-on-Avon
  BA15 23 E3
Newtown,
  Hampshire, RG20 15 G2
Newtown,
  Hampshire, SO43 18 D5
Newtown,
  Hampshire, SO51 18 D3
Newtown,
  Westbury BA13 65 D2
Newtown, Wiltshire 17 F2
Nibley 8 C5
Nicholson Cl SP4 21 F3
Niebull Cl SN16 37 C2
Nightingale Dr BA13 65 C2

Nightingale Rd,
  Swindon SN3 57 H1
Nightingale Rd,
  Trowbridge BA14 62 B6
Nightingale Way SN11 25 B2
Nightwood Copse SN5 54 A3
Nindum Rd SN3 57 E4
Nine Acre Dr SN13 28 B3
Nolan Cl SN25 51 F2
Nomansland 18 C4
Norcliffe Rd SN3 60 D3
Nore Marsh Rd SN4 68 B5
Noredown Way SN4 68 B4
Norfolk Cl SN3 56 C6
Norfolk Rd SP2 48 B3
Norman Rd SN2 55 H4
Normanton Down SP4 14 B6
Norridge Vw BA12 66 C4
Norrington Common 13 F2
Norris Rd BA14 63 H3
North Av SN13 28 F1
North Baddesley 19 E3
North Bank Rise SN4 68 C3
North Barrow 16 B2
North Bradley 13 F4
North Cadbury 16 C2
North Cerney 9 H1
North Charford 18 B3
North Cheriton 16 C2
North End 15 F2
North End SN11 25 B3
North Gorley 18 B5
North Keels SN6 29 A1
North La BA12 66 B3
North Meadow NNR 10 A3
North Meadow Rd SN6 29 A2
North Moreton 11 H4
North Newnton 14 B3
North Nibley 8 D3
North Oakley 15 H4
North Rd,
  Salisbury SP4 21 F4
North Rd,
  Warminster BA12 36 B4
North Row BA12 67 E3
North St, Calne SN11 25 B3
North St, Pewsey SN9 42 B2
North St, Salisbury SP1 48 D1
North St, Salisbury SP2 44 D3
North St,
  Warminster BA12 36 B5
North Stoke 12 D1
North Swindon
  District Centre SN25 51 E4
North Tidworth 14 C5
North View SN3 39 E3
North Vw SN6 34 B3
North Walk SP1 48 D2
North Wall SN6 29 B2
North Waltham 15 H5
North Wick 12 B2
North Widcombe 12 B3
North Wiltshire Golf Club
  SN10 13 H2
North Wootton,
  Dorset 16 C4
North Wootton,
  Somerset 12 A6
North Wraxall 9 E6
Northam 19 F5
Northbourne Rd SN25 51 F3
Northbrook Rd SN2 55 G4
Northcote SN11 25 B3
Northend 12 D1
Northern Rd SN2 55 F3
Northfield BA15 22 A2
Northfield Way SN3 57 E5
Northfields SN11 25 B3
Northgate Gdns SN10 30 C4
Northgate St SN10 30 C4
Northington 19 H1
Northleaze Cl SN2 55 E2
Northleigh Ter SP2 44 D3
Northmoor 11 F2
Northway SN11 25 B3
Northwick 8 A5
Northwood SN15 27 E1
Norton 9 F5
Norton Bavant 13 G5
Norton Dr SP4 47 E1
Norton Ferris 17 E1
Norton Gro SN3 60 A1
Norton Hawkfield 12 B2
Norton Malreward 12 B2
Norton St Philip 12 D4
Nortree Ct SN12 40 A2
Norwood Cl SN3 61 F3
Notton 13 F1
Noyes Cl,
  Chippenham SN14 26 A3
Noyes Cl,
  Swindon SN25 50 B6
Nuffield Cl SN5 54 B5
Nuneham Courtenay 11 H3

Nunney	12 D5
Nunton	18 B3
Nursery Cl, Salisbury SP4	21 C2
Nursery Cl, Swindon SN4	43 B6
Nursery Cl, Trowbridge BA14	63 G3
Nursery Gdns, Corsham SN13	28 E3
Nursery Gdns, Warminster BA12	36 C5
Nursery Rd SP2	48 B1
Nursling	19 E4
Nursteed Cl SN10	31 F6
Nursteed Ind Est SN10	31 F6
Nursteed Pk SN10	31 F6
Nursteed Rd SN10	31 E4
Nursteed Trading Est SN10	31 G6
Nuthatch Cl SN3	61 G1
Nuthatch Rd SN11	25 B2
Nutmeg Cl SN25	54 D1
Nyland Rd SN3	57 E6
Nympsfield	9 E2
Nythe Rd SN3	57 E4

O

Oak Ash Grn SP2	44 C5
Oak Cl SP9	41 E2
Oak Dr SN6	34 B3
Oak Gdn SN3	56 C1
Oak Lodge Cl SN14	26 D3
Oak Pl SP4	21 D1
Oak Rd SN14	26 A5
Oak Tree Av SN2	56 A2
Oak Tree Cl BA14	62 B5
Oak Tree Fld SP2	49 E6
Oakford Walk SN3	60 D1
Oakham Cl SN5	58 B2
Oakhill	12 C5
Oakhurst Way SN25	50 B4
Oakie Cl SN25	51 F5
Oaklands Av SP4	21 E2
Oaklands SN15	26 D1
Oakley	15 H4
Oakridge	9 G2
Oaksey	9 H4
Oaksey Rd SN2	51 H6
Oakway Rd SP1	47 E3
Oakwood Dr SN12	40 B4
Oakwood Rd SN5	54 B6
Oamaru Way SN10	31 F4
Oare	14 B2
Oasis Leisure Centre SN2	55 G6
Oate Hill SN15	27 G5
Oatfields BA14	62 D2
Oathills SN13	28 D3
Oberek La SN25	50 D4
Oberon Way SN25	51 F6
Oborne	16 C4
Ockwells SN6	29 B3
Ocotal Way SN1	56 A5
Odcombe	16 A4
Odcroft Cl SN15	27 G4
Odd Down	12 D2
Oddford Vale SP3	43 B3
O'Donnell Cl SN15	27 F1
Odstock	18 B2
Odstock Rd, Salisbury SP2	49 E5
Odstock Rd, Swindon SN2	51 H5
Offers Ct SN10	31 E4
Ogbourne Downs Golf Club SN8	10 C6
Ogbourne Maizey	14 C1
Ogbourne St Andrew	14 B1
Ogbourne St George	14 C1
Ogilvie Sq SN11	25 D4
O'Gormans Mews SN12	40 D1
Okebourne Pk SN3	61 F4
Okeford Cl SN3	57 E6
Okeford Fitzpaine	17 E5
Okus	10 B5
Okus Gro SN2	56 A1
Okus Ind Est SN1	59 G3
Okus Rd SN1	59 F3
Old Alexander Rd SN16	37 A3
Old Blandford Rd SP2	48 B5
Old Broughton Rd SN12	40 B2
Old Burghclere	15 G3
Old Castle Rd SP1	46 D2
Old Church Rd SP4	24 D2
Old Common Way SP11	35 D2
Old Court SN4	68 A4

Old Dilton Rd BA13	65 A6
Old Enburg Rd BA13	65 A5
Old George Mall SP1	48 D2
Old Granary La SP4	21 C3
Old Hardenhuish La SN14	26 C2
Old Hollow BA12	36 C4
Old Hospital Rd SN9	42 A1
Old Malmesbury Gdns*, Old Malmesbury Rd SN4	68 B2
Old Malmesbury Rd SN4	68 B2
Old Manor Hospital SP2	48 B1
Old Meadows Walk SP2	48 B3
Old Mill La SN3	60 A3
Old Railway Cl SN3	37 B2
Old Rd SN15	27 E3
Old School Ct SN3	61 E1
Old Shaft Rd SN13	28 A4
Old Shaftesbury Dro SP2	48 A5
Old Shaw La SN5	54 A5
Old Sodbury	8 D6
Old St SP2	48 B3
Old Town Gardens SN3	59 H3
Old Vicarage La SN4	57 H1
Old Wardour Castle SP3	17 G2
Oldbury Castle SN8	14 A1
Oldbury on the Hill	9 E4
Oldbury Prior SN11	25 C6
Oldbury Way SN11	25 B4
Oldbury-on-Severn	8 B4
Oldfield Pk BA13	65 A2
Oldfield Rd, Salisbury SP1	47 F3
Oldfield Rd, Westbury BA13	65 A3
Oldford	13 E4
Oldland	12 C1
Oldlands Walk SN3	60 D4
Olive Gro SN2	55 G2
Oliver Av SN13	28 D2
Oliver Cl SP2	45 H1
Oliver Rd, Salisbury SP2	44 B1
Oliver Rd, Swindon SN25	51 G4
Oliver's Battery	19 G2
Olivers La SN16	37 C4
Olveston	8 B5
Omdurman St SN4	55 H4
Orange Cl SN6	34 C2
Orchard Cl, Bradford-on-Avon BA15	22 C6
Orchard Cl, Calne SN11	25 C5
Orchard Cl, Devizes SN10	30 D6
Orchard Cl, Warminster BA12	67 F2
Orchard Cres SN14	26 C4
Orchard Ct, Malmesbury SN16	37 C5
Orchard Ct, Trowbridge BA14	64 D1
Orchard Ct, Westbury BA13	65 C3
Orchard End SP4	24 D3
Orchard Gdns, Bradford-on-Avon BA15	23 F3
Orchard Gdns, Melksham SN12	40 B4
Orchard Gro SN2	56 A1
Orchard Mead SN4	68 D3
Orchard Pl SP2	46 C6
Orchard Rd, Chippenham SN14	26 C4
Orchard Rd, Corsham SN13	28 E1
Orchard Rd, Marlborough SN8	39 E5
Orchard Rd, Morgans Vale SP5	33 F4
Orchard Rd, Salisbury SP2	46 A6
Orchard Rd, Trowbridge BA14	64 D1
Orchard Way, Westbury BA13	65 C3
Orchard Way, Salisbury SP4	21 D2
Orchard Way, Trowbridge BA14	64 D4
Orcheston	14 A5
Orchid Cl SN25	55 H2
Orchid Dr SP11	35 D3
Ordnance Rd SP9	41 D2
Orford Rd SP4	21 E4

Oriel Cl BA14	63 G2
Orlov Cl SN5	54 A5
Ormonde Ho SN14	26 A3
Orpington Way BA14	63 H5
Orrin Cl SN5	54 B3
Orwell Cl, Malmesbury SN16	37 C2
Orwell Cl, Swindon SN25	51 F6
Osborne Rd BA14	63 F3
Osborne St SN2	55 G5
Osprey Cl, Melksham SN12	40 D6
Osprey Cl, Swindon SN3	61 H1
Osterley Rd SN25	51 E5
Otter Way SN4	68 C3
Otterbourne	19 G3
Over	8 B5
Over Wallop	14 D6
Overbrook SN3	61 E3
Overhouse Dr SP3	43 B2
Overton	15 H5
Overton Gdns SN3	57 E3
Overtown Hill SN4	43 D6
Ovington	19 H2
Ower	19 E4
Owl Cl SN3	61 G1
Owlswood SP2	48 D5
Owslebury	19 H3
Oxenwood	14 D3
Oxford	11 H2
Oxford Rd, Calne SN11	25 C4
Oxford Rd, Swindon SN3	56 D4
Oxford St, Aldbourne SN8	20 C2
Oxford St, Malmesbury SN16	37 C4
Oxford St, St Martins SN8	39 E3
Ozleworth	9 E3

P

Packington Cl SN5	54 A5
Paddington Dr SN5	58 D1
Paddock Cl SN25	51 E6
Paddock La SN13	28 B4
Paddock Way SP1	47 H6
Padfield Gdns SN12	40 A6
Page Cl, Calne SN11	25 D4
Page Cl, Chippenham SN14	26 B4
Paget Cl SP9	41 C1
Pains Way SP4	21 D3
Painswick	9 F1
Painters Mead BA14	63 G4
Pakenham Rd SN3	61 E3
Palairet Cl BA15	23 G5
Palestine	14 D6
Palmer Dr BA15	23 G1
Palmer Rd, Salisbury SP2	46 B5
Palmer Rd, Trowbridge BA14	62 D4
Palmer St SN14	26 B4
Palomino Pl BA13	63 A4
Pampas Ct BA12	66 C3
Pans La SN10	31 E5
Parbrook	16 B1
Parhams Ct SN4	68 B4
Park Av, Chippenham SN14	26 C3
Park Av, Highworth SN6	34 C3
Park Cl, Calne SN11	25 D5
Park Cl, Malmesbury SN16	37 A3
Park Cl, Salisbury SP1	46 D4
Park Cl, Trowbridge BA14	64 D4
Park Gate	19 H5
Park La Ind Est SN13	28 B2
Park La, Britford SP5	49 G6
Park La, Chippenham SN15	27 E3
Park La, Corsham SN13	28 A4
Park La, Malmesbury SN16	37 A2
Park La, Salisbury SP1	46 D5
Park La, Swindon SN1	59 F1
Park Mead SN16	37 B3
Park Rd, Laverstock SP1	47 G6
Park Rd, Malmesbury SN16	37 A2
Park Rd, Tidworth SP9	41 D3
Park Rd, Tisbury SP3	43 B2
Park Springs SN5	58 C2
Park St, Salisbury SN1	46 D6
Park St, Swindon SN3	57 E3

Park St, Trowbridge BA14	64 C1
Park Ter SN15	26 D3
Park Vw SN10	30 B4
Parkend	8 B1
Parkers Cl SP5	32 A2
Parkfields, Chippenham SN15	26 D3
Parkfields, Devizes SN10	31 F2
Parklands Rd SN3	60 A2
Parklands, Malmesbury SN16	37 A3
Parklands, Trowbridge BA14	62 D3
Parkside, Chippenham SN15	27 E2
Parkside, Swindon SN3	56 D2
Parkview Dr BA13	65 A5
Parliament Row SN16	37 C5
Parliament St SN14	26 C4
Parsley Cl SN2	50 C6
Parsonage Cl SP1	46 B3
Parsonage Cl SN3	34 C3
Parsonage Down NNR SP1	13 H6
Parsonage Farm Cl SN6	29 B3
Parsonage Grn SP2	48 C3
Parsonage Rd, Salisbury SP4	21 C3
Parsonage Rd, Swindon SN3	56 C2
Parsonage Rd, Trowbridge BA14	63 G5
Parsonage Way Ind Est SN15	27 F1
Parsonage Way SN15	27 F1
Parsons Way SN4	68 B4
Partridge Cl, Chippenham SN14	26 C1
Partridge Cl, Corsham SN13	28 C3
Partridge Cl, Swindon SN3	61 H1
Passmore Cl SN3	57 G6
Pasteur Dr SN1	59 F3
Pasture Cl SN2	54 D6
Patchway	8 B5
Patchway SN3	26 C3
Patford St SN11	25 B4
Pathfinder Way SN25	50 A4
Patney	14 A3
Patney Walk SN2	51 G5
Paul St SN13	28 E2
Pauls Cft SN6	29 B3
Pauls Dene Cres SP1	47 E3
Pauls Dene Rd SP1	46 D3
Paulton	12 C4
Paveley Cl BA13	65 A2
Pavely Cl SN15	26 D4
Pavely Gdns BA14	63 G5
Paxcroft Way BA14	63 F5
Peaks Down SN5	54 A3
Pearce Cl SN2	52 B5
Pearce Way SP1	47 F2
Pearl Ho SP11	35 E3
Peasedown St John	12 D3
Peasemore	11 G6
Pecheron Pl BA13	65 A3
Peel Circus SN13	28 B3
Pembroke Cl SN14	64 D1
Pembroke Ct SP2	44 C3
Pembroke Gdns SN25	55 E2
Pembroke Ho SP1	48 D1
Pembroke Rd, Chippenham SN15	27 H6
Pembroke Rd, Melksham SN12	40 C3
Pembroke Rd, Salisbury SP2	45 H4
Pen Cl SN25	55 F1
Penallt	8 A1
Pencarrow Cl SN25	50 D5
Pendennis Rd SN5	58 A4
Pendlebury Ct SN5	54 A5
Penfold Gdns SN1	59 H3
Penhill Dr SN2	51 G5
Penleigh Cl SN13	28 D3
Penleigh Rd BA13	65 A3
Penn Ct SN11	25 C3
Penn Hill Rd SN11	25 C4
Penn Hill SN11	25 D3
Pennine Cl SN12	40 D3
Pennine Way SN25	51 E3
Penning Rd SP2	45 G3
Pennings Rd SP9	41 D1
Penny Bank La BA12	36 C5
Penny La SN3	56 C6
Penny Royal Cl SN11	25 A3
Pennycress Cl SN25	55 G6
Pennycress Dr SN12	40 C5
Pennyfarthing Row BA13	65 A5

Pennyfarthing St SP1	49 E1
Pennys La SP2	44 D3
Penruddock Cl SP2	45 H3
Penselwood	16 D1
Pensford	12 B2
Penton Mewsey	15 E5
Pentridge	17 H4
Pentridge Cl SN3	57 F6
Pentylands Cl SN6	34 C1
Pentylands La SN6	34 B1
Penwood Rd BA13	65 A2
Penzance Dr SN6	59 E2
Pepper Pl BA12	67 G2
Pepperacre La BA14	63 F4
Pepperbox Hill SN5	54 A3
Perch Cl SN11	25 B2
Percheron Cl SN5	54 A6
Percy St SN2	55 E6
Peregrine Cl SN3	57 G5
Peregrine Ct SN11	25 C2
Perham Cres SP11	35 E3
Perham Down	14 D5
Periwinkle Cl SN2	54 C1
Perretts Ct SN12	40 B3
Perriwinkle Cl BA12	66 B3
Perrys La SN4	43 B5
Peshawar Cl SP9	41 B2
Peter Furkins Ct SN1	59 F2
Petersfield Grn SP9	41 C3
Petersfield Rd SN3	61 E3
Petersfinger Rd SP5	49 H3
Peto Gro BA15	22 C6
Petter Cl SN4	43 C4
Petticoat La SP5	33 G3
Pettridge La BA12	36 C5
Pevensey Way SN5	58 B2
Pew Hill SN15	27 F2
Pewsey	14 B3
Pewsey Downs NNR SN8	14 B3
Pewsey Heritage Centre SP2	42 B2
Pewsey Ho SP9	41 D3
Pewsey Rd SN8	38 D6
Pewsham Lock SN15	27 F6
Pewsham Rd SN2	52 A6
Pewsham Way SN15	27 F5
Pheasant Bsns Pk SN14	26 C6
Pheasant Cl, Chippenham SN14	26 A5
Pheasant Cl, Swindon SN3	61 G1
Phelps Par SN11	25 C4
Philip Cl SN12	40 C1
Philip Ct SP2	46 A5
Philip Rd, Ditchampton SP2	44 B1
Philip Rd, Durrington SP4	24 B1
Philipp's House & Dinton Park SP3	17 H1
Phillip Cl SN10	31 F3
Phillips Cl SN14	26 A3
Phillips La SP4	46 B1
Phipps Cl BA13	65 B1
Phipps Ct SN14	26 D4
Phoebe Way SN25	50 A4
Phoenix Cl SN15	27 F5
Phoenix Gdns SN25	50 B4
Phoenix Rise BA13	65 A2
Phoenix Sq SN9	42 B2
Picked Mead SN13	28 C3
Picket Piece	15 F5
Picket Post	18 C6
Picketleaze SN14	26 B4
Pickford Way SN25	51 E4
Pickwick Cl SN2	52 A5
Pickwick Rd SN13	28 D2
Pickwick SN13	28 D2
Pictor Cl SN13	28 D2
Pigeon House La SN3	56 D2
Pike House Cl SN6	29 A2
Pilgrim Cl SN3	54 A5
Pilgrims Mead SP1	47 F3
Pilning	8 A5
Pilots Vw SP4	21 E3
Pilton	12 B6
Pimperne	17 G5
Pinckneys Way SP4	24 B1
Pine Cl SN12	40 A5
Pine View Cl SP5	33 F6
Pine Walk SP4	21 E2
Pinehurst Rd SN2	55 G4
Pinehurst Sports Centre SN2	55 G2
Pines Rd SN10	31 F5
Pinetree Ho SP9	41 E2
Pinetree Rise SN2	55 G2
Pinewood Cl SP2	45 H2
Pinewood Way SP2	45 H2
Pinhills SN11	25 B5
Pinnegar Way SN3	57 G6
Pinnocks Pl SN2	56 C1
Pintail Ct SN15	36 C3

Pintail Way BA13 65 C2
Pioneer Rd SN25 50 A4
Pipers Cl SN4 68 A5
Pipers Way SN1 59 H6
Pipitdene SN3 57 G5
Piplar Ground BA15 23 F5
Pippin Row SN11 25 C4
Pipsmore Rd SN14 26 B3
Pitchcombe 9 E1
Pitcombe 16 C1
Pitman Av BA14 64 B1
Pitman Cl BA14 64 B1
Pitton 18 C2
Pittsfield SN6 29 B3
Place Rd SN12 40 B3
Plaitford 18 D4
Plantation Rd, Chippenham SN14 26 C3
Plantation Rd, Tidworth SP9 41 D4
Plants Grn BA12 67 F4
Plassey Rd SP9 41 C2
Plastow Green 15 H3
Plattes Cl SN5 54 B5
Pleydell Rd SN1 59 H4
Pleydells SN6 29 B1
Plume of Feathers La SN8 39 E4
Plummer Cl SN4 43 B5
Plumpton Cl SN14 26 A5
Plush 16 D6
Plusterwine 8 B3
Poachers Way SN25 51 E3
Pockeredge Dr SN13 28 B4
Pockeridge Rd SN13 28 D4
Podimore 16 A3
Pointers Way SP4 21 E2
Polden Rd SP1 49 F2
Polonez Ct SN25 50 C4
Poltondale SN3 57 G6
Pond St SN25 51 E6
Pons Cl SN8 39 F3
Pontings SN26 51 H1
Pooksgreen 19 E5
Poole Keynes 9 H3
Poole Rd SN25 54 D1
Poores Rd SP4 24 C1
Pope Cl SN25 51 E5
Popham 15 H6
Poplar Av SN2 55 H3
Poplar Way SP1 47 F3
Popplechurch Dr SN3 57 H6
Poppy Cl SN11 25 A3
Port Fld SN8 39 E3
Port Hill SN8 39 E1
Portal Cl SN14 26 D1
Portal Pl SN15 36 C3
Portal Rd SN2 55 F3
Porte Marsh Ind Est SN11 25 C1
Porte Marsh Rd SN11 25 C2
Porters Mead SN13 28 D2
Porth Cl SN25 50 B4
Portland Av, Salisbury SP2 48 C5
Portland Av, Swindon SN1 59 F3
Portland Way SN11 25 D5
Portman Rd SN12 40 B1
Portmore Cl SN5 54 B3
Porton 18 C1
Porton Rd SP4 21 E1
Portskewett 8 A4
Portsmouth Ho SP9 41 C4
Portswood 19 F4
Portway La BA12 67 E2
Portway Mews BA12 67 E2
Portway, Chippenham SN14 26 C5
Portway, Salisbury SP4 47 E1
Portway, Warminster BA12 67 E3
Portwell SN6 29 B3
Post Office La SN13 28 E2
Poston Way BA15 22 A2
Potley La SN13 28 D4
Potterdown Rd SN2 51 H5
Potterne 13 H3
Potterne Rd, Devizes SN10 30 D6
Potterne Rd, Potterne SN10 42 B5
Potterne Wick 13 H3
Potters Walk SN4 68 A4
Potters Way SP1 49 G1
Poulsen Cl BA12 67 E4
Poulshot 13 G3
Poulton 10 A2
Poulton BA15 23 F4
Poulton Cres SN8 39 E3
Poulton Hill SN8 39 E3
Poulton La BA15 23 G5
Poulton St SN5 55 H5

Pound Cl SN15 36 B1
Pound Ct BA12 66 C4
Pound Farm Cl BA14 63 F2
Pound La, Bradford-on-Avon BA15 23 F3
Pound La, Swindon SN2 55 G3
Pound Mead SN13 28 D4
Pound Pill SN13 28 F2
Pound Rd SN6 34 B2
Pound Row BA12 66 C3
Pound St BA12 66 C4
Powell Rise SN16 37 C2
Poynder Rd SN13 28 D2
Poyntington 16 C3
Prescombe Down NNR SP3 17 H2
Preshute La SN8 38 B5
Preshute White Horse SN8 38 B5
Prestbury Dr BA14 67 F4
Prestleigh 12 B6
Preston La SN15 36 C2
Preston Vale SN15 36 D3
Preston, Gloucestershire 9 H2
Preston, Wiltshire 9 H6
Pretoria Rd SP11 35 F3
Priddy 12 A4
Priestley Gro SN11 25 D5
Primrose Cl, Calne SN11 25 C2
Primrose Cl, Swindon SN25 50 C6
Primrose Cnr BA14 62 D1
Primrose Dr SN12 40 D4
Primrose Hill, Chippenham SN14 26 D4
Primrose Hill, Salisbury SP2 44 D3
Primrose La SP5 33 E4
Primrose Rd, Andover SP11 35 D3
Primrose Rd, Salisbury SP2 46 A3
Primrose Walk BA12 66 C3
Primrose Way SN14 26 C1
Prince Charles Cl SP11 35 D2
Prince Charles Dr SN11 25 C5
Prince Maurice Ct SN10 31 G2
Prince Maurice Ho SN14 26 A3
Prince Rupert Ho SN14 26 A3
Princecroft La BA12 66 C4
Princes Cl SP5 33 G4
Princes Cotts SN3 60 D4
Princes Ct SP9 41 D2
Princes Hill SP5 33 G3
Princes Gdns, Swindon SN4 68 B4
Princes Gdns, Trowbridge BA14 63 E1
Princess Gdns, Warminster BA12 67 H4
Princess Mary Gdns SP11 35 C3
Priors Hill SN4 43 C6
Priorsfield SN8 39 F4
Priory Cl, Bradford-on-Avon BA15 23 F2
Priory Cl, Salisbury SP2 44 B5
Priory Grn SN6 34 D3
Priory New Rd SN13 28 D1
Priory Pk BA15 23 F2
Priory Rd SN3 60 D3
Priory St SN13 28 D1
Priston 12 C3
Pritchard Cl SN2 52 B5
Privet Way SN13 28 C3
Proby Pl BA14 63 G5
Prospect Pl, Trowbridge BA14 62 D4
Prospect Pl, Warminster BA12 36 A5
Prospect SN13 28 F4
Prospect Sq BA13 65 C3
Prospero Way SN25 50 C5
Proudman Rd SN10 31 F3
Providence La SN13 28 E2
Pucklechurch 8 D6
Pulham 16 D5
Pullman Dr SP2 45 G4
Pulsar Rd SN25 50 A4
Purbeck Cl SN3 57 E6
Purbeck Pl SN11 25 D5
Purcells Ct SN8 39 E4
Purleigh Rd SN13 28 C2
Purley Av SN3 60 D4
Purley Cl SN4 43 C5
Purley Rd SN4 61 H6
Purlyn Acre SN8 39 E2
Purse Caundle 16 C4
Purslane Cl SN4 54 C1

Purton Rd SN6 29 B3
Purton Stoke 10 A4
Purton, Gloucestershire 8 C2
Purton, Wiltshire 10 A4
Purvis Cl SP4 21 F2
Pusey 11 E3
Pylle 12 B6

Q

Quakers Walk SN10 30 D3
Quantock Cl, Melksham SN12 40 D3
Quantock Cl, Warminster BA12 67 E1
Quarley 14 D6
Quarr Barton SN11 25 B4
Quarry Cl SN10 31 F4
Quarry Cres SN6 34 C2
Quarry Dale Cl SN11 25 C5
Quarry Mews SN1 59 H4
Quarry Rd SN1 59 H3
Quarrybrook Cl SN3 53 G6
Quarryfield Ind Est BA12 36 A5
Quarterway La BA14 63 E5
Quavey Rd SP5 33 G4
Queen Alexandra Rd SP2 46 A5
Queen Camel 16 B3
Queen Charlton 12 B2
Queen Elizabeth Dr SN25 50 B6
Queen Manor Rd SP1 49 G2
Queen Mary Rd SP2 46 A4
Queen Rd SP1 46 D6
Queen St, Salisbury SP1 49 E1
Queen St, Salisbury SP2 44 D2
Queenborough SN5 58 B3
Queens Av, Corsham SN13 28 D1
Queens Av, Swindon SN6 34 C2
Queens Cl SP11 35 C3
Queens Club Gdns BA14 62 A5
Queens Cres SN14 26 B5
Queens Dr SN3 60 B1
Queens Falls SP4 21 B2
Queens Gdns BA14 63 E1
Queens Rd, Devizes SN10 30 D5
Queens Rd, Salisbury SP3 43 C2
Queens Rd, Swindon SN4 68 B4
Queens Rd, Trowbridge BA14 62 D4
Queens Rd, Warminster BA12 36 C4
Queens Rd, Westbury BA13 65 A3
Queens Sq, Chippenham SN15 27 F5
Queens Sq, Westbury BA13 65 A2
Queens Way SN8 39 F4
Queensberry Rd, Amesbury SP4 21 D1
Queensberry Rd, Salisbury SP1 46 D5
Queensfield SN2 52 A6
Queensgate SN1 60 A2
Queensway, Melksham SN12 40 C3
Queensway, Warminster BA12 67 H4
Queenswood Ho SP1 48 D2
Quentin Rd SN3 60 A4
Quemerford 13 H1
Quemerford SN11 25 C6
Quenington 10 B2
Quidhampton, Hampshire 15 G4
Quidhampton, Wiltshire 18 A2
Quilling Cl BA14 64 F1

R

Rabley Wood Vw SN8 39 E2
Radcliffe Rd SP2 48 D4
Radcot 10 D3
Radley 11 H3
Radley Cl SN3 57 E6
Radnor Cl SN10 31 E6
Radnor Pl SN12 40 B5
Radnor Rd SP1 46 D4
Radnor St SN1 59 F2

Radstock 12 C4
Radstock Av SN3 61 E1
Radway Rd SN3 56 C2
Raffin La SN9 42 B3
Raglan Cl SN3 60 B4
Ragleth Gro BA14 63 F4
Railway Village Museum SN3 59 G1
Rainer Cl SN3 57 E2
Rainham Rd SN3 51 E4
Raleigh Av SN3 56 C6
Raleigh Cres SP4 21 F3
Rambler Cl BA14 62 B5
Rambridge Cres SP2 45 G2
Ramleaze Dr, Salisbury SP2 45 H1
Ramleaze Dr, Swindon SN5 54 A6
Rampart Rd SP1 49 E1
Rampisham 16 A6
Ramsbury 14 D1
Ramsbury Av SN2 51 G5
Ramsbury Walk BA14 64 E2
Ramsdell 15 H3
Ramsthorn Cl SN2 54 C1
Randall Cres SN5 54 A5
Randall Ct SN13 28 C2
Randalls Croft Rd SP2 44 B5
Randolph Cl SN3 60 C1
Randwick 9 E1
Rangeworthy 8 C5
Rannoch Cl SN5 54 A5
Ransome Cl SN5 54 A5
Ratcoombe Rd SN5 54 A3
Ratfyn Rd SP4 21 C1
Ravenglass Rd SN5 58 B1
Ravens Walk SN4 68 B3
Ravenscroft Gdns BA14 63 F4
Ravenscroft, Salisbury SP2 48 D5
Ravenscroft, Swindon SN3 57 F5
Rawlence Rd, Bemerton Heath SP2 45 H3
Rawlence Rd, Bulbridge SP2 44 B5
Rawlings Cl SN3 57 G1
Rawlings Ct SP11 35 D3
Rawlings Well La SN8 39 E3
Rawlins Rd SN9 42 A2
Rawston Cl SN3 61 F1
Ray Cl, Chippenham SN15 27 G6
Ray Cl, Swindon SN25 51 F6
Raybrook Cres SN2 55 E6
Rayfield Gro SN2 55 G4
Read St SN1 59 F2
Recreation Rd, Amesbury SP4 21 B3
Recreation Rd, Durrington SP4 24 B1
Recreation Rd, Ludgershall SP11 35 D2
Rectory Cl BA12 67 E2
Rectory La SN6 29 C2
Rectory Rd SP2 48 C1
Red Lion La SN6 29 C2
Redbridge Cl SN5 59 E2
Redbook 8 A1
Redcap Gdns SN5 54 A6
Redcliffe St SN2 59 E1
Redford Cl SP1 47 F5
Redgrave Cl BA14 64 E1
Redhorn Gdns SN10 31 E6
Redhouse Way SN25 50 B3
Redland 8 B6
Redland La BA13 65 B3
Redland SN14 26 C3
Redlynch Cl SN2 51 H5
Redlynch, Somerset 16 C1
Redlynch, Wiltshire 18 C3
Redman Rd SN11 25 C1
Redposts Dr SN1 59 E2
Redruth Cl SN2 51 E2
Redwick 8 A5
Redwing Av SN14 26 C1
Reed Cl SN4 31 F4
Reed Walk SP4 24 D2
Reeds Cl SN8 39 F4
Reeds Cnr SN8 39 F4
Reeds Farm Rd SN16 37 C3
Reeds SN8 29 A2
Reeves Rd SN16 31 F6
Regal Ct BA12 67 E3
Regent Cl SN1 59 H1
Regents Pl, Bradford-on-Avon BA15 23 F4
Regents Pl, Swindon SN1 56 B4
Regents Pl, Trowbridge BA14 64 A2
Regil 12 A3
Regimental Museum SN2 48 D2

Rendcomb 9 H1
Rendells Ct SN10 30 D4
Renoir Cl SN25 51 F3
Retingham Way SN3 52 B6
Revell Cl SN2 52 B6
Reynolds Way SN25 51 F3
Rhine Cl SN5 59 E3
Rhuddlan SN5 58 B3
Ricardo Rd SN15 27 E3
Richard Jefferies Museum SN3 61 E5
Richards Cl SN4 68 A5
Richards Way SP2 48 B3
Richmond Cl, Devizes SN10 31 H1
Richmond Cl, Trowbridge BA14 62 B6
Richmond Rd, Calne SN11 25 A3
Richmond Rd, Salisbury SP2 46 C6
Richmond Rd, Swindon SN2 55 F4
Rickfield BA15 23 E3
Rider Cl SN10 31 H1
Ridge 17 G1
Ridge Grn SN5 54 A5
Ridge Nether Moor SN3 61 G5
Ridge SP4 21 D3
Ridgemead SN11 25 B3
Ridgeway Cl SN2 55 E2
Ridgeway Rd, Salisbury SP1 47 E5
Ridgeway Rd, Swindon SN2 52 B6
Ridgmount SP4 39 E4
Riding School Yd SN8 39 E4
Rimpton 16 B3
Ringwood 18 B6
Ringwood Av SP4 21 D3
Ringwood Cl SN3 56 D6
Rinsdale Cl SN5 54 B3
Ripley Rd SN1 59 H3
Ripon Cl SN4 26 B6
Ripon Way SN3 60 D4
Ripple Fld SN5 58 B2
Risingham Mead SN5 58 B2
Rivar 14 D3
Rivenhall Rd SN5 58 B2
River Pk SN8 38 D5
River Ray Est SN1 54 D6
River St SN9 42 B2
River Vw SN16 37 B3
River Way SP4 24 C1
Riverbourne Rd SP1 49 G1
Riverdale Cl SN1 59 H5
Riverdale Walk SN1 59 H5
Rivergate SN5 54 C5
Rivermead Dr SN5 54 B5
Rivermead Ind Est SN5 54 C5
Rivers Way SN5 34 B2
Riverside Av SP4 21 A3
Riverside Cl SP1 47 G6
Riverside Dr, Chippenham SN15 27 G4
Riverside Dr, Melksham SN12 40 B2
Riverside Rd SP1 47 G6
Robbins SP4 21 D3
Roberts Cl SN4 43 C6
Roberts Rd SP2 46 A5
Robin Cl BA12 67 F3
Robin Hill La SP4 24 C2
Robinia Cl SN9 42 C1
Robins Cl, Chippenham SN15 26 C1
Robins Cl, Swindon SN4 68 C3
Robinsgreen SN3 57 G6
Robinson Cl SN3 61 G1
Rochdale Av SN11 25 C2
Roche Cl SN3 61 G3
Roche Court Sculpture Park SP5 18 D1
Rocher Cl BA13 65 B3
Rochester Cl SN5 58 A3
Rock La BA12 67 G4
Rock Rd BA14 64 C1
Rockbourne 18 A4
Rockdown Ct SN2 52 A6
Rockhampton 8 B3
Rockley 14 B1
Rodbourne 9 G5
Rodbourne Grn SN5 55 B3
Rodbourne Rd SN2 55 H5
Rode 13 E4
Rodley 8 D1
Rodmarton 9 G3
Rodwell Cl SN3 60 C3
Rodwell Pk BA14 63 E4
Roebuck Dr SN4 68 C4
Roebuck Mdw SN8 39 F4

Rogers Cl, Salisbury SP2 45 F4
Rogers Cl, Swindon SN3 56 C6
Rogers Mdw SN8 39 E2
Rollestone St SP1 49 E1
Roman Cres SN1 59 G4
Roman Mdw SP5 32 C4
Roman Rd SP2 46 A6
Roman Way, Chippenham SN15 27 H6
Roman Way, Swindon SN6 34 B4
Romer Rd SP2 48 D4
Romney Way SN5 58 A1
Romsey 19 E3
Romsey Rd SP4 21 E4
Romsey St SN2 55 E1
Ron Rolding Cl SN16 37 C2
Rookes La SN10 42 A6
Rooks Nest Cl SN15 27 G6
Rope Walk SN12 40 B4
Rope Yard Walk SN4 68 C6
Rope Yd SN4 68 A4
Rose Ct SN4 68 D6
Rose St SN2 55 E6
Rose Walk SN25 51 E6
Rosebrook Gdns SN12 40 C5
Rosedale Gdns BA14 62 A5
Rosedale Rd SN3 66 D3
Rosedean SP5 33 G4
Rosefield Way BA13 65 B2
Roseland Av SN10 31 E5
Rosemary Cl, Calne SN11 25 A3
Rosemary Cl, Salisbury SP1 47 G6
Rosemary Cl, Swindon SN2 50 C6
Rosemary La SP1 48 D2
Rosemary Steps BA15 23 F2
Rosemary Walk BA15 23 F3
Rosetta Cl SN25 50 A3
Rosewood Ct SP9 41 E2
Ross Gdns SN3 52 D6
Rossett Gdns BA14 62 B6
Rothe Rise BA13 65 B5
Rother Cl SN25 51 E6
Rotherstone SN10 30 D3
Rougemont Cl SP1 49 E1
Round Ho SN11 25 D6
Roundhills Mead SN6 34 C1
Roundponds SN12 40 A1
Roundway 13 H2
Roundway Down SN5 58 B4
Roundway Gdns SN10 31 E2
Roundway Pk SN10 31 E2
Roves Farm SN6 10 C5
Rowan Cl, Durrington SP4 24 B1
Rowan Cl, Pewsey SN9 42 C1
Rowan Cl, Salisbury SP2 45 G3
Rowan Cotts SN13 28 C1
Rowan Cl, Melksham SN12 40 B5
Rowan Cl, Tidworth SP9 41 E1
Rowan Dr SN4 68 B5
Rowan Ho SN1 59 G1
Rowan Rd SN2 55 F2
Rowbarrow Cl SP2 49 E4
Rowbarrow Gdns SP2 49 E5
Rowde 13 H2
Rowden Hill SN15 26 C5
Rowden La, Bradford-on-Avon BA15 23 F5
Rowden La, Chippenham SN15 26 C5
Rowden Rd SN15 26 D5
Rowe Mead SN15 27 F6
Rowland Hill Cl SN3 61 H3
Rowley Pl SN12 40 C3
Rownhams 19 F4
Royal Cl SN15 27 E5
Royal Cres SP9 41 E2
Royal Gloucestershire, Berkshire & Wiltshire Regimental Salisbury Museum SP1 48 C2
Royal Oak Cl SN15 27 F5
Royal Oak Cl SN10 34 D4
Royston Rd SN3 60 D3
Rubens Cl SN25 51 F2
Ruckley Gdns SN3 56 D3
Rudge 13 E4
Rudgeway 8 B5
Rudloe 13 F1
Rumble Dene SN15 27 F6
Rupert Cl SN10 31 H1
Rural Gdns SN15 27 F5
Rushall 14 B4
Rushall Cl SN2 51 G6

Rushton Rd SN3 60 D4
Ruskin Av, Melksham SN12 40 C3
Ruskin Av, Swindon SN2 56 C2
Ruskin Dr, Swindon SN4 68 C2
Ruskin Dr, Warminster BA12 66 B4
Ruspidge 8 B1
Russell Rd SP2 46 B6
Russell Sq SN8 38 D4
Russell St SP2 44 D3
Russell Ter SP2 44 D3
Russell Walk SN3 60 B1
Russett Ct BA12 66 B3
Rutland Cl SN12 40 C4
Rutland Cres BA14 64 D1
Rutland Rd SN3 60 C2
Ruxley Cl SN4 68 A5
Ryan Av SN14 26 B4
Ryan Cl SN5 54 B3
Rycote Cl SN5 58 A1
Rydal Cl SN25 51 E6
Ryeland Way BA14 64 F1
Ryeleaze SN10 42 B6
Rylands Way SN4 68 B3
Ryme Intrinseca 16 B5
Rysy Ct SN25 50 D4

S

Sackville Cl SN3 56 C6
Saddleback Cl SN11 25 C5
Saddlers Mead SP2 44 C3
Sadler Walk SN3 60 C2
Sadlers Mead SN15 27 F3
Saffron Cl, Swindon SN25 54 D1
Saffron Cl, Wootton Bassett SN4 68 B2
Saffron Mdw SN11 25 A4
Sage Cl SN12 50 C6
Sailsbury Arts Centre SP1 49 E1
St Albans Cl, Salisbury SP1 47 G3
St Albans Cl, Swindon SN2 55 E6
St Aldhelm Rd, Bradford-on-Avon BA15 23 G4
St Aldhelm Rd, Malmesbury SN16 37 B3
St Aldhelms Cl SN16 37 B3
St Ambrose Cl SN3 57 G6
St Andrews Cl, Salisbury SP2 44 B5
St Andrews Cl, Swindon SN4 43 C5
St Andrews Ct, Blunsdon SN25 51 E3
St Andrews Ct, Swindon SN4 43 C4
St Andrews Grn SN3 57 G6
St Andrews Rd, Melksham SN12 40 C2
St Andrews Rd, Salisbury SP2 46 A6
St Andrews Rd, Tidworth SP9 41 C2
St Andrews Rd, Warminster BA12 66 B4
St Andrews SP1 47 G6
St Ann Pl SP1 49 E2
St Ann St SP1 49 E2
St Annes Cl, Salisbury SP4 21 D2
St Annes Cl, Trowbridge BA14 64 A4
St Arvans 8 A3
St Augustines Rd BA14 62 B6
St Austell Way SN2 59 E1
St Barbaras Rd SN13 28 B3
St Bedes Cl SN3 47 G3
St Birinus Rd SP5 33 F4
St Brendans Cl SP1 47 F3
St Briavels 8 A2
St Bridget Cl SN10 31 G4
St Catherine 12 D1
St Catherines Cl SN13 25 D3
St Catherines Cl SN4 43 C6
St Christophers Cl SP1 47 F3
St Clair Rd SP2 49 E4
St Clements Ct SN14 26 C3
St Clements Walk SP1 47 F3
St Davids Cl SP1 47 F3
St Davids Way SN8 39 E3
St Dennis Rd SN16 37 C4
St Devizes Rd SN10 30 A2
St Dunstan Cl SN11 25 B2
St Dunstan Ct SN11 25 B2
St Ediths Cl SN5 44 C5

St Edmunds Church St SP1 49 E1
St Francis Av SN15 26 D5
St Francis Rd SP1 46 D4
St Georges Cl SP9 41 C3
St Georges Rd, Salisbury SP2 48 A3
St Georges Rd, Tidworth SP9 41 C3
St Gregorys Av SP2 46 A5
St Helens Vw SN1 59 E3
St Ives 18 B6
St Ives Ct*, Broadmead Walk SN3 57 E6
St James Cl, Salisbury SP1 47 G3
St James Cl, Swindon SN2 52 A5
St James SN8 20 C4
St James St SP11 35 C2
St John Rd SN4 43 B5
St John St SP1 49 E2
St Johns Cl, Marlborough SN8 38 D3
St Johns Cl, Pewsey SN9 42 C2
St Johns Cl, Salisbury SP1 49 G2
St Johns SP3 43 B3
St Johns Cres BA14 64 A2
St Johns Ct, Devizes SN10 30 D4
St Johns Ct, Salisbury SP2 44 C3
St Johns Hospital BA14 64 C2
St Johns Rd BA12 67 G4
St Johns Sq SP2 44 C3
St Johns St, Devizes SN10 30 D4
St Johns St, Malmesbury SN16 37 C5
St Josephs Cl SP1 47 F3
St Josephs Dr SN15 26 D5
St Josephs Rd SN10 30 C4
St Judes Cl SP1 47 G3
St Julians Cl SN3 57 G1
St Katharine & St Peter Church SN4 10 A6
St Katherines Grn SN3 57 G6
St Katherines Quay BA15 23 F4
St Laurence Rd BA15 23 G4
St Laurences Church BA15 23 F7
St Lawrence Cl SP1 46 B3
St Leonards 18 A6
St Leonards Cl SP4 24 E3
St Lukes Cl SP1 47 G3
St Lukes Dr SN15 26 D5
St Margarets Cl, Calne SN11 25 A3
St Margarets Cl, Salisbury SP1 49 F2
St Margarets Cl, Trowbridge BA14 64 B2
St Margarets Gdns, Chippenham SN15 26 D5
St Margarets Gdns, Melksham SN12 40 C2
St Margarets Grn SN3 57 G2
St Margarets Hill BA15 23 F3
St Margarets Mead SN8 39 F4
St Margarets Pl BA15 23 F3
St Margarets Rd SN1 60 A4
St Margarets Rd BA15 23 F3
St Margarets Steps BA15 23 F3
St Margarets Villas BA15 23 F3
St Marks Av SP1 47 E5
St Marks Rd SP1 46 D6
St Martins Church St SP1 49 E2
St Martins SN8 39 E3
St Mary Bourne 15 F4
St Mary St SN15 26 C4
St Mary the Virgin Church BA14 13 G3
St Mary's Cathedral SP1 48 D2
St Mary's Church SN5 10 A4
St Marys Cl, Bulbridge SP2 44 B5
St Marys Cl, Devizes SN10 42 B6
St Marys Cl, Redlynch SP5 33 H6
St Marys Cl, Trowbridge BA14 63 F1
St Marys Gdns BA14 63 E2
St Marys Gro SN2 55 G4
St Marys La SN16 37 B3

St Marys Pl SN15 27 E3
St Marys Rd SP2 48 C3
St Marys St SN16 37 B3
St Matthews Cl SP1 47 G3
St Mellion Cl SN15 27 G4
St Michaels & All Angels Church SN6 10 C3
St Michaels Av, Swindon SN6 34 B2
St Michaels Av, Tidworth SP9 41 C3
St Michaels Church SN8 20 B2
St Michaels Cl, Marlborough SN8 20 B2
St Michaels Cl, Salisbury SP2 44 B5
St Michaels Cl, Trowbridge BA14 63 G3
St Michaels Rd, Melksham SN12 40 B4
St Michaels Rd, Salisbury SP2 45 H2
St Michaels Rd SN15 36 B5
St Nicholas Church of St Nicholas Hardenhuish SN14 26 C1
St Nicholas Church SN15 13 G2
St Nicholas Cl, Andover SP11 35 F3
St Nicholas Cl, Bradford-on-Avon BA15 22 A2
St Nicholas Cl, Calne SN11 25 D3
St Nicholas Cl, Salisbury SP2 44 B5
St Nicholas Rd SP1 48 D3
St Osmonds Cl SP1 48 D3
St Patricks Av SP9 41 B3
St Paul St SN15 27 E3
St Pauls Dr SN3 57 F6
St Pauls St SN2 55 H4
St Peters Cl, Chippenham SN15 26 C5
St Peters Cl, Salisbury SP2 44 B5
St Peters Rd SP1 47 F3
St Phillips Rd SN2 56 B1
StTeresas Cl SP1 47 F3
StTeresas Dr SN15 26 D5
StThomas Pass BA14 62 D5
StThomas Rd BA14 63 E5
StThomas Way SP1 47 F3
St Ursulas Cl SP1 47 F3
Saintes Cl SP1 47 F2
Salcombe Gro SN3 60 B2
Salisbury 18 B2
Salisbury & South Wiltshire Golf Club SP2 18 A2
Salisbury & South Wiltshire Museum SP2 48 D2
Salisbury Arts Centre SP1 49 E1
Salisbury Bsns Pk SP1 49 G3
Salisbury Cl, Chippenham SN14 26 B5
Salisbury Cl, Westbury BA13 65 A5
Salisbury Ct SN2 55 H6
Salisbury District Hospital SP2 49 E6
Salisbury Hill BA13 39 F5
Salisbury Ho SP9 41 D2
Salisbury Leisure Centre SP1 46 C5
Salisbury Playhouse SP2 48 D1
Salisbury Racecourse SP2 18 A2
Salisbury Rd, Amesbury SP4 21 C2
Salisbury Rd, Boscombe Down SP4 21 F4
Salisbury Rd, Bulford SP4 24 D3
Salisbury Rd, Marlborough SN8 39 E4
Salisbury Rd, Pewsey SN9 42 B3
Salisbury Rd, Quidhampton SP2 45 E3
Salisbury Rd, Wick SP5 32 A1
Salisbury Retail Pk SP1 47 E2
Salisbury St, Devizes SN10 30 B4
Salisbury St, Salisbury SP4 21 B2
Salisbury St, Warminster BA12 36 B5
Salmons Leap SN11 25 B2
Salt La SP1 49 E1
Saltersford La SN14 26 B6

Saltford 12 C2
Saltram Cl SN3 61 E1
Salzgitter Dr SN25 51 F2
Sambourne Chase BA12 66 D3
Sambourne Gdns BA12 67 E3
Sambourne Rd BA12 66 D4
Sams La SN26 51 H1
Sand Cl BA15 23 G2
Sand Pit Rd SN11 25 D2
Sandalwood Ct SN3 56 D1
Sandalwood Rd BA13 65 A4
Sandbourne Rd SN25 50 C5
Sanders Rd BA14 62 D4
Sandes Cl SN15 26 D4
Sandford Ct*, Springfield Rd SN1 59 H4
Sandford on Thames 11 H2
Sandford Orcas 16 B3
Sandgate Mews SN3 57 E4
Sandgate SN3 57 E4
Sandle La BA13 65 A5
Sandown Av SN3 60 B3
Sandown Centre BA14 64 F4
Sandown Dr SN14 26 A6
Sandpiper Bri SN3 57 H6
Sandpiper Gdns SN14 26 A6
Sandridge Rd SN12 40 C2
Sandringham Ct*, Devizes Rd SP2 46 C6
Sandringham Rd, Swindon SN3 60 C3
Sandringham Rd, Trowbridge BA14 64 B3
Sandstone Rd SN25 51 E4
Sandwood Cl SN5 54 B3
Sandy La, Salisbury SP5 33 G3
Sandy La, Swindon SN1 59 G3
Sandy Lane 13 G2
Sandy Leaze SN3 23 E3
Sandy Ridge SN11 25 B2
Sangster Av SN12 40 C4
Sapperton 9 G2
Sarisbury 19 G5
Sarsen Cl SN1 59 E3
Sarsen Stones SN8 14 B1
Sarum Av SN12 40 B5
Sarum Cl SP2 46 B5
Sarum Dr SN10 31 E6
Sarum Gdns BA13 65 C1
Sarum Rd SN14 26 B5
Sarum Way SN11 25 A4
Sassoon Cl BA12 66 B4
Sassoon Walk SN8 38 C4
Saul 8 D1
Saunders Gro SN13 28 C1
Savernake Av SN12 40 D1
Savernake Cl BA12 67 E2
Savernake Cres SN8 39 G4
Savernake Ct, Marlborough SN8 39 E4
Savernake Ct, Swindon SN1 59 H2
Savernake Dr SN11 25 A4
Savernake Ho SP9 41 D2
Savernake Hospital SN8 39 H5
Savernake Rd SN13 29 E4
Savill Cres SN4 43 A4
Savoy Cl SN11 25 B3
Sawyer Cl SN25 51 G4
Sawyers Cres SN13 28 B3
Saxby Rd SN15 27 F1
Saxifrage Bank SN12 40 D4
Saxon Cl, Cricklade SN6 29 B3
Saxon Cl, Westbury BA13 65 B2
Saxon Ct SN1 60 A3
Saxon Dr BA14 63 E1
Saxon Hurst SP5 32 C3
Saxon Mdw SN3 32 C4
Saxon Rd SP2 48 C4
Saxon St SN14 26 C3
Saxon Way SN15 22 B2
Saxons Acre BA12 66 B3
Saxton Walk SN5 54 B5
Scamells Rd SP2 46 D6
Scarborough Rd SN3 55 E4
Scarlet Cl SN25 51 E3
School Cl SN16 37 C5
School Dr SP4 24 C2
School La, Marlborough SN8 38 A5
School La, Salisbury SP4 21 C2
School La, Westbury BA13 65 A5
School Lane Cl BA14 62 D1
School Rd, Calne SN11 25 A2

School Rd, Durrington SP4 24 C1
School Rd, Redlynch SP5 33 H6
School Row SN25 54 D1
School Vw SN9 42 A1
School Walk SN14 26 B4
Science Museum SN4 10 B6
Scotby Av SN3 60 A4
Scotchel Grn SN9 42 B1
Scotland Rd SN12 40 B2
Scotney Cres SN25 51 E5
Scots La SP1 48 D1
Scotts Cl SP5 32 A2
Seacole Cres SN1 59 F4
Seagrim Rd SP2 44 C5
Seaton Cl SN25 51 E6
Sedbury 8 A4
Sedgebrook SN3 61 F5
Sedgefield Gdns SN10 31 E3
Sedgefield Way SN14 26 A5
Sedgehill 17 F2
Seend 13 G3
Seend Cleeve 13 G3
Sefton Rd SN25 50 B4
Selby Cres SN5 58 A2
Seldon Cl SN3 60 B1
Sells Green 13 G2
Semington 13 F3
Semington Rd SN10 42 A6
Semley 17 F2
Semley Walk SN2 55 H1
Senior Dr SP2 49 E4
Seth Ward Dr SP1 47 F5
Sevenfields SN6 34 D1
Sevenhampton 10 C4
Severn Av SN25 51 F6
Severn Beach 8 A5
Severn Cl SN11 25 B2
Severn Rd SN12 40 B1
Seymour Ct BA14 62 C5
Seymour Rd, Chippenham SN15 27 G3
Seymour Rd, Swindon SN3 60 B1
Seymour Rd, Trowbridge BA14 62 D5
Shackleton Rd SN10 31 F5
Shady Bower Cl SP1 49 F2
Shaftesbury 17 F3
Shaftesbury Av SN3 61 E4
Shaftesbury Ct BA14 62 C5
Shaftesbury Gro SP2 48 B5
Shaftesbury Rd, Salisbury SP2 44 A3
Shaftesbury Rd, Warminster BA12 36 C6
Shails La Ind Est BA14 62 C5
Shakespeare Dr SN8 38 C4
Shakespeare Path SN2 56 C1
Shakespeare Rd, Salisbury SP1 46 C4
Shakespeare Rd, Swindon SN4 68 C3
Shalbourne 15 E2
Shalbourne SN2 51 G5
Shanklin Rd SN25 54 D1
Shaplands SN3 56 D3
Shapwick 17 G6
Shapwick Cl SN3 57 F6
Sharp Cl SN5 54 B6
Sharpness 8 C2
Sharrat Av SP1 47 F3
Shaw Rd, Shaw SN5 54 B6
Shaw Rd, Westlea SN5 58 C1
Shaw Ridge Leisure Complex SN5 58 A1
Shaw, West Berkshire 15 G2
Shaw, Wiltshire 13 F2
Shawford 19 G3
Shearman St BA14 64 E1
Shearwater Way SN13 28 C4
Shearwood Rd SN5 54 A3
Shedfield 19 H4
Sheen Cl SP2 45 H1
Sheep St, Devizes SN10 31 E4
Sheep St, Swindon SN6 34 C3
Sheepcote Barton BA14 64 E1
Sheepscombe 9 F1
Sheepscroft Cl SN13 36 C3
Sheerwold Cl SN3 57 E1
Shelburne Rd SN11 25 C5
Sheld Dr SN15 36 C3
Sheldon Rd SN14 26 C4
Shelfinch SN5 58 C3
Shelley Av SN4 68 C3
Shelley Dr SP1 46 C4
Shelley Gdns SN12 40 B4
Shelley Way BA12 66 B4
Shellingford 10 D3
Shenton Cl SN3 56 D2

Shepherds Breach SN4 68 B4
Sheppard Cl, Chippenham SN15 27 G6
Sheppard Cl, Devizes SN10 30 C3
Shepperdine 8 B3
Shepperton Way SN25 51 E5
Shepton Mallet 12 B5
Shepton Montague 16 C1
Sherborne 16 B4
Sherborne Rd BA14 62 A5
Sherbourne Pl SN3 57 E6
Sherfield English 18 D3
Sherfields SN4 68 B5
Sherford Rd SN25 54 D1
Sheridan Dr SN4 68 C3
Sheridon Gdns BA14 64 A2
Sherrington 13 G6
Sherston 9 F5
Sherston Av SN2 51 H6
Sherston Rd SN16 37 A3
Sherwood Av SN12 40 D1
Sherwood Cl BA12 67 E2
Sherwood Rd SN3 61 E3
Shetland Cl, Swindon SN5 51 E5
Shetland Cl, Westbury BA13 65 A4
Shifford 11 E2
Shillingford 11 H4
Shillingstone 17 E5
Shilton 10 D1
Shipley Dr SN25 51 E5
Shippon 60 B1
Shipton Bellinger 14 C5
Shipton Gro SN3 60 B1
Shipton Moyne 9 F4
Shire Cl SN5 54 A6
Shire Cl SN1 59 F2
Shire Way BA13 65 A4
Shirley 19 F4
Shirley Cl SN3 56 C6
Shirrell Heath 19 H4
Shoddesden La SP11 35 H3
Sholing 19 G5
Shore Pl BA14 62 A5
Shoreland Cl BA13 65 B3
Shorncote 9 H3
Short St, Andover SP11 35 D3
Short St, Melksham SN12 40 D1
Shortlands SP2 44 B3
Shoscombe 12 D4
Showfield SN4 68 A2
Shrewsbury Rd SN3 60 C1
Shrewton 14 A6
Shrewton Cl BA14 64 E2
Shrewton Walk SN2 51 H6
Shrivenham 10 C4
Shrivenham Rd, Highworth SN6 34 C4
Shrivenham Rd, Swindon SN1 56 A6
Shropshire Cl, Salisbury SP2 45 H2
Shropshire Cl, Swindon SN5 54 A6
Shurnhold SN12 40 A2
Sidbury Circular Rd SP9 41 B1
Sidbury Hill Av SP9 41 D1
Siddington 9 H3
Sidmouth St SN10 31 E4
Sidney St SP2 46 C6
Sigerson Rd SN25 50 B6
Signal Way SN3 60 A4
Silbury Cl, Chippenham SN14 26 B6
Silbury Cl, Westbury BA13 65 A4
Silbury Hill SN8 14 A1
Silbury Mews SN25 54 D1
Silbury Rd SN11 25 B4
Silchester Way SN5 58 B1
Silman Cl SN13 28 B2
Silto Ct SN2 51 H6
Silton 17 E2
Silver Birch Gro BA14 64 B3
Silver Mdws BA14 64 B2
Silver St, Bradford-on-Avon BA15 23 F2
Silver St, Calne SN11 25 B6
Silver St, Devizes SN10 42 B5
Silver St, Malmesbury SN16 37 C4
Silver St, Salisbury SP1 48 D2
Silver St, Salisbury SP2 44 D3
Silver St, Warminster BA12 66 D3
Silver Street La BA14 64 B2
Silverless St SN8 39 E3
Silverton Rd SN3 61 E1
Silverwood Dr SP1 47 H5
Silveston Way SN16 37 A3

Simmance Way SP4 21 D3
Simonds Rd SP11 35 C3
Siston 8 C6
Sixpenny Handley 17 H4
Skew Bridge Rd SP2 46 A6
Skew Rd SP2 45 G4
Skye Cl SN6 34 B1
Slab La SP5 32 D3
Slad 9 F1
Slade Dr SN3 56 D4
Sladesbrook BA15 23 G2
Sladesbrook Cl BA15 23 G1
Slag La BA13 65 A1
Slater Rd SN9 42 B2
Slaughterford 13 E1
Slessor Rd SN15 36 B3
Slimbridge 8 D2
Slowgrove Cl BA14 63 F6
Smallbrook Gdns BA14 63 E1
Smallbrook La BA12 67 G5
Smallbrook Rd BA12 67 F5
Smeaton Rd SP2 48 B1
Smitan Brook SN3 57 G6
Smithfield St SP4 21 C2
Smiths Cl SN9 42 A1
Smiths Yd SN13 28 E2
Smithywell Cl BA14 63 F5
Snail Creep SP5 32 C2
Snails La SN10 30 C4
Snappersnipes BA13 65 C3
Snarlton La SN12 40 D2
Snowberry La SN12 40 C5
Snowdon Pl SN2 52 B6
Snowdrop Cl SN25 50 C6
Snows Hill SP3 43 C1
Snowshill Cl SN25 51 F6
Snowy Ter SN10 31 E4
Snuff St SN10 30 D4
Solstice Rise SP4 21 C2
Somerdale Cl SN5 58 B1
Somerford Cl SN2 56 A1
Somerford Keynes 9 H3
Somerley Rd SN10 40 C4
Somerset Cres SN10 40 C4
Somerset Dr BA13 65 C1
Somerset Rd, Salisbury SP1 47 E5
Somerset Rd, Swindon SN2 55 F4
Somerville Rd SN3 60 B1
Somme Rd SP11 35 A4
Sopworth 9 E5
Sorley Cl SN8 38 C4
Sorrell Cl, Melksham SN12 40 C5
Sorrell Cl, Swindon SN4 68 B2
Sorrell Cl, Trowbridge BA14 64 E2
Sound Copse SN5 54 A3
Soundwell 8 C6
South Av SN2 28 F2
South Barrow 16 B2
South Cadbury 16 C3
South Cerney 9 H3
South Cheriton 16 D3
South Fawley 11 F6
South Gorley 18 B5
South Horrington 12 B5
South La SP5 32 B3
South Leigh 11 F1
South Marston 10 C4
South Marston Pk Ind Est SN3 53 E4
South Mill Cl SP4 21 C3
South Mill Cl SP4 21 C3
South Moreton 11 H4
South Newton 18 A1
South Pl, Calne SN11 25 C5
South Pl, Corsham SN13 28 E2
South St, Aldbourne SN8 20 C2
South St, Avebury SN8 20 B5
South St, Corsham SN13 28 E3
South St, Salisbury SP2 44 C4
South St, Warminster BA12 66 C5
South Tidworth 14 C5
South View Av SN3 60 B1
South View Pl SN8 39 E3
South Vw Rd BA14 64 E2
South Western Rd SP2 48 C1
South Widcombe 12 B3
South Wonston 19 G1
South Wraxall 13 E2
Southampton 19 F4
Southampton Ho SP9 41 C4
Southbank Glen SN4 68 C4
Southbourne Rd SN8 36 C6
Southbrook Gdns BA12 36 D6
Southbrook Rd SN12 40 A1

Southbrook St SN2 55 G5
Southbroom Rd SN10 31 E5
Southcott Rd SN9 42 C3
Southdown Dr SN2 54 D4
Southerwicks SN13 28 E3
Southey Cl SN25 51 F3
Southfield SN8 20 C3
Southgate Cl SN10 31 E5
Southgate SN10 30 D5
Southleigh BA15 23 E4
Southleigh Vw BA12 67 F4
Southmead La SN8 20 C3
Southmill Hill SP4 21 C4
Southmoor 11 F3
Southrop 10 C2
Southstoke 12 D3
Southville Cl BA15 23 H4
Southville Rd BA15 23 G4
Southward La SN8 20 C3
Southway BA14 64 E1
Southway Rd BA15 23 F5
Southwell Cl SN14 26 B6
Southwick 13 E4
Southwick Av SN2 51 G6
Southwick Country Park BA14 64 A3
Southwold Cl SN25 50 B5
Southwood 16 A1
Southwood Rd BA14 63 F6
Spa Cl SN6 34 D2
Spa Ct SN12 40 B4
Spa Rd SN12 40 B4
Spackman La SN13 28 D3
Spanbourn Av SN3 27 E3
Sparcells Dr SN5 54 A3
Sparkford 16 B2
Sparrick La BA13 65 A5
Sparrow La SN4 68 A4
Sparsholt, Hampshire 19 F1
Sparsholt, Oxfordshire 11 E4
Speedwell Cl, Melksham SN12 40 C5
Speedwell Cl, Swindon SN25 50 D5
Speedwell Cl, Trowbridge BA14 64 E2
Speen 15 G2
Spencer Cl SN12 40 A1
Spencers Orchard, Bradford-on-Avon BA15 23 F5
Spencers Orchard, Swindon SN4 43 C6
Spenser Cl SN3 56 C6
Speresholt SN5 58 C3
Spetisbury 17 F6
Spindle Tree Ct SN2 55 G3
Spinners Cft BA14 64 E1
Spinners Way BA12 36 C4
Spinney Cl SN14 26 B5
Spirthill 9 H6
Spital La SN6 29 C3
Spitfire Way SN3 53 E4
Spode Cl SN5 50 D4
Sprats Barn Cl SN4 68 A3
Spray Leaze SP11 35 F3
Spring Gdns SN13 28 E2
Spring La BA13 28 A3
Spring Mdws BA14 64 B3
Spring Vws SN3 60 D2
Springers Cl SN10 31 F4
Springfield BA15 23 G3
Springfield Bldgs SN15 27 E3
Springfield Cl BA14 63 E4
Springfield Cres, Salisbury SP5 33 F6
Springfield Cres, Swindon SN25 50 D5
Springfield Dr SN11 25 A3
Springfield Leisure Centre SN13 28 D2
Springfield Pk, Salisbury SP3 43 A3
Springfield Pk, Trowbridge BA14 63 E4
Springfield Rd, Swindon SN1 59 H4
Springfield Rd, Warminster BA12 36 C5
Springfield Westbury BA13 65 B4
Springhill Cl SN5 58 B2
Spruce Ct SN2 55 G3
Spur Way SN2 56 B1
Squarey Cl SP5 32 C4
Squires Copse SN5 54 A3
Squires Hill Cl SN4 68 C4
Squirrel Cres SN4 68 C3
Stackpole Cres SN25 50 B3
Stainers Way SN14 28 B1
Stalbridge 16 D4
Stalbridge Weston 16 D4

Stamford Cl SN5 58 B2
Stanbridge 17 H6
Stanbridge Pk SN5 54 A6
Stancomb Av BA14 64 B3
Stancombe Pk SN5 58 C2
Standen Way SN25 51 E3
Standlake 11 F2
Standon 19 F2
Stanford Ct*, Sheep St SN10 31 E4
Stanford Dingley 15 H1
Stanford in the Vale 11 E3
Stanford Rd SN25 50 B5
Stanier Rd SN11 25 C1
Stanley Honey Ct SN3 60 C1
Stanley La SN15 27 H6
Stanley Little Rd SP2 45 G3
Stanley St SN1 59 C6
Stanley Ter SN10 31 E5
Stanmore 11 G6
Stanmore St SN1 59 F2
Stansfield Cl SN5 58 C3
Stanton Cl BA14 64 D2
Stanton Cl SN3 53 F3
Stanton Drew 12 B2
Stanton Fitzwarren 10 B4
Stanton Harcourt 11 F2
Stanton Prior 12 C2
Stanton St Bernard 14 A2
Stanton St Quintin 9 F6
Stanton Wick 12 B3
Stanway Cl SN3 60 C2
Stapehill 18 A6
Stapleford 18 A1
Stapleford Cl SN2 51 G5
Stapleford Way SN1 51 G5
Stapleton 8 B6
Stapleton Cl SN6 34 B3
Stardust Cres SN16 50 A4
Starfield Ct BA13 29 C5
Startley 9 G5
Station App, Ludgershall SP11 35 C3
Station App, Melksham SN12 40 A2
Station App, Swindon SN3 60 A3
Station App, Westbury BA13 65 A1
Station Cotts SP4 21 D7
Station Hill SN15 27 E3
Station Rd Ind Est SN11 25 B5
Station Rd, Calne SN11 25 B5
Station Rd, Corsham SN13 28 E2
Station Rd, Devizes SN10 30 C4
Station Rd, Highworth SN6 34 B3
Station Rd, Salisbury SP3 43 B2
Station Rd, Swindon SN4 68 A4
Station Rd, Tidworth SP9 41 D3
Station Rd, Trowbridge BA14 29 C4
Station Rd, Warminster BA12 67 F3
Station Rd, Westbury BA13 65 A1
Station Ter, Bulford SP4 24 D3
Station Ter, Salisbury SP2 48 C1
Staverton 13 F3
Staverton Rd BA14 29 A6
Staverton Way SN2 51 H5
Steam Museum of the Great Western Railway SN2 55 F6
Stedham Walk SN3 60 D3
Steele Cl SN3 31 F4
Steep St BA12 36 C4
Steeple Ashton 13 G3
Steeple Langford 13 H6
Stenbury Cl SN25 51 F4
Stenness Cl SN5 54 B3
Stephens Cl SP2 48 B3
Stephens Rd SN3 56 D4
Stephens Way BA12 66 D1
Stephenson Rd, Salisbury SP2 48 B3
Stephenson Rd, Swindon SN25 52 A4
Stert 13 H3
Stevenson Rd SN25 50 C6
Steventon, Hampshire 15 H5
Steventon, Oxfordshire 11 G4
Stewart Cl SN25 51 G5
Stickleback Rd SN11 25 B2
Stillman Cl BA14 29 C6

Stinchcombe 8 D3
Stirling Cl SN4 43 B5
Stirling Rd SN3 53 F5
Stock La SN8 20 A3
Stockbarrow SP4 21 D3
Stockbridge 19 E1
Stockbridge Copse*, Ratcombe Rd SN5 54 A3
Stockcross 15 F2
Stockham Cl SN6 29 C2
Stockley 13 H2
Stockton 17 G1
Stockton Rd SN2 55 H1
Stockwell Rd SN10 53 F3
Stockwood Cl SP1 47 F5
Stockwood Rd SN14 26 C5
Stoford, Somerset 16 B4
Stoford, Wiltshire 15 F4
Stoke 15 F4
Stoke Charity 15 G6
Stoke Gifford 8 B6
Stoke St Michael 12 C5
Stoke Trister 16 D2
Stokehill BA14 63 G5
Stokes Cft SN11 25 C3
Stokes Cl SN10 31 H1
Stokes Rd SN13 28 E3
Stokesay Dr SN5 58 B2
Ston Easton 12 B4
Stone 8 C3
Stone Avenue SN8 20 D5
Stone Cl SN13 28 E3
Stonebridge Cl SN8 39 F4
Stonebridge La SN8 39 E3
Stonecrop Way SN25 50 D5
Stonefield Cl, Bradford-on-Avon BA15 23 G4
Stonefield Cl, Eastleaze SN5 54 B6
Stonefield Dr SN6 34 C4
Stonehenge Rd, Amesbury SP4 21 A2
Stonehenge Rd, Durrington SP4 24 A2
Stonehenge Way SN4 14 A6
Stonehill Grn SN5 58 C1
Stonehouse 9 E2
Stonehurst Rd SN3 56 D4
Stonelea BA14 63 G3
Stonelea Cl SN14 26 C3
Stoneover La SN4 68 C4
Stones La SN6 29 A2
Stoney Cross 18 C5
Stoney Cross SP11 35 C3
Stoney Stratton 12 C6
Stonybeck Cl SN5 58 C1
Stour Provost 17 E3
Stour Row 17 E3
Stour Walk SN25 55 G1
Stourhead (NT) BA12 16 D1
Stourpaine 17 F5
Stourton 17 E1
Stourton Caundle 16 C4
Stourton House Garden BA12 17 E1
Stourton Pk BA14 63 H3
Stowell 16 C3
Stranks Cl SN6 34 C4
Stratford Cl SN5 58 C2
Stratford Ct SP1 46 D5
Stratford Rd SP1 46 B5
Stratford Tony 18 A2
Stratton Ct SN3 56 D2
Stratton Orchard SN3 56 D3
Stratton Rd, Pewsey SN9 42 B2
Stratton Rd, Swindon SN1 56 C5
Stratton St Margaret 10 B5
Stratton St Margaret By-Pass SN3 51 H3
Stratton-on-the-Fosse 12 C4
Strattons Walk SN12 40 B3
Streatley 11 H6
Stroat 8 B3
Stroma Way SN6 34 B2
Stroud 9 F2
Stroud La SN10 42 D6
Stuart Cl, Swindon SN3 60 C1
Stuart Cl, Trowbridge BA14 63 E2
Stuart Grn BA12 67 E4
Stubbington 19 H6
Stubhampton 17 G4
Stubsmead SN3 61 F2
Stuckton 18 B4
Studland Cl SN3 60 D3
Studland Pk BA13 65 C4
Studley 13 G1
Studley Rise BA14 64 D1
Sturminster Newton 16 D4

Sudgrove 9 G1
Suffolk Rd SP2 48 B4
Suffolk St SN1 55 H5
Summer Rd BA13 65 B2
Summerdown Ct BA13 65 C2
Summerdown Walk BA14 64 C3
Summerhouse Rd SN4 43 B5
Summerleaze, Corsham SN13 28 B2
Summerleaze, Trowbridge BA14 64 A1
Summerlock App SP1 48 D1
Summers St SN2 55 E6
Sumsions Dr SN13 28 C2
Sun La BA13 65 A5
Sunningdale Cl SN15 27 F4
Sunningdale Rd SN3 11 G2
Sunnyhill Rd SP1 47 E4
Sunnyside Av SN1 59 F2
Supermarine Rd SN3 53 F3
Surrey Pl BA14 64 C1
Surrey Rd SN2 55 F4
Sussex Rd SP2 48 B4
Sussex Wharf SN10 30 C4
Sutton Benger 9 G6
Sutton Courtenay 11 G4
Sutton Mandeville 17 G2
Sutton Montis 16 B3
Sutton Rd SN26 51 H1
Sutton Pl SN10 31 E5
Sutton Rd SN3 61 F3
Sutton Scotney 15 G6
Sutton Veny 13 F6
Sutton Waldron 17 F4
Sutton, Oxfordshire 11 F1
Sutton, Somerset 16 B1
Swaddon St SN11 25 C3
Swallow Cl, Tidworth SP9 41 D3
Swallow Cl, Warminster BA12 66 C5
Swallow Dr BA14 62 D6
Swallowcliffe 17 H2
Swallowdale SN3 57 F6
Swallowfield Av SN15 60 B2
Swallowmead SP3 48 D5
Swallows Mead SN4 68 D4
Swan Cl, Durrington SP4 24 C2
Swan Cl, Salisbury SP2 48 D4
Swan Dr BA14 62 D1
Swan Mdw SN9 42 B3
Swan Rd, Corsham SN13 28 C2
Swan Rd, Pewsey SN9 42 B2
Swanage Walk SN25 54 D2
Swanbrook SN3 57 F5
Swanmore 19 H4
Swanwick 19 H5
Swattons Cl SN3 24 E3
Swayne Cl SN15 27 F6
Swayne Rd SP2 44 B5
Swaynes Cl SP1 46 D6
Swaythling 19 F4
Sweetbriar Rd SN12 40 C4
Swift Av SN25 51 F4
Swift Down SP2 48 D5
Swift Mead BA12 66 C5
Swinburne Pl SN4 68 B2
Swindon 10 B4
Swindon & Cricklade Railway SN25 10 A4
Swindon Arts Centre SN1 60 A3
Swindon Ho SN1 41 D2
Swindon Museum & Art Gallery SN3 59 H3
Swindon Rd, Avebury SN8 20 C4
Swindon Rd, Cricklade SN6 29 C2
Swindon Rd, Highworth SN6 34 B6
Swindon Rd, Lower Stratton SN1,3 56 D4
Swindon Rd, Malmesbury SN16 37 C5
Swindon Rd, Marlborough SN8 39 E3
Swindon Rd, Wootton Bassett SN4 68 C2
Swindon Rd, Wroughton SN4 43 D4
Swindon St SN6 34 C3
Swinford 11 G1
Sword Gdns SN1 59 E3
Sycamore Cl, Chippenham SN15 36 D2
Sycamore Cl, Tidworth SP9 41 E2
Sycamore Dr SP1 47 F3

Sycamore Gro, Swindon SN2 55 H2
Sycamore Gro, Trowbridge BA14 64 C2
Sycamore Gro, Westbury BA13 65 A3
Syde 9 G1
Sydmonton 15 G3
Sydney Wood Ct SN14 26 D4
Symonds SN5 58 A4
Syon Cl, Corsham SN13 28 D3
Syon Cl, Swindon SN25 51 F5
Syringa Ct SP2 48 A1
Sywell Rd SN3 57 F5

T

Tadden 17 H6
Talbot Cl, Melksham SN12 40 D2
Talbot Cl, Salisbury SP1 47 F4
Talbot Rd BA14 64 B1
Tall Trees SN15 26 D4
Tallis Walk SN5 58 A2
Tamar Cl SN25 55 G1
Tamar Rd SN12 40 B1
Tamarisk Cl SN15 25 C6
Tamworth Dr SN5 54 A6
Tangley 15 E4
Tanis SN10 30 A1
Tanner Cl SN15 27 G6
Tanners Cl SN4 68 A3
Tanners Fld SP4 21 E3
Tansley Moor SN3 61 G4
Taplow Walk SN3 60 D3
Taramah Gdns SP3 43 B2
Targetts Mead SP3 43 C1
Tarka Cl SN25 55 H3
Tarlton 9 G2
Tarragon Cl SN2 54 B1
Tarrant Crawford 17 G6
Tarrant Gunville 17 G5
Tarrant Hinton 17 G5
Tarrant Keyneston 17 G6
Tarrant Launceston 17 G5
Tarrant Monkton 17 G5
Tarrant Rawston 17 G5
Tarrant Rushton 17 G6
Tascroft BA12 66 A5
Tasker Cl SN13 28 D3
Tatry Rd SN15 50 D4
Tattershall SN5 58 B4
Taunton Cl SN14 26 A6
Taunton St SN1 59 G1
Tavistock Rd SN3 61 E1
Tawny Owl Cl SN3 57 E5
Taylor Cres SN3 52 D6
Taylors Cl SN16 37 C4
Taylors Row BA15 23 F3
Teal Av SN25 55 G1
Teal Cl BA13 65 A3
Tealsbrook SN3 57 G5
Teasel Cl SP11 35 C3
Techno Trading Est SN2 56 B3
Tedder Cl SN2 55 G3
Teddington Ct BA12 66 D3
Tees Cl SN25 51 F6
Teeside BA14 64 A4
Teeswater Cl SN5 54 A6
Teffont Evias 17 H2
Teffont Magna 17 H1
Teichman Cl BA12 67 F4
Telford Pool SN2 55 E4
Telford Rd SP2 48 B2
Telford Way SN5 58 D3
Tellcroft Cl SN13 28 E4
Tellisford 13 E4
Temperence Row SP3 43 B2
Tempest Rd SP4 21 F3
Templars Firs SN4 68 B6
Templars Way Ind Est SN4 68 A6
Templars Way SN4 68 B6
Temple Cloud 12 B3
Templecombe 16 D3
Tenby Cl SN3 60 C4
Tench Rd SN11 25 B1
Tennyson Cl, Marlborough SN8 38 B4
Tennyson Cl, Warminster BA12 66 C4
Tennyson Rd SN4 68 C3
Tenzing Gdns SN25 55 H1
Tern Cl SN11 25 D4
Terncliff SN3 57 F6
Testwood 19 E4
Tetbury 9 F4
Tetbury Hill Gdns SN16 37 B2
Tetbury Hill Ind Est SN16 37 B2
Tetbury Hill SN16 37 B1

Tetbury Upton 9 F3
Thackeray Cl SN3 61 G3
Thackeray Cres SN3 48 B3
Thames Av SN25 50 D6
Thames Cl, Cricklade SN6 29 C2
Thames Cl, Warminster BA12 67 E5
Thames Cres SN12 40 B1
Thames La SN6 29 C2
Thamesdown Dr SN25 50 D5
Thatcham 15 H2
Thatcham Cl SN11 25 A3
The Acorns SN3 60 D5
The Activity Centre SN16 37 A4
The Archers SN6 34 C3
The Ark SN10 30 D5
The Avenue, Durrington SP4 24 B1
The Avenue, Fugglestone St Peter SP2 45 E3
The Avenue, Salisbury SP1 49 F1
The Avenue, Tisbury SP3 43 B2
The Avenue, Warminster BA12 67 E3
The Avenue, Westbury BA13 65 B3
The Battens SN14 26 B2
The Beeches, Salisbury SP1 49 F2
The Beeches, Trowbridge BA14 63 F4
The Beeches, Warminster BA12 66 D4
The Birches SN3 60 D5
The Borough SP5 32 A3
The Boulevard SN25 50 B5
The Bourne Centre SP1 49 G3
The Brambles SP1 47 F6
The Bramptons SN5 54 A5
The Breach SN10 30 D5
The Bridge SN15 27 E4
The Brittox SN10 30 D4
The Brow SN25 54 D1
The Bungalows SN2 55 G2
The Buntings SN3 57 G5
The Burlongs SN4 68 A4
The Butts, Chippenham SN15 27 F4
The Butts, Devizes SN10 42 A6
The Butts, Marlborough SN8 20 B3
The Butts, Westbury BA13 65 C4
The Camp 9 F1
The Causeway, Chippenham SN15 27 F4
The Causeway, Salisbury SP3 43 B2
The Centre SP4 21 C2
The Chesters SN5 58 C1
The Chestnuts SN25 50 B5
The Circle SN2 55 H2
The City SN12 40 A2
The Cleeve SN13 28 E3
The Cloisters SN15 26 D5
The Close, Chippenham SN15 27 F5
The Close, Melksham SN12 40 B4
The Close, Salisbury SP5 33 F3
The Close, Swindon SN5 56 D2
The Close, Warminster BA12 67 E3
The Common 18 D1
The Common, Marlborough SN8 38 D3
The Common, Trowbridge BA14 29 C4
The Copse SN26 51 G1
The Corn Market SP1 67 E3
The Court SN4 43 C4
The Courts Gardens (NT) BA14 29 B5
The Courts Gdns BA14 29 B5
The Courtyard SN15 27 F4
The Crays SN12 40 C2
The Crescent, Pewsey SN9 42 B2
The Crescent, Salisbury SP1 49 E1
The Crescent, Westbury BA13 65 B3
The Croft, Bradford-on-Avon BA15 22 C6

The Croft, Devizes SN10 31 F4
The Croft, Trowbridge BA14 64 D2
The Crofts Sports Centre SN3 60 A4
The Cross SP3 43 B1
The Crusaders SP1 47 F3
The Cullerns SN6 34 C3
The Dorcan Complex SN3 61 H1
The Dormers SN6 34 D2
The Down BA14 63 E4
The Downlands BA12 67 F2
The Downs SN8 20 B3
The Drive SN3 57 E6
The Drove, Amesbury SP4 21 C2
The Drove, Warminster BA12 36 A5
The Drove, Woodfalls SP5 33 F5
The Elms, Bradford-on-Avon BA15 23 E1
The Elms, Highworth SN6 34 C3
The Elms, Trowbridge BA14 29 B4
The Fairway SN10 30 D6
The Ferns SN2 55 H5
The Fiddle SN6 29 A2
The Fields BA12 36 C4
The Firs SN14 26 B5
The Folly SN14 26 B2
The Forty SN6 29 B3
The Forum SN5 58 B2
The Fox Talbot Museum SN15 13 G2
The Friars SN12 40 C1
The Friary SP1 49 E2
The Gallery SN1 60 A1
The Gardens, Greenmeadow SN25 55 F1
The Gardens, Kingsdown SN2 52 B5
The Garlings SN8 20 B3
The Glebe SN11 25 C4
The Gravel BA14 29 C5
The Great Western Hospital SN3 61 G6
The Green 17 F2
The Green, Aldbourne SN8 20 B2
The Green, Calne SN11 25 C5
The Green, Chippenham SN15 36 B1
The Green, Highworth SN6 34 C4
The Green, Marlborough SN8 39 E3
The Grove BA12 67 E3
The Groves SN25 55 G2
The Hamlet SN15 27 E2
The Hardings SP2 46 C6
The Harriers SN3 57 F5
The Hawthorns SN16 37 A5
The Headlands SP5 32 A3
The Heathlands BA12 66 C5
The Heights SN1 59 F3
The Hollows SP2 44 B3
The Homelands BA12 66 C5
The Kilns SN11 25 D3
The Kingsway SP2 44 D2
The Knap BA14 63 G3
The Knapp SN11 25 C4
The Knoll, Marlborough SN8 20 C1
The Knoll, Swindon SN1 59 H4
The Knoll, Westbury BA13 65 D1
The Knowle SN13 28 D3
The Laggar SN13 28 E1
The Lane SN2 55 E2
The Laurels BA15 22 C6
The Lawns SN4 68 A3
The Leaze SP4 24 E3
The Links SN9 42 A2
The Lynch BA12 36 C6
The Mall, Swindon SN1 59 G3
The Mall, Tidworth SP9 41 A4
The Mallards SP3 43 B3
The Maltings Shopping Centre SP1 48 D1
The Maltings, Bradford-on-Avon BA15 23 F4
The Maltings, Malmesbury SN16 37 C4
The Maltings, Swindon SN4 68 A4
The Maltings, Warminster BA12 66 D3

The Manor Apartments SN25 50 D4
The Maples SP2 46 C6
The Market Pl SN10 30 D4
The Marsh, Swindon SN4 61 H5
The Marsh, Wootton Bassett SN4 68 B1
The Mead, Bradford-on-Avon BA15 22 B2
The Mead, Warminster BA12 67 E2
The Mead, Westbury BA13 65 B1
The Meadows SP1 49 G2
The Meads Bsns Centre SN5 58 D1
The Mews, Highworth SN6 34 C3
The Mews, Malmesbury SN16 37 B3
The Mews, Warminster BA12 67 E3
The Midlands BA14 29 B5
The Mill Ho BA15 23 G3
The Moorlands SN10 30 C5
The Mount SN4 63 E4
The Mountings SN4 43 C4
The Mulberrys SN4 68 A4
The Narth 8 A1
The Nestings BA14 64 A3
The Nurseries SN1 59 G2
The Nursery SN10 30 C3
The Oakbournes SP1 47 F3
The Oaks, Chippenham SN15 27 E1
The Oaks, Warminster BA12 67 E1
The Old Batch BA15 23 G2
The Old Farmyard SP3 43 C2
The Old Orchard SN16 37 B1
The Old School SN1 60 A1
The Olympiad Leisure Centre SN15 27 F3
The Orangery SN13 28 C1
The Orbit Centre SN5 58 D1
The Orchard, Salisbury SP1 47 F6
The Orchard, Swindon SN3 60 C6
The Owlets SN3 57 H6
The Packway SP4 24 A2
The Paddock, Salisbury SP3 43 C2
The Paddock, Warminster BA12 67 F4
The Paddocks, Chippenham SN15 27 E5
The Paddocks, Highworth SN6 34 C3
The Paddocks, Marlborough SN8 20 C2
The Paddocks, Swindon SN3 56 D3
The Paddocks, Trowbridge BA14 63 F5
The Paddocks, Warminster BA12 36 C5
The Parade SN8 39 E4
The Pastures BA15 22 B6
The Patchway SN10 31 G4
The Pippin SN11 25 C4
The Pippins BA12 66 D3
The Pitchens SN4 43 C6
The Planks SN3 60 A3
The Poplars, Chippenham SN15 26 B1
The Poplars, Trowbridge BA14 64 B3
The Portway SP1 46 C3
The Pound BA12 36 C5
The Precinct SN13 28 E2
The Priory SN6 29 C1
The Quadrangle SN15 26 D5
The Quadrillion SN5 54 D6
The Quarries SN1 59 H4
The Quarry 8 D2
The Quarry SN11 25 C6
The Ridge, Bradford-on-Avon BA15 23 G2
The Ridge, Salisbury SP5 33 F6
The Ridge, Swindon SN26 51 G1
The Ridgeway BA12 67 E3
The Ridgeway Hospital SN4 43 C5
The Ropewalk*, Newtown BA15 23 F3
The Rosary SN4 68 B3
The Row, Salisbury SP5 33 G3

The Row, Swindon SN2 56 A3
The Rowans SN16 37 B3
The Sanctuary SN8 14 A2
The Seasons SN2 52 B5
The Shambles BA15 23 F2
The Sidings, Devizes SN10 30 C4
The Sidings, Salisbury SN9 32 D2
The Slades SN11 25 D3
The Slipway BA14 62 D1
The Spitfire Retail Pk BA14 64 D3
The Square, Blunsdon SN25 51 E5
The Square, Calne SN11 25 B4
The Square, Marlborough SN8 20 B2
The Square, Pewsey SN9 42 A2
The Square, Stratton St Margaret SN3 56 D1
The Square, Warminster BA12 36 B5
The Stables, Corsham SN13 28 C1
The Stables, Westbury BA13 65 C3
The Star BA13 29 B6
The Steadings, Salisbury SP4 47 G1
The Steadings, Swindon SN4 58 B4
The Strand SN11 25 B4
The Street, Blunsdon SN25 51 E5
The Street, Swindon SN25 54 D2
The Street, Trowbridge BA14 29 B5
The Studio SN1 60 A1
The Teasels BA12 66 D3
The Thatchers SN25 51 H4
The Thorns SN8 39 E2
The Tinings SN15 27 G3
The Turnpike SN15 27 H6
The Tynings, Corsham SN13 28 E3
The Tynings, Westbury BA13 65 B4
The Uplands BA12 66 F2
The Valley SP2 45 H1
The Walk BA14 29 B5
The Weavers SN3 60 A3
The Were SN11 25 C3
The Wharf SN11 25 B5
The White Ho SP9 41 D3
The Wilderness BA15 23 F2
The Willows SN6 34 D3
The Woodlands BA12 67 E1
The Wynd SN11 25 C3
The Yews BA12 36 C4
Theobold St SN1 59 E1
Thestfield Dr BA14 62 D2
Thetford Way SN25 50 B6
Thickwood 13 E1
Thirlmere SN3 61 G4
Thirsk Cl SN14 26 B6
Thistlebarrow Rd SP1 47 E4
Thomas Cl SN11 25 C6
Thomas Mead SN15 27 F6
Thomas St SN2 55 F6
Thompson Cl SP2 48 C5
Thomson Way SN8 38 C4
Thorley Ct SN25 51 F5
Thorn Leigh SN12 40 B4
Thornbank SN12 40 B4
Thornbridge Av SN3 60 C3
Thornbury 8 B4
Thornbury Rd BA13 65 B2
Thorne Rd SN3 61 F3
Thornford 16 B5
Thornford Dr SN5 58 C2
Thornhill 19 G5
Thornhill Dr SN25 51 F3
Thornhill Ind Est SN3 57 G1
Thornhill Rd, Swindon SN3 57 G3
Thornhill Rd, Warminster BA12 66 B5
Thornicombe 17 F6
Thoulstone Park Golf Club BA13 13 F5
Three Legged Cross 18 A5
Three Lions Mews BA14 29 C5
Thresher Dr SN25 51 H4
Throughamn 9 F1
Thrupp 9 F2
Thrushel Cl SN25 55 E1
Thruxton 14 D5

Thurlestone Rd SN3 60 B2
Thurlow Cl SP4 21 F3
Thursday Rd SN25 50 C4
Thyme Cl SN2 54 C2
Tichborne 19 H2
Tickle Belly La BA13 65 B5
Tidcombe 14 D3
Tidenham 8 A3
Tidpit 18 A4
Tidworth Cl SN5 59 E3
Tidworth Garrison Golf Club SP9 14 C5
Tidworth Leisure Centre SP9 41 D3
Tidworth Rd SP11 35 A4
Tilley Cl SN10 31 F4
Tilleys La SN3 56 C3
Tilshead 13 H5
Tilshead Walk SN2 51 G6
Timandra Cl SN25 51 F5
Timber St SN15 27 F4
Timbrell St BA14 62 D5
Timbrells Pl SN15 26 C5
Timor Rd BA14 65 A4
Timsbury, Bath & NE Somerset 12 C3
Timsbury, Hampshire 19 E3
Tin Pit SN8 39 E3
Tinkers Fld SN4 68 A4
Tinkers Mead SN9 42 C3
Tinneys Cl SP5 33 F6
Tintagel Cl SN3 58 B3
Tintern Parva 8 A2
Tintern Rd SN10 31 E6
Tintinhull 16 A3
Tippet Av SN25 50 D3
Tisbury 17 G2
Tisbury & District Sports Centre SP3 43 A1
Tisbury Cl SN2 51 H5
Tisbury Rd, Amesbury SP4 21 E1
Tisbury Rd, Bulford SP4 24 D4
Tisbury Row SP3 43 D1
Tismeads Cres SN1 59 H5
Titchfield 19 G6
Tithe Barn Cres SN1 59 F3
Tiverton Rd SN2 55 H4
Tockenham 10 A6
Tockenham Way SN2 51 G5
Tockenham Wick 9 H5
Tockington 8 B5
Todber 17 E3
Toghill Cres SN13 28 A3
Tollard Cl SN3 61 F1
Tollard Royal 17 G4
Tollbar Cl SN10 42 A5
Toller Whelme 16 A6
Tollgate Rd SP1 49 E2
Toot Baldon 11 H2
Toothill, Hampshire 19 E4
Toothill, Swindon 10 B5
Toppers Cl SN25 55 G2
Tor Ho BA13 65 B2
Torino Cl SN10 31 F3
Tormarton 9 E6
Torridge Cl SN25 55 E1
Tortworth 8 C3
Tortworth Rd SN25 50 B3
Torun Way SN25 50 C5
Tory BA15 23 E3
Tory Pl BA15 23 E3
Totterdown Cl SN3 57 G6
Totton 19 E4
Tournament Rd SP2 46 A5
Tovey Rd SN2 55 F3
Towcester Cl SN14 26 A6
Towcester Rd SN3 57 E5
Tower Cl BA14 64 B1
Tower Mews SP1 47 E6
Tower Rd, Melksham SN12 40 D3
Tower Rd, Swindon SN5 54 A3
Town Mews SN15 27 F5
Town Mill SN8 39 E4
Townsend Cl BA12 36 B5
Townsend Fm SN12 40 A5
Townsend Pl SN14 26 A3
Towpath Rd BA14 63 E1
Tracy Cl SN25 51 F5
Trajan Rd SN3 57 F4
Transfer Bridge Ind Est SN2 56 A5
Tree Courts Rd SN2 55 G3
Treenwood Ind Est BA15 23 F5
Treforest Cl SN25 50 B4
Tregantle Walk SN3 61 E1
Trenchard Cl SN14 26 B5
Trenchard Rd SN15 36 B3
Trenchard Way SN12 40 C6

Trent 16 B4
Trent Cres SN12 40 B1
Trent Rd SN25 55 F1
Trentham Cl SN3 60 D3
Tresham 9 E4
Trickett's Cross 18 A6
Trinity Pk SN11 25 D6
Trinity St SP1 49 E2
Trinty Cl SN3 60 D4
Tropenell Cl SN13 28 D3
Trow Green 8 B1
Trowbridge 13 F3
Trowbridge Community Hospital BA14 62 D4
Trowbridge Ho SP9 41 D2
Trowbridge Lodge Residential Pk BA14 63 F6
Trowbridge Museum BA14 62 D5
Trowbridge Rd, Bradford-on-Avon BA15 23 F3
Trowbridge Rd, Trowbridge BA14 63 G4
Trowbridge Rd, Westbury BA13 65 C1
Trowbridge Sports Centre BA14 62 D5
Trowle BA14 62 A3
Trowle Common 13 E3
Trudoxhill 12 D6
Truman Cl SN3 61 F3
Truro Path SN5 58 B3
Truro Walk SN14 26 A5
Truscott Av SN25 50 C3
Truslow Cotts SN8 20 B5
Tryhorn Dr SP1 47 F2
Tryon Cl SN3 61 G5
Tubney 11 F3
Tuckers Cl SP4 21 D3
Tuckingmill Rd SP3 43 A3
Tudor Cres SN3 56 D3
Tudor Dr BA14 63 E1
Tudor Walk SN3 60 C1
Tugela Rd SN15 27 E2
Tukman Rd SN13 28 D2
Tuke Walk SN1 59 F3
Tulip Tree Cl SN2 55 H3
Tupman Rd SN13 28 D2
Turnberry Cl SN15 27 G4
Turner Cl SP2 48 B3
Turner St SN1 59 F2
Turnham Grn SN8 58 A3
Turnpike Rd, Blunsdon SN26 51 G2
Turnpike Rd, Highworth SN6 34 C2
Turnpike SN8 20 C2
Turnworth 17 E5
Turpin Way SN14 26 A4
Tweed Cl SN25 51 E6
Twerton 12 D2
Twickenham Way SN15 27 E2
Twineham Rd SN25 50 B3
Twinhoe 12 D3
Twyford 19 G3
Twyford Cl SN3 60 D1
Twynham Cl SN5 32 C4
Twynnoy Cl SN16 37 C2
Tyburn Cl SN5 58 A2
Tydeman St SN2 56 A4
Tylees Ct SN10 31 E5
Tylers Cl SP2 48 B3
Tyneham Rd SN3 57 E6
Tyning Cl BA14 62 A6
Tyning Pk SN11 25 C6
Tyning Rd BA15 22 B2
Tynings Way BA15 22 B6
Tytherington, South Gloucestershire 8 C4
Tytherington, Wiltshire 13 G6
Tytherton Lucas 9 G6

Ubley 12 A3
Uffcott 10 B6
Uffington 11 E4
UGC Cinema SN5 58 A1
Uley 9 E3
Ullswater Cl SN3 61 G4
Ulysses Rd SN25 50 A3
Underdown Mead BA12 36 C4
Underhill BA12 36 A5
Underwood Dr SP4 21 E4
Union Rd, Chippenham SN15 27 E3
Union Rd, Salisbury SP3 43 B3
Union St SN12 40 B3
Unity St SN14 26 D4

Up Cerne 16 C
Up Somborne 19 F
Up Sydling 16 B
Upavon 14 B
Upavon Ct SN2 51 H
Upavon Golf Club SN9 14 E
Upfield SN3 61 G
Upham 19 H
Upham Rd SN3 60 A
Upland Rise BA13 65 C
Upper Basildon 11 H
Upper Bucklebury 15 H
Upper Church Flds SN8 58 D1
Upper Chute 14 D
Upper Clatford 15 E
Upper Folly SP2 44 B
Upper Framilode 8 D
Upper Green 15 E
Upper Inglesham 10 C
Upper Isbury SN8 39 E
Upper Lambourn 11 E
Upper Marsh Rd BA12 67 E
Upper Mill BA15 23 G
Upper Minety 9 H
Upper Potley SN13 28 C
Upper Regents Pk BA15 23 F
Upper Seagry 9 G
Upper Soudley 8 C
Upper St SP2 48 B
Upper Street 18 B
Upper Studley BA14 64 A
Upper Swainswick 12 D
Upper Upham 10 C
Upper Water St BA12 36 C
Upper Westwood BA15 22 A
Upper Woodford 14 B
Upton Cheyney 12 C
Upton Cl, Swindon SN25 51 E
Upton Cl, Warminster BA12 66 D
Upton Lovell 13 G
Upton Noble 12 D
Upton Scudamore 13 F
Upton, Hampshire, SO16 19 E
Upton, Hampshire, SP11 15 E
Upton, Oxfordshire 11 H
Urchfont 13 E
Urchfont Ho SP9 41 E
Urchfont Way SN2 51 H
Ursa Way SN25 50 B
Utah Cl SN3 59 E
Utterson Vw SN15 26 D

V
Vale Ct SN6 29 B2
Vale Rd, Pewsey SN9 42 A2
Vale Rd, Salisbury SP5 33 F4
Vale Vw SN4 68 A5
Valley Cl SP5 33 F
Valley Rd SN13 28 D2
Valley Vw SN11 25 B8
Valleyside SN1 59 F3
Van Diemens Cl SN8 39 E4
Vanbrugh Gate SN3 60 C6
Vanessa Av SP1 50 B3
Vega Cl SN25 50 B3
Ventnor Cl SN25 54 D1
Ventry Cl SP1 47 E6
Verney Cl SN3 61 G1
Vernham Dean 15 E4
Vernham Street 15 E4
Vernon Cl SP4 21 F2
Verny Cl SP4 21 E2
Verona Rd SP1 46 C4
Verulam Cl SN3 57 F4
Verwood 18 A5
Verwood Cl SN3 60 D2
Vespasian Cl SN3 57 F5
Vicarage Cl, Calne SN11 25 C4
Vicarage Cl, Marlborough SN8 39 E3
Vicarage Gdns SN16 37 C5
Vicarage La SN6 34 C3
Vicarage Pk SP5 33 F4
Vicarage Rd, Salisbury SP3 43 B2
Vicarage Rd, Swindon SN2 55 E4
Vicarage St BA13 66 D3
Victoria Cl SP2 44 C3
Victoria Cross Rd SN4 43 A4
Victoria Ct SP1 46 D4
Victoria Dr SN15 36 D2
Victoria Gdns BA14 62 C3
Victoria Hospital SN1 59 G3
Victoria Mews BA12 66 C3

Victoria Rd, Devizes SN10 31 E3
Victoria Rd, Salisbury SP1 46 D5
Victoria Rd, Trowbridge BA14 63 E3
Victoria Rd, Warminster BA12 66 A4
Victoria Rd, Wilton SP2 44 B3
Victoria Ter SN11 25 B4
Victory Flds BA15 23 F4
Victory Row SN4 68 A4
Viking Cl SN25 51 E4
Viking Way SP2 49 E5
Village La SN25 50 B5
Village St SN25 50 A4
Villiers Cl SN15 27 G4
Villiers Ho SN14 26 B3
Vincent Cl SN12 40 D3
Vincients Rd SN14 26 A3
Vincients Wood SN14 26 A4
Vine Cotts BA15 23 E2
Virginia Cl SP4 21 F2
Virginia Dr BA12 66 B3
Viscount Way SN3 53 F5
Vista Ct BA13 65 C3
Vistula Cres SN25 50 D4
Vobster 12 D5
Vockins Cl SP9 41 C1
Vorda Rd SN6 34 C2
Vowley Vw SN4 68 C5
Voyager Dr SN25 50 A4

W

Wade Mews SN15 27 F2
Waggoner Cl SN25 51 G4
Wagtail Cl SN3 57 E5
Waiblingen Way SN10 30 C3
Wain-a-Long Rd SP1 49 F1
Wainwright Cl SN3 61 G3
Wakefield Cl SN5 58 A3
Walcot 10 B5
Walcot Rd SN3 60 A2
Walden Lodge Cl SN10 31 E6
Wallingford 11 H4
Wallingford Cl SN5 58 B4
Wallis Dr SN25 51 F3
Wallsworth Rd SN3 60 C2
Walmesley Chase BA14 63 G5
Walnut Cl SN9 42 C2
Walnut Gro BA14 64 C2
Walnut Tree Cl SN3 57 E2
Walsingham Rd SN3 60 C1
Walter Sutton Cl SN11 25 A4
Waltham Chase 19 H4
Walton Cl SN3 60 C2
Walwayne Fld SN3 52 D6
Wanborough 10 C5
Wanborough Rd, Covingham SN3 57 G6
Wanborough Rd, Stratton St Margaret SN3 57 F4
Wansdyke Dr SN11 25 B4
Wanshot Cl SN4 43 D6
Wanstrow 8 C2
Wanswell 8 C2
Wantage 11 E4
Wapley 8 D6
Warbler Cl BA14 62 B6
Warburton Cl BA14 64 B2
Wardley Cl SN3 60 D3
Wardour Cl SN3 60 A2
Wardour Pl SN12 40 B5
Wardour Rd SN14 26 B5
Wareham Cl SN5 58 A2
Warminster 13 F5
Warminster Av SN2 51 H5
Warminster Community Hospital BA12 67 G4
Warminster Ho SP9 41 D2
Warminster Rd, Salisbury SP2 44 C1
Warminster Rd, Westbury BA13 65 B5
Warminster Sports Centre BA12 67 G4
Warneford Cl SN5 58 C3
Warner Cl SN3 57 E1
Warren Cres SN11 25 C3
Warrener Cl SN25 51 G4
Warsash 19 G6
Warwick Cl, Chippenham SN14 26 A6
Warwick Cl, Salisbury SP1 46 C5
Warwick Cres SN12 40 B4
Washbourne Rd SN4 68 B4
Washern Cl SP2 44 B5
Wasing 15 H2
Wastfield SN13 28 E3
Watchfield 10 D4

Water Ditchampton SP2 44 B2
Water Furlongs SN6 29 B3
Water Mdws SN16 37 C5
Water Mint Way SN11 25 A3
Water St BA12 66 C3
Watercrook Mews SN5 58 C2
Waterdown Cl SN3 50 B6
Waterford Beck BA14 64 A1
Watergate La SP4 24 B3
Waterlip 12 C5
Waterloo Rd SP1 49 F2
Watermead SN3 57 E2
Waters Edge SN15 27 F6
Waters Rd SP1 46 D4
Waterside Pk SN10 31 H2
Waterside SP5 32 C3
Waterside Way SN3 61 G6
Watersmead BA13 65 C2
Watersmeet Rd SP2 48 D4
Waterworks Rd BA14 64 C1
Watling Cl SN2 59 E1
Watt Rd SP2 48 B2
Wavell Rd, Salisbury SP2 48 D4
Wavell Rd, Swindon SN2 55 G3
Wavell Rd, Tidworth SP9 41 B1
Waverley Cl SN13 28 E3
Waverley Gdns SN12 40 B4
Waverley Rd SN3 57 E4
Waylands, Cricklade SN6 29 B3
Waylands, Devizes SN10 31 F5
Wayne Cl SN25 51 F6
Wayside Cl SN3 54 D6
Weaveland Rd SP3 43 B1
Weavern Ct SN14 26 B4
Weavers Cft SN12 40 A2
Weavers Cl, Chippenham SN14 26 A4
Weavers Cl, Malmesbury SN16 37 C2
Weavers Dr BA14 64 E1
Webb Cl SN15 27 F6
Webbers Ct BA14 64 A2
Webbington Rd SN15 27 F6
Webbs Ct SN15 36 B1
Webbs Way SN16 37 C2
Webbs Wood SN5 54 A3
Wedgewood Cl SN5 55 F5
Wedhampton 14 A3
Wedmore Av SN15 26 D2
Weedon Rd SN3 56 D4
Weir Hayes Av SN13 28 A3
Weir Pl BA15 23 F3
Weirside Av SN4 43 C5
Weirside Mill BA15 23 G3
Welbeck Cl SN3 60 C2
Welcombe Av SN3 60 D2
Welford 15 F1
Welford Cl SN13 57 E5
Weller Rd SN13 28 D2
Wellhead BA12 36 B4
Wellhead La BA13 65 B4
Wellington Dr SN14 40 D6
Wellington Pl SN8 38 D4
Wellington St SP9 41 E2
Wellington Sq SN12 40 D6
Wellington Way SP2 46 A5
Wellow 12 D3
Wells 12 A5
Wells Cl SN14 26 B5
Welton Rd SN5 58 C1
Wembley St SN2 55 F5
Wenhill Heights SN11 25 A6
Wenhill La SN11 25 A6
Wensleydale Cl SN5 54 A6
Wentworth Cl SN15 27 G4
Wentworth Pk SN5 58 A2
Were Cl BA12 66 C3
Wesley Ct SN4 68 C3
Wessex Cl, Calne SN11 25 D4
Wessex Cl, Devizes SN10 31 F4
Wessex Cl, Melksham SN12 40 C4
Wessex Rd, Bulbridge SP2 44 B5
Wessex Rd, Chippenham SN14 26 C3
Wessex Rd, Salisbury SP1 49 F1
Wessex Walk BA13 65 B2
Wessex Way SN6 34 D1
Wessington Av SN11 25 C6
Wessington Ct SN11 25 D6
Wessington Pk SN11 25 D6
West Ashton 13 F4
West Bradley 16 A1
West Camel 16 B3

West Cepen Way SN14 26 A5
West Challow 11 E4
West Chelborough 16 A6
West Coker 16 A4
West Compton 12 B6
West Dean 18 D2
West End Rd, Salisbury SP2 46 B6
West End Rd, Swindon SN3 56 C3
West End, Hampshire 19 G4
West End, Melksham SN12 40 B4
West End, Oxfordshire 11 F2
West End, Westbury BA13 65 C2
West Ginge 11 F5
West Grafton 14 C3
West Grimstead 18 C2
West Hagbourne 11 G4
West Hanney 11 F4
West Harptree 12 A4
West Hendred 11 F4
West Highland Rd SN25 51 E4
West Horrington 12 B5
West Ilsley 11 G5
West Kennet Av SN8 20 D5
West Kennet Long Barrow SN8 14 A2
West Kennet Stone Avenue SN8 20 D5
West Kennett 14 B1
West Kington 9 E6
West Knoyle 17 F1
West Lavington 13 H4
West Littleton 8 D6
West Lydford 16 A1
West Manton SN8 38 A5
West Mill La SN6 29 A2
West Moors 18 A6
West Orchard 17 E4
West Overton 14 B2
West Par BA12 66 C3
West Park Rd SN13 28 C2
West Pennard 12 A6
West St, Malmesbury SN16 37 B4
West St, Marlborough SN8 20 B2
West St, Salisbury SP2 48 C1
West St, Warminster BA12 66 C3
West St, Wilton SP2 44 A3
West Stour 17 E3
West Stowell 14 B2
West Street Pl BA12 66 C3
West Swindon Centre SN5 58 B1
West Tytherley 18 D4
West View Cres SN10 30 C5
West Walk SP1 48 D2
West Wellow 18 D4
West Wiltshire Golf Club BA12 67 E1
West Winterslow 18 C1
West Woodhay 15 F2
West Woodlands 13 E5
Westbourne Cl SP1 49 F1
Westbourne Cl SN2 55 E6
Westbourne Rd BA13 65 C3
Westbrook Cl SN14 26 B4
Westbrook Rd SN2 55 F4
Westbury 13 F5
Westbury BA13 65 A1
Westbury Community Hospital BA13 65 C4
Westbury Ho SP9 41 D3
Westbury Ind Est BA13 65 A1
Westbury Leigh 13 F5
Westbury on Trym 9 A6
Westbury Pk SN4 68 A5
Westbury Rd, Swindon SN2 51 H6
Westbury Rd, Warminster BA12 66 A1
Westbury Vw SN12 40 D3
Westcombe 12 C6
Westcott Pl SN1 59 F2
Westcott St SN14 26 B6
Westcroft SN14 26 B6
Westcroft St BA14 62 C4
Westerham Walk SN11 25 D5
Westerleigh 8 C6
Westerleigh Cl SN14 26 C5
Western Way, Melksham SN12 40 A3
Western Way, Salisbury SP2 45 G3
Westfield BA15 23 E2
Westfield Chase SN8 20 B3

Westfield Cl, Durrington SP4 24 A1
Westfield Cl, Laverstock SP1 47 G6
Westfield Cl, Trowbridge BA14 64 A1
Westfield Rd BA14 64 A1
Westfield Way SN2 54 C1
Westhill Cl SN6 34 B4
Westland Cl SP4 21 F2
Westlea Dr SN5 58 B1
Westlecot Rd SN1 59 G4
Westleigh BA12 66 C3
Westmead Cres BA14 64 C3
Westmead Dr SN5 54 C6
Westmead Ind Est SN5 54 D6
Westmead La SN15 27 F5
Westmead Ter SN15 27 F5
Westminster Ct SN5 58 B3
Westminster Gdns SN14 26 C4
Westminster Rd, Salisbury SP2 46 C5
Westminster Rd, Swindon SN5 58 B3
Weston, Bath & NE Somerset 12 D2
Weston, West Berkshire 15 F1
Westonbirt 9 F4
Westpoint Bsns Pk SN14 26 A2
Westridge SN10 30 D4
Westrop SN6 34 C2
Westview Walk SN3 57 E6
Westwell 10 C1
Westwood 13 E3
Westwood Manor House (NT) BA15 22 C6
Westwood Rd, Bradford-on-Avon BA15 22 D6
Westwood Rd, Salisbury SP2 45 G2
Westwood Rd, Swindon SN2 51 H5
Westwood Rd, Trowbridge BA14 62 A5
Westwood Sports Centre SP2 45 G2
Wetherby Cl SN14 26 B6
Wexcombe 14 D3
Wey Cl SN5 55 G1
Weyhill 14 D5
Weyhill Cl SN3 60 D2
Weymouth St BA12 67 E4
Whaddon 18 B2
Whaddon La BA14 63 G2
Whalley Cres SN4 43 B5
Wharf Ct SN12 40 B4
Wharf Rd, Swindon SN3 58 A6
Wharf Rd, Wroughton SN4 43 A4
Wharf St SN10 30 D3
Whatcombe 17 E6
Whatley 12 D5
Wheatlands SN25 54 D1
Wheatley 11 H1
Wheatstone Rd SN3 61 G3
Wheeler Av SN2 56 A2
Wheeler Cl SN9 42 A1
Wheelwright Mews SP5 32 A3
Whelan Way SP4 21 E2
Whelford 10 B3
Wherwell 15 E6
Whilestone Way SN3 57 E4
Whistley Rd SN10 42 A5
Whitbourne Av SN3 60 C2
Whitbread Rd SP2 45 H1
Whitbred Cl SN5 54 A6
Whitby Gro SN2 55 E4
Whitchurch, Bath & NE Somerset 12 B2
Whitchurch, Hampshire 15 G5
White Beam Ct SN2 55 G3
White Castle SN5 58 B3
White Eagle Rd SN25 50 C5
White Edge Moor SN3 61 G4
White Horse Bsns Pk BA14 64 E3
White Horse Cl BA14 64 E2
White Horse Leisure Centre SN11 25 C6
White Horse Rd, Bradford-on-Avon BA15 22 B2
White Horse Rd, Cricklade SN6 29 B2
White Horse Way, Calne SN11 25 C6

White Horse Way, Westbury BA13 65 B2
White Horse, Avebury 14 A1
White Horse, Marlborough Downs 10 B6
White Horse, Milk Hill 14 B3
White Horse, Pewsey 14 B3
White Horse, Preshute 13 F4
White Horse, Westbury 13 F4
White Lion Pk SN16 37 A3
White Rd, Marlborough SN8 39 H6
White Rd, Warminster BA12 36 C4
White Row Hill BA14 64 B3
Whitebeam Ct SP9 41 D3
Whitebridge Rd SP1 49 G1
Whitebrook 8 A1
Whitecroft 8 B1
Whitefriars Rd SP1 49 E2
Whitehall Gdns SN11 25 B4
Whiteheads La BA15 23 F2
Whitehill BA15 23 F2
Whiteland Rise BA13 65 D3
Whitelands Rd SN3 56 D4
Whiteman St SN2 55 H5
Whitemarsh BA12 36 C6
Whiteparish 18 D3
Whiterow Pk BA14 64 A2
Whiteshill 9 F1
Whiteshoot Hill SP5 33 F6
Whiteshoot SP5 33 H6
Whitethorn Cl SN4 68 B2
Whiteway 9 G1
Whitfield 8 C4
Whitfield Cl BA12 67 G3
Whitley 13 F2
Whitley Golf Club SN12 13 F2
Whitley Rd SN8 20 B3
Whitminster 8 D1
Whitsbury 18 A3
Whittington Rd SN5 58 B1
Whittle Cl SN14 26 B3
Whittonditch 14 D1
Whitworth Rd, Chippenham SN15 27 F6
Whitworth Rd, Swindon SN25 55 F2
Wibdon 8 B3
Wichelstok Cl SN1 59 H4
Wick La, Covingham SN3 61 H1
Wick La, Devizes SN10 30 D6
Wick La, Liden SN3 61 G5
Wick La, Salisbury SP5 32 A2
Wick, Bath & NE Somerset 12 D1
Wick, West Berkshire 18 B3
Wickdown Av SN25 55 E2
Wickfield SN10 30 D6
Wickham, Hampshire 19 H5
Wickham, West Berkshire 15 F1
Wicks Cl SN25 51 E6
Wicks Dr SN15 27 G6
Wickwar 8 D4
Widbrook Hill, Bradford-on-Avon BA15 23 H6
Widbrook Hill, Trowbridge BA14 62 A3
Widbrook Mdw BA14 62 A6
Widbrook Vw BA15 23 H4
Widhill La SN26 51 F1
Wigbeth 18 A5
Wigmore Av SN3 60 B3
Wilcot 14 B3
Wilcot Av SN2 52 A6
Wilcot Cl, Salisbury SP4 21 F4
Wilcot Cl, Trowbridge BA14 64 D2
Wilcot Rd SN9 42 A1
Wilcox Cl SN2 55 H3
Wildern Sq SN3 56 D1
Wildhern 15 E4
Wiley Ter SP2 44 D3
Wilkins Cl SN2 52 C5
William Cl SP1 49 G1
William Rd SN10 31 F6
William Robbins Ct SN25 55 E2
William St, Calne SN11 25 C3
William St, Swindon SN1 59 F2
William Stumpes Cl SN16 37 B2
Williams Gro SN13 28 E3
Williamson Cl SP11 35 C3
Willington Rd SN25 50 D4
Willoughby Rd BA13 65 A4

Entry	Ref
Willow Cl, Marlborough SN8	39 G4
Willow Cl, Melksham SN12	40 A4
Willow Cl, Salisbury SP1	47 G6
Willow Cres, Corsham SN13	28 C3
Willow Cres, Warminster BA12	67 F4
Willow Dr, Devizes SN10	31 G2
Willow Dr, Salisbury SP4	24 A1
Willow Gro, Chippenham SN15	27 E1
Willow Gro, Trowbridge BA14	64 B2
Willow Gro, Westbury BA13	65 A3
Willow Mews SP9	41 E2
Willow View Cl SN8	37 B3
Willow Walk SN4	43 C6
Willowbank SN14	26 B1
Willowherb Cl SN25	50 D5
Willows Av SN2	55 H2
Wills Av SN1	56 B5
Wilman Way SP2	48 C5
Wilsford, Wiltshire, SN9	14 A3
Wilsford, Wiltshire, SP4	14 B6
Wilson Ho SP9	41 C1
Wilson Rd SN25	51 E4
Wilson Sq BA12	67 G2
Wilton Dr BA14	64 D2
Wilton House SP1	44 D4
Wilton Rd SP2	45 F3
Wilton Walk SN2	51 H5
Wilton Windmill SN8	14 D3
Wilton, Wiltshire, SN8	14 D3
Wilton, Wiltshire, SP2	18 A1
Wiltshire Av SN2	55 F4
Wiltshire Cres SN12	40 C4
Wiltshire Dr BA14	64 D2
Wiltshire Music Centre BA15	23 E1
Wiltshire Rd SP2	48 B3
Wiltshire Way BA13	65 C2
Wimborne St Giles	17 H5
Wimpole Cl SN3	60 D3
Win Green Hill SP7	17 G3
Wincanton	16 C2
Winchester	19 F2
Winchester Cl, Chippenham SN14	26 B5
Winchester Cl, Salisbury SP4	21 E4
Winchester Cl, Swindon SN3	57 E4
Winchester Ho SP9	41 C4
Winchester St SP1	49 E1
Windbrook Mdw SN12	56 C1
Windermere Rd BA14	63 E4
Windermere SN3	61 G4
Windflower Rd SN25	50 D5
Winding Way SP2	45 H3
Windlass Way SN15	27 F6
Windlesham Rd SP1	47 E4
Windmill Cl SN8	20 C1
Windmill Hill (NT) SN4	14 A1
Windrush Rd SN25	55 F2
Windrush SN6	34 B3
Windsor Av SN12	40 B5
Windsor Cl SN14	26 B5
Windsor Dr, Devizes SN10	31 G2
Windsor Dr, Trowbridge BA14	64 B3
Windsor Dr, Westbury BA13	65 D2
Windsor Mews SP4	24 B1
Windsor Rd, Durrington SP4	24 B1
Windsor Rd, Salisbury SP2	48 C1
Windsor Rd, Swindon SN3	60 B4
Windsor Rd, Trowbridge BA14	64 E4
Windsor St SP2	48 C1
Windy Ridge BA15	22 B6
Wine St, Bradford-on-Avon BA15	23 E2
Wine St, Devizes SN10	30 D4
Wine Street Ter BA15	23 E3
Winford	12 A2
Wingate Par SN2	55 F3
Wingfield	13 E3
Wingfield Av SN2	51 H5
Wingfield SN3	52 C6
Winifred St SN3	60 A4
Winlaw Cl SN5	54 B6
Winnipeg Gdns SP4	24 F2
Winsley	13 E3
Winsley Cl SN4	51 H6
Winsley Rd BA15	22 C2
Winson	10 A1
Winston Rd SN12	40 A6
Winstone	9 G1
Winterborne Clenston	17 F6
Winterborne Houghton	17 E6
Winterborne Stickland	17 F6
Winterbourne Bassett	14 A1
Winterbourne Dauntsey	18 B1
Winterbourne Earls	18 B1
Winterbourne Gunner	18 C1
Winterbourne Monkton	14 A1
Winterbourne Stoke	14 A6
Winterbourne, South Gloucestershire	8 C6
Winterbourne, West Berkshire	15 F1
Wintergreen SN11	25 A4
Wintershill	19 H4
Winterslow Rd, Swindon SN2	51 G6
Winterslow Rd, Trowbridge BA14	64 C3
Winton Cl SP9	41 D4
Winton Rd SN3	56 D1
Winwick Rd SN5	58 A3
Wirral Way SN25	51 F4
Wise Cl SN2	56 B2
Wiseman Cl SN3	57 G6
Wishart Way SN15	27 F6
Wishford Rd SP2	44 B1
Witchampton	17 G6
Witham Friary	12 D6
Witham Way SN2	52 C6
Withering Rd SN1	59 F4
Withy Cl, Swindon SN4	68 A2
Withy Cl, Trowbridge BA14	63 E3
Witney	11 E1
Wittenham Vw SP4	21 D3
Woburn Cl, Swindon SN25	51 E5
Woburn Cl, Trowbridge BA14	62 A5
Wolferstan Dr SP1	47 F3
Wolsely Av SN3	60 C3
Wolvercote	11 G1
Wolverton	15 H3
Wolverton SN14	26 A5
Wonston, Dorset	16 D5
Wonston, Hampshire	15 G6
Wood La SN15	27 F4
Wood Pk SP11	35 E3
Wood St, Calne SN11	25 C4
Wood St, Swindon SN1	60 A3
Wood St, Wootton Bassett SN4	68 A4
Woodbine Ter SN3	61 H5
Woodborough	14 B3
Woodborough Cl BA14	64 E3
Woodborough Rd SN13	28 F4
Woodbury Gdns SP2	49 E4
Woodchester	9 E2
Woodchester SN12	58 C2
Woodcock Gdns BA12	67 G4
Woodcock Ind Est BA12	67 G3
Woodcock La BA12	67 F3
Woodcock Pk BA12	67 G3
Woodcock Rd BA14	67 F3
Woodcombe SN12	40 D1
Woodcroft	8 A3
Woodcutters Mews SN25	51 H4
Woodeaton	11 H1
Woodfalls	18 C3
Woodford	8 C3
Woodford Cl SN2	51 H5
Woodford Rd SP2	46 A1
Woodford Valley SP4	14 B6
Woodgreen	18 C4
Woodhall Dr SN2	54 C1
Woodhenge SP4	24 A3
Woodhill Av SN11	25 D3
Woodhill Rise SN11	25 D3
Woodhouse Gdns BA14	63 H4
Woodhouse Rd SN3	60 C2
Woodland Ind Est BA13	65 B3
Woodland Pk SN11	25 C5
Woodland Rd BA12	66 C3
Woodland Vw, Calne SN11	25 C6
Woodland Vw, Swindon SN4	59 G6
Woodland Way, Devizes SN10	30 D6
Woodland Way, Salisbury SP1	47 G5
Woodlands Edge BA14	63 F6
Woodlands Rd Ind Est BA12	36 C6
Woodlands Rd, Chippenham SN14	26 C4
Woodlands Rd, Marlborough SN8	39 H2
Woodlands Rd, Pewsey SN9	42 C3
Woodlands Rd, Warminster BA12	36 C6
Woodlands St Mary	15 E1
Woodlands SN13	28 D1
Woodlands, Dorset	18 A5
Woodlands, Hampshire	18 D5
Woodman Mead BA12	66 D3
Woodmancote	9 H1
Woodmancott	15 H6
Woodmand BA14	29 C5
Woodmarsh BA14	64 D4
Woodmill Ter BA14	63 G3
Woodminton	17 H3
Woodpecker Mews SN14	26 A1
Woodroffe Sq SN11	25 D4
Woodrow Rd SN12	40 C1
Woodsage Way SN11	25 A4
Woodsend	10 C6
Woodshaw Mead SN4	68 C4
Woodside Av SN3	60 B2
Woodside Rd, Salisbury SP2	45 H3
Woodside Rd, Swindon SN3	53 E4
Woodsman Rd SN25	51 G5
Woodspring Ct*, Grovelands Av SN1	59 H4
Woodstock Gdns SN12	40 B5
Woodstock Rd, Salisbury SP1	47 E6
Woodstock Rd, Swindon SN3	57 E4
Woodville Rd SP1	47 F3
Woodyates	17 H4
Wookey	12 A5
Wookey Hole	12 A5
Woolaston	8 B3
Woolford Grange SN4	68 D3
Woolhampton	15 H2
Woolland	16 D5
Woollaston Cl SN5	58 A2
Woolley Cl BA15	23 G2
Woolley Dr BA15	23 G2
Woolley Grn BA15	23 H1
Woolley St BA15	23 F2
Woolley Ter BA15	23 G2
Woolpack Mdws BA14	64 E1
Woolston	19 F5
Woolstone	10 D4
Woolton Hill	15 F3
Woolverton	12 D4
Wootton	11 G2
Wootton Bassett	10 A5
Wootton Bassett Museum SN4	68 A4
Wootton Bassett Rd SN5	59 E2
Wootton Bassett Way SN1,5	58 D2
Wootton Rivers	14 C2
Wootton St Lawrence	15 H4
Wordsworth Cl SN4	68 C3
Wordsworth Dr SN2	56 C1
Wordsworth Rd SP1	47 E6
World's End	11 G6
Worlidge Dr SN5	54 B5
Worminster	12 A6
Worsted Cl BA14	64 E1
Wortheys Cl SN16	37 C2
Wortley	8 D4
Worton	13 G3
Wotton-under-Edge	9 E3
Wrag Barn Golf & Country Club SN6	34 C6
Wraxhall	16 B1
Wrde Hill SN6	34 B4
Wren Cl BA12	66 C5
Wren Ct BA14	62 B6
Wrenscroft SP2	48 D5
Wrenswood SN3	57 G5
Wright Cl SN25	51 F3
Wroughton	10 B6
Wychurch Rd SN16	37 C2
Wyke	17 E2
Wyke Rd BA14	63 E1
Wyld Ct SN25	51 E3
Wylye	17 H1
Wylye Cl, Salisbury SP2	45 F4
Wylye Cl, Swindon SN25	55 E1
Wylye Cl, Warminster BA12	66 D4
Wylye Rd, Tidworth SP9	41 D2
Wylye Rd, Warminster BA12	66 D5
Wyndham Cl SN15	27 G3
Wyndham Rd, Salisbury SP1	46 D6
Wyndham Rd, Swindon SN2	55 F5
Wyndham Ter SP1	46 D6
Wynndale Cl SN3	52 D6
Wynwards Rd SN25	51 F5
Wytham	11 G1
Wyvern Av SN11	25 D4
Wyvern Cl, Devizes SN10	31 H1
Wyvern Cl, Swindon SN1	59 H5
Wyvern Walk BA13	65 A2
York Cl, Corsham SN13	28 E1
York Pl SN8	39 E3
York Rd SN15	36 D2
Yorkley	8 C1

Z

Entry	Ref
Zakopane Rd SN25	50 C5
Zander Rd SN11	25 B2
Zeals	17 E1
Zoar Cl SN4	43 B6
Zouch Av SP9	41 C1
Zouch Cl SP9	41 C1
Zouch Farm Rd SP9	41 C2

Y

Entry	Ref
Yard Ct BA12	67 F3
Yardley Cl SN2	55 E2
Yarlington	16 C2
Yarmouth Cl SN5	58 A3
Yarn Ter BA14	64 E1
Yarnbury Castle SP3	13 H6
Yarrow Cl SN2	54 C2
Yate	8 C5
Yatesbury	14 A1
Yattendon	15 H1
Yatton Keynell	9 F6
Yeats Cl SN25	51 F3
Yelde Hall Museum SN15	27 E4
Yelford	11 E2
Yellowhammer Cl SN3	57 F5
Yenston	16 C3
Yeoman Way BA14	64 C1
Yeovil	16 A4
Yeovil Cl SN3	61 E2
Yeovil Marsh	16 A3
Yeovilton	16 A3
Yersin Ct SN1	59 G3
Yetminster	16 B5
Yew Tree Cl, Calne SN11	25 A4
Yew Tree Cl, Salisbury SP4	24 D2
Yew Tree Gdns SN3	57 H1
Yew Way SN13	28 C3
Yewstock Cres East SN15	26 D2
Yewstock Cres West SN15	26 D2
Yiewsley Cres SN3	57 E3
Yockney Cl SN3	28 D3
York Bldgs BA14	62 D4
York Cl, Chippenham SN14	26 B5